Walter Scott

The Miscellaneous Works

Volume XXVIII.

Walter Scott

The Miscellaneous Works
Volume XXVIII.

ISBN/EAN: 9783741180163

Manufactured in Europe, USA, Canada, Australia, Japa

Cover: Foto ©Andreas Hilbeck / pixelio.de

Manufactured and distributed by brebook publishing software (www.brebook.com)

Walter Scott

The Miscellaneous Works

THE PROSE WORKS
OF
SIR WALTER SCOTT, BART.
VOL. 28

THE

MISCELLANEOUS WORKS

OF

SIR WALTER SCOTT, BART.

VOL. XXVIII.

TALES OF A GRANDFATHER—VII.
HISTORY OF FRANCE.

EDINBURGH:
ADAM AND CHARLES BLACK.
1861.

NOTICE.

This Volume concludes the Collected Works of Sir Walter Scott, which have reached, in Monthly issues, the term of seven years and four months, an extent for the writings of one individual unprecedented in English literature.

Various communications have been received, urging additions to the series now brought to a close. There cannot be a doubt that several volumes could have been added to this long line of books; but, with every respect to those who press its extension, it is right to state that not a few subscribers have already complained of its bulk. The Proprietors, besides, have it not in their power to add some of the works alluded to in various letters—Sir Walter Scott's Sketch of the History of Scotland, for example, which he contributed to Lardner's Cyclopædia, and which belongs to the Proprietors of that work. Moreover, even if the power to insert it had been attained, it is doubtful if the public would have relished two Histories of Scotland, particularly as the one now alluded to is incomplete, extending only to the year

NOTICE.

1603, whereas that embraced in the far more celebrated Tales of a Grandfather brings us down to the close of the rebellion of 1745—thus comprehending by far the most picturesque and interesting period of Scottish annals, which the other does not touch upon.

The Letters on Demonology, too, could not have been included in this collected edition without injury to the Proprietors of the Family Library, in which Miscellany they still continue to circulate.

A volume might have been added of Miscellaneous Contributions, but the number having already exceeded by four the promise of the early announcements, some consideration was due to this pledge

1st August, 1836.

TALES OF A GRANDFATHER.—FRANCE.

CHAP. XVI.—Homage paid by Edward III. to Philip of France in the Cathedral of Amiens—Edward subdues Scotland, and resolves to assert his Claim (in right of his Mother) to the Crown of France—obtains the consent of his Parliament for an Invasion of France—Naval Engagement at the entrance of the Harbour of Sluys, in which the English are victorious—Siege of Saint Omer—Siege of Tournay—a Truce for one year concluded, and Edward returns to England—Prolongation of the Truce—Dispute concerning the Succession to the Dukedom of Bretagne—The French King espouses the part of Charles of Blois, who had been dispossessed of the Duchy by John de Montfort—De Montfort taken, and imprisoned—the masculine Courage of his Countess—English Succours, under Sir Walter Manny, thrown into the Town, by whose gallantry the Siege is raised—Prosecution of the War—Hennebon again besieged, and the siege again raised—a Truce concluded—Renewal of the War—Edward takes the Field, and is opposed by John, the son of Philip—Truce concluded—Fresh Rupture between the Kings of France and England—Campaign under the Earl of Derby—Siege of Auberoche raised by the gallantry of Sir Walter Manny—Military Tactics at this period—Feudal Chivalry—Free Companions—English Bows and Bills—Italian Crossbowmen—French Infantry—Mercenaries, ... 1

CONTENTS.

CHAP. XVII.—Edward III. loses several of his adherents in the Low Countries—his Interest is espoused by Godfrey of Harcourt—Invasion of Gascony—Philip marches to the defence of Rouen, which is threatened by the English—Manœuvres of Edward, by which he accomplishes a passage across the Seine—He crosses the Somme—Battle of Cressy, ... 15

CHAP. XVIII.—Siege of Calais—War in Bretagne—Siege of Roche-d'Arien—Anxiety of the two Monarchs, Edward and Philip, to obtain the Alliance of the Flemings—The People of Flanders favourable to Edward, and their Earl to Philip—Attempt of Philip to raise the Siege of Calais—Its Surrender—Noble Conduct of Eustace de Saint Pierre, and five other Burgesses—they are ordered for Execution by him, but saved by the intercession of his Queen, Philippa—Measures of Edward for securing possession of Calais—Sir Emeric of Pavia treats with Sir Geoffrey Charny to betray the place to the French—his Treachery discovered—Sir Emeric delivers Sir Geoffrey to an Ambuscade of the English under Sir Walter Manny, by whom the French Party are defeated, and their Leader, Sir Geoffrey, taken Prisoner—Edward's treatment of the Prisoners—Pestilence rages in France and England—Submission of Godfrey of Harcourt to the French King—Death of Philip VI. 62

CHAP. XIX.—Accession of John the Good—Truce with England violated, but renewed—Intrigues of Charles King of Navarre—Charles assassinates the Constable of France, and extorts his pardon from the King—Edward and his son, the Black Prince, invade France—the Black Prince winters at Bourdeaux—King John assembles a large army, and marches into Poitou—Battle of Poitiers—King John taken Prisoner—his Reception by the Black Prince—Return of the Prince, with his Prisoner, to England, ... 91

CHAP. XX.—Consequences to France of the Battle of Poitiers—Disputes between the Dauphin and the States-General—Suppression of an Insurrection under Sir Godfrey Harcourt,—Siege of Rennes— Truce concluded—Capture of the Castle of Evreux by Sir William Granville—Escape of Charles of Navarre from Prison—he organises the Faction of the Navarrois—Insolence of Marcel, Provost of Paris—Insurrection of the Peasantry, called Jac querie—

CONTENTS.

	PAGE
Partial Success of the Regent against the English—Treaty for the ransom of King John—the states of France refuse to sanction this treaty, and Edward again invades France—Siege of Rheims—Peace of Bretigny—Death of King John, and Accession of the Dauphin Charles,	109
CHAP. XXI.—War in Normandy—Battle of Cocherel—War in Bretagne, between the adherents of De Montfort and De Blois—Battle of Aurai—Financial Difficulties of King Charles—Sumptuary Laws—Free Companions—Charles's Plan of removing them from France—their leader Du Guesclin marches upon Avignon, and exacts a Fine from the Pope—he next engages in a war against Don Pedro the Cruel, King of Castile, and drives him from his Kingdom—Pedro solicits assistance from the Black Prince, and is by him reinstated in his Dominions—Du Guesclin, having been taken Prisoner, is ransomed—Tax upon Chimneys, called Fouage, imposed in Gascony by the Black Prince—Unpopularity of this Tax,	135
CHAP. XXII.—Don Pedro of Castile taken prisoner, and assassinated by his brother Henry—Charles of France fosters the disaffections in Gascony—Mutual Preparations for War—The Earl of Pembroke wastes Poitou—he is enclosed by the French in the village of Puyrenon, and rescued by Sir John Chandos—Ineffectual attempt of Chandos to recover Saint Salvin—Skirmish at the Bridge of Lusac, in which Chandos is slain—Edward III. sends an army under his Son, John of Gaunt, to Calais—The Duke of Burgundy, son of the King of France, marches to oppose him, but, being unsuccessful, returns to Paris—Predatory expedition of Sir Robert Knolles—Adventure of a Knight in Knolles's army,	151
CHAP. XXIII.—Revolt of Limoges to the French—the Black Prince besieges and re-captures it—Death of the Black Prince—Bertrand du Guesclin made Constable of France—the Constable defeats the English at Pont Volant—Marriage of the Duke of Lancaster to a daughter of Don Pedro the Cruel, by which alliance Henry, the Reigning King of Castile, is rendered an enemy to England—Defeat of the English Fleet by the Spanish, off Rochelle—Rochelle delivered by the Mayor to the French—the Constable captures Poitiers—Thouars besieged, and surrenders to the French—King Charles drives the Count de Montfort from Bretagne, and declares his duchy	

forfeited to the French Crown—the Breton Lords rise in insurrection, and drive the French from their country—Death of the Constable du Guesclin, while besieging Chateauneuf de Randun—Charles of Navarre deprived of the Dominions he held in France—Horrible Death of Charles of Navarre—Death of Charles V., surnamed the Wise,... 177

CHAP. XXIV.—Accession of Charles VI., when only six years of age—Regency of the Duke of Anjou, who seizes the Treasures of Charles V., which he afterwards employs in advancing his own claim to the Crown of Sicily and Naples—An English army, under the Duke of Buckingham, sent to the assistance of the Duke of Bretagne, who promises to support them, but makes a Peace with France—Disorders in Flanders—Insurrection of the Ghentois, under Artavelde—The French espouse the part of the Earl of Flanders, and the English that of the Insurgents—Defeat of the Insurgents at Rosebecque—Marriage of Charles VI.—Expedition of the Bishop of Norwich—the Bishop worsted, and compelled to retreat to Calais—Expedition of the Duke of Anjou to establish his claims to the Throne of Naples—his Failure, and Death—Adventures of two Captains of Free Companions, Geoffrey Tête-noir and Amerigot Marcel—Unsuccessful Attempt of the Duke of Lancaster to conquer Castile—Wreck of a French Fleet assembled in the Harbour of Sluys for the Invasion of England—Arrest of Oliver de Clisson, Constable of France, by the Duke of Bretagne—his Imprisonment, and Ransom.. 201

CHAP. XXV.—Charles VI. takes the Government into his own hands—his choice of Counsellors—Attempt of Peter de Craon to assassinate Oliver de Clisson, Constable of France—the Assassin takes refuge in Bretagne, whose Duke, John de Montfort, had been privy to his design—King Charles, in marching towards Bretagne, to avenge himself upon the intended Murderer, is struck with Insanity, whereupon the Expedition is abandoned—Accident at a Masque, in which the King, during one of his lucid Intervals, performed a part—The Duke of Burgundy appointed Regent, in opposition to the claims of the Duke of Orleans—Burgundy drives Oliver de Clisson from Court, who retires to Bretagne, and engages in a war with De Montfort—Peace concluded between them

—Death of John de Montfort, Duke of Bretagne—Death of Oliver de Clisson—Administration of the Duke of Burgundy—Assistance afforded by France to the Scots—Expedition to protect Hungary from the Turks—the French and Hungarians defeated by the Sultan Bajazet near Nicopolis—Massacre of the Prisoners—State of France at the Close of the Fourteenth Century,...... 213

CHAP. XXVI.—Factions of Orleans and Burgundy—Threatened Rupture with England—The Duke of Orleans appointed Regent, and again deprived of that office—Death of Philip of Burgundy—John the Fearless succeeds him, and the Dissensions with Orleans continue—Reconciliation of the two Dukes—their hatred again bursts out—Murder of Orleans—Burgundy, who instigated this crime, obtains a full pardon, but, having gone to quell an Insurrection at Liege, the Doom of Treason is pronounced against him—Burgundy advances upon Paris—The Adherents of Burgundy termed Cabochins, those of Orleans Armagnacs—the Armagnacs obtain assistance from England—King Charles, during an Interval of his Malady, manifests the utmost indignation at this League with England, and marches in person against the Armagnacs—the French Nobles assemble in Paris, and compel the Armagnacs and Cabochins to be reconciled to each other—On an Insurrection of the Parisians, the Dauphin calls to his assistance, and re-organises, the Orleans Party—Burgundy retires from Paris, but is recalled by the Dauphin—On the approach of Burgundy, the Dauphin again invites the Armagnacs to join him—Charles, partially recovered, marches against Burgundy, and compels him to sign a Pacification—State of England—Conclusion,.. 260

GENERAL INDEX,.. 283

TALES OF A GRANDFATHER.

CHAPTER XVI.

Homage paid by Edward III. to Philip of France in the Cathedral of Amiens—Edward subdues Scotland, and resolves to assert his Claim (in right of his Mother) to the Crown of France, to which course he is incited by Robert of Artois, the exiled Minister of Philip—Edward obtains the consent of his Parliament for an Invasion of France, and sets sail—Naval Engagement at the entrance of the Harbour of Sluys, in which the English are victorious—Siege of Saint Omer—the Besiegers dispersed by a sally of the Defenders—Siege of Tournay—a Truce for one year concluded, and Edward returns to England—Prolongation of the Truce—Dispute concerning the Succession to the Dukedom of Bretagne—The French King espouses the part of Charles of Blois, who had been dispossessed of the Duchy by John de Montfort—De Montfort taken, and imprisoned—the masculine Courage of his Countess—she holds out Hennebon against Charles of Blois and his French Auxiliaries—English Succours, under Sir Walter Manny, thrown into the Town, by whose gallantry the Siege is raised—Prosecution of the War—Hennebon again besieged, and the Siege again raised—a Truce concluded—Renewal of the War—Edward himself takes the Field, and is opposed by John, the son of Philip—Truce concluded—Fresh Rupture between the Kings of France and England—Campaign under the Earl of Derby—Siege of Auberoche raised by the gal-

luntry of Sir Walter Manny—Military Tactics at this period—Feudal Chivalry—Free Companions—English Bows and Bills—Italian Crossbowmen—French Infantry—Mercenaries.

[1327-1342.]

ALTHOUGH the States of France had formally recognised the right of inheritance of Philip de Valois, yet Edward III., the young King of England, was far from acquiescing in a decision that deprived him of a succession, which, in every other kingdom but France, would have made him unquestioned heir to his maternal uncle, Charles the Fair.

Edward was young, brave, ambitious, full of talent, and at the head of a mighty nation Yet, even in early youth, he was capable of listening to prudent counsel; and he felt that, considering the revolutions which England had lately undergone—considering his own bondage, as it might be termed, under the guardianship of his mother and her favourite, Mortimer—considering also the unanimity of France under the present King, this was not a time to prefer a claim so important, and which must be followed by inevitable war. His decision was hurried by a summons from the King of France, requiring him to appear and do homage for the dukedom of Aquitaine, the neglect of which requisition must have instantly been followed by a declaration of forfeiture, which Edward was as yet in no condition to provoke. He therefore resolved to yield obedience to the summons for the present. - But, to avoid the inference, that, by rendering this homage for his French possessions, he acknowledged the right of Philip of Valois as King of France, King Edward, in his own secret council, entered a solemn protest, that such homage as he should at this time pay to Philip should not prejudice his own hereditary right to the kingdom of France, in virtue of his mother, Isabella. Under this private protestation, Edward went to France with a noble train of knights and peers, where Philip met him with an attendance and retinue suited to the occasion, to receive the homage which the other came to pay. It may be well supposed, that every ceremony applicable to the rendering of such fealty was nicely disputed between such august personages. The meeting of the Sovereigns was in the cathedral of Amiens. The English King appeared clad in a robe of crimson velvet, embroidered with leopards of gold. He wore a royal crown on his head, was girt with his sword, and had his golden spurs buckled upon his heels. The King of France received him seated in a chair, before which a cushion was laid for the King of England to kneel upon. As he refused that act of humiliation, the Grand Chamberlain of France insisted, not only that that posture should be adopted, but that the King of England should lay aside the regal ornaments, and that the homage should be rendered by him kneeling, bare-headed, without sword and girdle, and without spurs. Edward was extremely angry at being compelled to divest himself, in such an assembly, of the usual marks of his rank. He was, however, obliged to do so; and it is probable his hatred to

Philip of Valois was greatly increased by his being subjected to this public affront.

This unpleasing ceremony being performed, and the English possessions in France so far secured, Edward returned to England, where he dispossessed his mother and her lover, Mortimer, of the administration, and took the government of the kingdom into his own hands.

This revolution effected, the young King, perceiving Scotland deprived by death of her heroic deliverer, Robert Bruce, and of his great captains, Randolph, Douglas, and others, thought the time opportune for renewing his grandfather's and father's attempts upon the liberty of that nation. With this purpose, he invaded that country—first, by means of the disinherited Barons, as the English lords were called (lords, that is, who had lost estates in Scotland, granted to them by Edward I. and II.), and afterwards by his own royal armies —and soon reduced the Scots to nearly the same state of reluctant subjection which they experienced in the time of his grandfather Edward I.

As, however, the natives of the north continued to show the same indomitable opposition to the English yoke; as the young King and Queen of that nation had found refuge in France, when there was no corner of safety left for them in their own country; as French money, and even French troops, were sent at different times to keep up the spirits of the Scottish insurgents, Edward, now in nearly complete possession of the island of Britain, began to meditate the assertion of his own claim of inheritance upon France, that so he might put an end at once, and for ever, to the troublesome interference of that powerful nation, in his Scottish wars.

To this resolution the King of England was urged by the counsels of a hot-tempered and disappointed man, who fled about this time from the court of France to that of England. This was no other than Robert, Count of Artois, a high prince of the blood, and an especial counsellor, till this period, of Philip of Valois. This nobleman was grandson to a Robert Count of Artois, slain at the battle of Courtray, after having had a son, named Philip, who died before him. The slaughtered Count left a daughter named Matilda, besides this Robert of Artois, son of Philip, who was entitled, as male-heir, to the succession of his grandfather. But Matilda, the daughter of the elder Count Robert, being married to Otho of Burgundy, and two daughters, whom she had by that marriage, being married to two sons of Philip the Fair, that King of France adjudged the county of Artois to the heir-female, which was confirmed by a judgment of Philip the Long. In this decision the Salic Law was set aside, it being alleged that the peculiar customs of inheritance, observed from time immemorial in Artois, did not permit its application.

By these judgments, Robert of Artois, the grandson, conceived himself highly injured, and began to employ his political sagacity in the way which he thought most likely to favour his own interest in

the county of Artois. In the debate concerning
the succession, upon the death of Charles the Fair,
Robert of Artois declared zealously for the party
of Philip of Valois, both because Philip's right,
being that of an heir male, favoured his own claim
upon the county of Artois, and because he was himself
brother-in-law and friend of the claimant.

Philip, who was greatly indebted to this prince
for smoothing his access to the crown, by his important
services and eloquent representations,
received him into his highest favour, conferred
upon him the earldom of Beaumont le Roger,
and consulted him in almost all important business
which he had to transact, until Robert, thus
distinguished, begun to think the period was favourable
for again trying the question respecting
the succession of his grandfather, no longer indeed
with his aunt Matilda, who was dead, but with her
successors. After obtaining, therefore, many marks
of the King's favour and confidence, he was so secure
of his interest, as to propose to Philip of Valois,
to review and alter the decisions of his predecessors,
Philip the Fair and Philip the Long, which
took from Robert the county of Artois. The King
eluded his minister's request, by replying, that he
had no power to disturb the decisions of his predecessors,
and that Robert ought to remain satisfied
with such possessions as he had obtained from the
kindness of the King. This refusal drove D'Artois
to still more unlawful expedients, to obtain the end
on which he had determined. He forged, or
caused to be forged, a testament of his grandfather,

settling the county of Artois in his favour, and produced it to the King, as a document affording sufficient room for reviewing and recalling the judgments of which he complained. Philip of Valois, looking upon the deed produced, of which he instantly recognised the falsehood, sternly exhorted his minister to desist from a pursuit so unjust, and to beware how he prejudiced his own honour, and insulted his sovereign, by claiming faith for forged deeds. Robert of Artois replied with fury, that he would support the truth of the testament with his lance in the lists, against whosoever impugned it. The King, highly offended at a defiance in which he thought his own person was included, answered sternly, "I will impugn it, and will know how to punish the fabricator."

The King and his minister parted in great displeasure on both sides, and Robert of Artois was heard to drop these dangerous words :—" He who placed the crown upon Philip's head, knows how to deprive him of it again."

This imprudent speech being reported to Philip, he published a sentence against his late minister, condemning him for forgery; declaring him degraded from his honours, banishing him from France, and pronouncing his property confiscated. At the same time, a female of the house of Bethune was burnt alive, as the actual forger of the testament in question, and as guilty also of sorcery. By this usage, in which, perhaps, the King, in forgetting former services, followed the dictates of offended dignity farther than prudence would have

counselled, Robert of Artois was driven to despair.
Philip's displeasure even extended to the exile's
wife, whom he imprisoned, although she was his
own sister; and he showed similar rancour, by
interfering to prevent Robert from finding refuge
in Brabant, where his friends were prohibited from
protecting him, under pain of the King of France's
vengeance. This inflexible severity drove the
exiled statesman to seek refuge with Edward,
who was Philip's most formidable enemy, both
from situation, and recollection of the scene of
homage which he had been constrained to perform
at Amiens.

In the year 1337, Robert of Artois fled to England in disguise, and being a near relation of Edward, received there welcome
and protection; and, from his character for policy,
speedily found the road to the King's ear. He
employed his influence, which soon became great,
to persuade Edward of the practicability of asserting his title to the crown of France in right of his
mother. Edward, flattered by the prospects displayed by so sagacious a counsellor, resolved upon
a war with France, founded on the sweeping and
general assertion, that he himself was the lawful
heir of that kingdom, in despite of the Salic law
on which Philip reposed his right.

Availing himself of the wealth which his subjects readily placed at their King's command, in a
point where their sense of national glory was so
strongly interested, Edward commenced, at very
great expense, to form a confederacy with the

Emperor, Louis of Bavaria, the Dukes of Brabant and Gueldres, the Archbishop of Cologne, and other petty princes of the Low Countries, for the formation of an army which should support the title which he intended to assume as King of France. For the levying and keeping on foot this army, he engaged to pay large subsidies to the Princes of the confederacy.

Edward III., however, experienced what has been since often felt, that it is easier for England, by her wealth, to induce continental powers to take up arms in her behalf, than to inspire them with vigour and spirit in an enterprise to which money alone had induced them to accede. Philip took the field, with an army of one hundred thousand men, to face this gathering storm, but cautiously avoided a combat, in which a defeat might have cost him his throne; and the allied princes trimmed, shuffled, procrastinated, and delayed assembling their forces, till the summer passed away without any remarkable event. In the spring, 1340, Edward returned to hold his par- _{A.D. 1340.} liament, which was called chiefly for the purpose of requiring new subsidies from his subjects, having exhausted those formerly granted among his allies to little purpose. His parliament were, however, complaisant; and, having settled his affairs at home, the King resolved to return to the Continent, although the French fleet, amounting to four hundred sail, with forty thousand men on board, who had been already troublesome to the English coasts and commerce, were prepared, by their master's order, to intercept Edward upon the sea.

These vessels were hired from the republic of Genoa, and manned with mariners from that state.

A.D. 1340. On 22d June, 1340, the King of England set sail with two hundred and sixty vessels, well manned with archers and men-at-arms. Other vessels conveyed English ladies and gentlewomen, who went over to pay their respects to the Queen, whom Edward had left behind him in Flanders as a pledge of his return. When the English approached the harbour of Sluys, which they had fixed for disembarkation, they beheld it occupied by so many vessels, that their masts and streamers seemed like a great wood. The King demanded of the master of his vessel, "what he conceived this navy to be."—"They are," answered the master, "ships fitted out by the French King to despoil your Majesty's coasts, and interrupt your commerce. They have already done you, in this way, much harm; and now, if they may, it is their object to take your person."—"Ha!" said the King, "I have long desired to meet them, and now I will make them dearly abye the displeasures they have done to me." Acting as admiral in person, the King commanded his fleet to cast anchor for the night.

On the next morning, having arranged the vessels bearing the ladies at such a distance that they might see the conflict without danger, Edward, with his ships of war, held a course in moving towards the fight which was calculated to gain the wind of the enemy, in which manœuvre he succeeded. This conduct also seemed to the French to evince timidity on the part of Edward, and induced them to leave the harbour to attack the English fleet,—another object which the King of England had in view. The battle commenced at ten in the morning, and lasted nine long hours, during which the Genoese sailors, by whom the French ships were manned, plied the English with their crossbows, to which the English replied with the long-bow, a much more effective weapon, and which had been a favourite in England ever since the Norman Conquest. When the missiles on each side were expended, the ships approached close to each other, and grappled or secured themselves to their opponents by means of iron chains or hooks, by which the contending vessels were held together. The men-at-arms on both sides thus fought on the decks hand to hand, with their swords and axes, as if on shore. The English, animated by the presence and example of Edward, obtained at length, after a bloody battle, a most complete victory, the first distinguished naval success of England, which has since gained so many. In consequence of which, the whole French navy being taken, dispersed, or destroyed, King Edward achieved his landing with all glory and victory; and the splendour of his conquest induced his allies to show an activity which they had not yet manifested. The King, in conjunction with them, formed the siege of Tournay, a strong town, which was valiantly defended by the assistance of a French garrison.

At this time the country of Flanders was divided betwixt two factions. The earl of that country adhered faithfully to King Philip, whose vassal he was, and was followed by the nobles and gentry. But the towns of Flanders were at all times inhabited by a mutinous body of citizens, manufacturers, and the like, who were not disposed to submit to the Earl or his nobility, and were often engaged in actual rebellion against him, and in insurrection against his dependent nobles. A brewer, of the name of Van Artavelde, had raised himself to the rank of a principal demagogue among these artisans, and, holding a close intercourse with Edward III was of course hostile to the French party, which had been embraced by the Earl.

An army of these insurgent Flemings, amounting in number to forty thousand men, with the auxiliary aid of five thousand English archers, took the field under Robert of Artois, who, acting as the commander of this second and somewhat tumultuary army, laid siege to Saint Omer, while the more regular part of the allied troops besieged Tournay. Saint Omer, however, was well defended; and in an attack upon the suburbs of the place, the besieged made a strong sally upon the Flemings while in disorder, slew about three or four thousand men, and impressed upon the rest a panic terror, which manifested itself in an extraordinary way that very night. About midnight, there fell upon the undisciplined besiegers a strange consternation, and groundless fear, which impelled them to cut down their tents and pavilions, and fly from before the place. Their leaders in vain endeavoured to argue with them, asking, " Why they fled? whom they feared?" and such like questions, to which the Flemings made no answer, but dispersed themselves in confusion, never again to be assembled as an army.

One part of King Edward's plan for the campaign was frustrated by this singular accident; nor was the siege at Tournay more successful, though it was more regularly conducted, and more honourably raised, than that of Saint Omer. King Edward maintained the siege of the former place for nine weeks and upwards, still hoping that he might be able to compel Philip, who lay with a royal army within three or four leagues of the place, to hazard a battle for its relief.

In this, however, he failed. In consequence of which disappointment, and scarcely knowing in what way to bring the war to an end, Edward despatched a personal challenge, defying King Philip to let the controversy be decided either by the Kings themselves in single fight, or by a hundred champions on each side. Philip had too much wisdom to accept of this defiance. He returned for answer, that a King accepted not a challenge from a vassal, and upbraided Edward with being perjured after the oath which he had taken when he paid him homage at Amiens.

The German and Dutch confederates of England were again becoming weary of the war, which was marked by so little good fortune; and, what may be considered as a simultaneous occurrence, Edward's means of continuing the subsidies to these venal allies were gradually diminishing.

When matters were in this critical posture before Tournay, the Pope and his cardinals urged strongly the necessity of peace betwixt the two Christian monarchs, the most powerful in Europe, in order that they might engage in a joint effort against the infidels. This gave an apology, at least, to Edward's pride, for entering into terms. Robert, King of Sicily, was equally anxious in the same cause of mediation; but especially the Lady Jane of Valois, Countess Dowager of Hainault, mother-in-law to the King of England, and sister to Philip of France, did her utmost, by affectionate remonstrances and judicious arguments, to prevail upon the contending monarchs to negotiate for a truce. This was concluded in September, 1340, to continue for one year, and affording, it was supposed, sufficient leisure for adjusting a definitive peace.

A.D. 1340.

Edward returned to England in very bad humour, deserted by his mercenary confederates, and convinced that he himself was mistaken in supposing he could conquer France by the aid of princes, who, one by one (the Emperor himself not excepted), made peace with his enemy when the subsidies of England failed. On the other hand, notwithstanding his loss in the great sea action, Philip of France carried away all the advantages of the campaign. He had saved Tournay from ruin, and obliged the King of England, who had threatened to dethrone him, to retreat from his dominions without having been able to gain so much as a single village of France, and was therefore, undoubtedly, in every sense, possessed of the effective fruits of victory.

The truce, of course, terminated the war for the present; but still the ground of mortal quarrel remained betwixt the two countries, rankled deep in each, and afforded a ready pretence for either nation, when they should again choose to take up arms. Neither could a more solid peace between the crowns be now achieved, although Edward required nothing more than a release from the rendering of homage for Gascony; a condition greatly short of his original high pretensions. The truce, therefore, was prolonged for another year, as the only way of avoiding the revival of a war which endangered Christendom. Thus stood matters, when an unexpected event took place, which revived Edward's hopes of obtaining possession of the crown of France, much abated as they had been by the event of the late unsatisfactory campaigns. This was a dispute concerning the succession of the Duke of Bretagne, which originated as follows.

Arthur, the second duke, had, by his first wife three sons, John, Guy, and Peter; by his second wife he left one son, named John de Montfort, being the title of his mother's family. At his death, Duke Arthur was succeeded by his eldest son, John III. This prince died 30th April, 1341, without issue; Guy, the second son of Duke Ar-

thur, had been dead about ten years before, leaving
one daughter, Jane, who, by desire of her uncle,
was married to Charles de Blois, nephew to the
King of France. During Duke Arthur's lifetime
and reign, Peter, the third son of that prince, had
died young and childless, while the aforesaid John
de Montfort, son of Arthur, by his second wife,
was still alive. Thus standing the succession, Duke
John III. had prevailed upon the States of Bretagne to recognise the right of his niece, Jane, and
her husband, Charles de Blois, as his presumptive
heir and successor in the duchy, in preference to
John de Montfort, who was unquestionably the
heir-male, and had, as such, a considerable party
among the Bretons. This expression of the Duke's
will met with no direct opposition. But upon the
death of Duke John III., the Earl de Montfort determined to dispute the destination in which he
had hitherto acquiesced. He entered into a close
correspondence with Edward III., and easily prevailed upon him to forward his pretensions to the
dukedom of Bretagne, agreeing, at the same time,
to assert those of Edward to the kingdom of France.
De Montfort seized on the treasure of the deceased
Duke, gained possession of Nantes, and several
other towns of Bretagne, and made every effort to
support his claim. To draw his connexion with
England still closer, he visited that country, made
a formal alliance with its sovereign, and did homage
to Edward as King of France, for the dukedom of
Bretagne.

These proceedings gave great and natural offence to the King of France, who, upon the complaint of Charles of Blois, summoned De Montfort to appear before his Parliament of Paris. The Earl, somewhat incautiously, obeyed the summons; but, finding himself charged with the feudal offence of acknowledging Edward as his superior, and commanded to remain in the city of Paris for fifteen days, he became alarmed, and returned privately into Bretagne, before the French King knew of his departure.

The Parliament of Paris proceeded, in the absence of the Count de Montfort, to adjudge the duchy to Charles of Blois and his wife, as legal heirs to the deceased Duke, adding, at the same time, that De Montfort, even had he ever possessed an interest in the fief, had forfeited it, both by doing homage to the King of England, and by breach of his arrest, contrary to King Philip's orders.

The King of France, at the same time, commanded his eldest son, the Duke of Normandy, to assist Charles of Blois in regaining possession of those towns in Bretagne which De Montfort had taken and garrisoned. A vigorous effort was instantly made for the recovery of Bretagne, and Charles of Blois, by the assistance of a French army, in which a distinguished warrior, called Louis de la Cerda, more commonly Louis of Spain, acted as marshal of the host, had the good fortune to retake the capital of Nantes, in which De Montfort himself was made prisoner. He was sent to Paris, and imprisoned in the Louvre, where he long remained, entirely lost to his party. In most cases, therefore, the war would have been at an end ere it was well begun; and the scheme of Edward to obtain access to France, by the way of Bretagne, must have been totally frustrated. This was, however, prevented, by the masculine courage of the Countess Jane de Montfort, wife of the imprisoned Earl, and sister to the Earl of Flanders.

This lady, who, says Froissart, " had the courage of a man and the heart of a lion," being in the city of Rennes when her lord was taken, scorned to yield to the grief with which that event oppressed her; but, assembling her friends, presented to them her young son, John, as successor to his rights, who, by the grace of God, should be the means of restoring his father unto his family and friends. She undertook also to pay the soldiers regularly, and inspired a spirit of resistance into her party, which, but for her exertions, would have been utterly extinguished by her husband's misfortune.

Notwithstanding the resistance of the Countess, Rennes was yielded to Charles of Blois, and there seemed little chance of any effectual stand being made, till she threw herself into Hennebon, a strong town in Bretagne, situated on the sea-coast, in which she was accompanied by the flower of her partisans, and where she prepared for a gallant defence. She herself wore armour, and rode through the streets on a mettled charger, exhorting the citizens to resistance. Her women were not excepted from martial labour, for she caused them to cut short their gowns, that they might be more active, and carry stones and other missiles to the walls to make good the defence.

The French having attempted to carry the town, by a general assault upon one side, the Countess made a sally on the other, and set fire to the Frenchmen's camp, while they were engaged in the assault; and upon this and other occasions did great damage to the besiegers. Notwithstanding this, and the valour and military skill which she displayed in making good the defence, the town suffered severely in the progress of the siege. The walls were so much shattered by the engines, that the Bishop of Léon, who visited the place in person, as a friend of Charles of Blois, pressed the conductors of the defence very much to come to terms with the besiegers. His arguments, and the desperate condition of the place, made considerable impression upon several of its defenders. The valiant Countess now became alarmed for the defection of her followers, and piteously entreated them to hold out, were it but for the space of three days only, during which time she asserted she was certain that the town would be relieved. Nevertheless, on the second day the Breton lords of her party again met in council with the Bishop of Léon, adjusting terms for the capitulation of Hennebon; and Charles of Blois, who was with the besiegers in person, had approached the walls with a strong party, to be in readiness to take possession of the place.

At this critical moment, the valiant Countess, in a state wellnigh approaching to despair, cast an

almost hopeless glance upon the sea, from a lofty
window of the castle, when, what was her joy to
discover the horizon covered with the masts of a
large squadron steering towards Hennebon. She
exclaimed joyfully, "The Red Cross! the Red
Cross! the succours of England are in sight!"

The Breton lords speedily changed their purpose
of surrender, and dismissed the Bishop of Léon, to
whom they were formerly disposed to listen, while
Charles of Blois, incensed at his disappointment,
approached to the walls the greatest engine the besiegers
had in their camp. The English, who had
been forty days delayed on the sea by contrary
winds, now landed at Hennebon. They formed
a small army, commanded by Sir Walter Manny,
a Flemish lord in the service of King Edward, and
one of the most renowned warriors of that period.
The very next day after his arrival, he expressed
his wish to come to action. "I have a great desire,"
he said, "to issue from the town, and to break down
yonder great engine, which they have brought so
near us." The Breton lords within the place
gladly assented. They burst forth from the gates,
broke the engine to pieces, and pursued those who
guarded it to the camp of the besiegers. The host
of the French now began to get under arms, to
protect the fugitives; and Sir Walter, seeing their
main body advancing, turned against them, with
the chivalrous protestation, "May I never be beloved
of my lady, if I refuse to break a lance with
these pursuers!" He turned accordingly, and
many a knight was unhorsed, and deed of arms

done. With prudence equal to his valour, Sir Walter Manny, after a gallant skirmish, drew off his forces under cover of the ditches, which were lined with English archers, and returned to Hennebon, where the Countess de Montfort, as we are informed by the chronicle, kissed him and his brave companions twice or thrice, like a valiant lady. The siege of Hennebon was accordingly raised.

A.D. 1342.

Many skirmishes were fought, in which the English courage, and the excellence of their archers, gained an ascendency, which was exceedingly mortifying to Charles of Blois, and to Don Louis of Spain, who acted as marshal of his army.

The latter was a general of great courage and conduct, but nevertheless was tinged with the vindictive and cruel temper which was supposed peculiar to the Spanish nation. Moving along the coast of Bretagne with a strong force of Spaniards and Genoese, he destroyed a seaport town, called Guerande, where he spared neither man, woman, nor child. Taking shipping at this place, Don Louis reached Quimperlé, another haven, where he landed, and, burning, sacking, and destroying the whole surrounding country, collected a great spoil. But while he was thus engaged, Sir Walter Manny, who had put to sea in pursuit of him, arrived at Quimperlé, with three thousand English archers, and a sufficient number of men-at-arms. The English instantly seized upon the French ships and booty, which remained unprotected in the port of Quimperlé, while Don Louis himself, with his soldiers, continued to ravage the neighbourhood; and Sir Walter Manny, landing with his forces, set off in pursuit of his enemy. They met, and engaged with fury. The English archers displayed their usual superiority. Don Alphonso, the nephew of Don Louis, was killed on the spot; the Genoese and Spaniards dispersed themselves, and were destroyed by the Bretons, as they fled in different directions. Don Louis, much wounded, with great difficulty made his escape in a swift-sailing skiff, which held only a few of his followers.

Notwithstanding these successes on the part of the Countess de Montfort and her auxiliaries, the forces of Charles of Blois daily increased; and it became obvious, that although the troops of Sir Walter Manny were sufficient to deliver the Countess, and to protect her person, yet more numerous and effectual succours were necessary for obtaining success in her undertaking, and maintaining Bretagne against the power of France. Charles of Blois had succeeded in taking the important towns of Vannes and Karhuis, and had resolved again to attack Hennebon, which might be considered as the principal seat of the war, since the Countess and her son resided there, secure in the strength of the place, which was protected by strong trenches, to which the sea was admitted, and no less secure in the valour of Sir Walter Manny, and the English auxiliary forces.

Determined, therefore, to renew the siege, Charles of Blois and Don Louis of Spain reared up against Hennebon sixteen engines of the largest size, with which they cast great stones into the place, and ruined the walls and defences. The besieged, however, strengthened their defences with a great number of woolpacks, which broke the force of the stones; this encouraged the Countess and her auxiliaries so much, that they upbraided the besiegers by calling from the walls, " Why bring you not up the troops whom you carried from hence to Quimperlé?" This insult was particularly directed against Louis of Spain, whose pride was highly offended at being thus reminded of his shameful defeat, the loss of his army, his own wounds and flight, and the death of a beloved nephew. He chose a mode of revenge which accorded ill with the honourable sentiments by which men of his rank were then expected to guide themselves.

Passing to the tent of Charles of Blois, Louis of Spain desired of him a boon, in requital of all the service which he had done him; this was readily granted. When his request came to be explained, he demanded the persons of two gallant English knights, who had been made prisoners, when wounded, that he might do with them according to his pleasure; declaring at the same time that, in revenge of the insults of the people of Hennebon, and of the defeats he had suffered from the English, it was his purpose to strike off the heads of the prisoners within sight of the walls. Charles of Blois, who was a courteous and accomplished knight, answered the Spaniard that his boon should be readily granted, were it not asked for a purpose which would dishonour Don Louis himself, and occasion the English generals to use retaliation on the prisoners of their party. Don Louis to this expostulation sullenly replied, that if Charles did not grant him the boon he required, he would instantly renounce both his cause and his company. Charles of Blois, unable to dispense with the Spaniard's services, thought himself obliged to deliver up the two English prisoners, who were named Sir John Butler and Sir Matthew Trelawney, to be used as Don Louis pleased. Nor could any entreaty of those around divert the Spaniard from his savage and unknightly resolution of having them publicly executed shortly after dinner upon the same day.

Sir Walter Manny, being informed of the imminent danger in which the two valiant knights stood, addressed his followers thus:—" Great honour were it to us should we able to save the lives of yonder knights; and even the attempt, though unsuccessful, will be praised by our good King Edward, and by all men of worth who shall hear thereof." With this resolution, which was adopted with acclamation by all who heard the proposal, the greater part of the garrison, being six thousand archers, and three hundred men-at-arms, under the command of a gallant Breton knight, Sir Aymery of Clisson, sallied forth suddenly, and with great vigour, against the camp of the French, which they furiously assailed. The besiegers immediately took to arms, and the battle became very hot. In the mean time, Sir Walter Manny, taking a hundred men-at-arms and five hundred archers, whom he had reserved for the purpose, and sallying from a private postern, fetched a circuit, and fell upon the camp of the enemy, in a quarter where he met so little opposition, that he penetrated to the tent where the two knights were confined. Here he found them bound, and prepared for instant execution. He cut their bonds, mounted them on horseback, and carried them off in triumph, thus delivering them from the destiny allotted to them by Louis of Spain.

After sustaining this insult, Charles of Blois and his party, finding no chance of possessing themselves of Hennebon, raised the siege, and withdrew, after having established a truce with the Countess de Montfort, which was to endure to the 15th of May following, when the weather would permit the campaign to be opened anew.

In the winter season the heroic Countess herself, with some of her principal partisans, made a visit to England, where she kept her Christmas in high state, honoured by all, as became her courage and celebrity.

Early next year, an auxiliary army was raised in England for the service of Bretagne, and Robert of Artois, already mentioned, was appointed its commander. He put to sea about A.D. 1343. the middle of May, in which month the truce with Charles of Blois expired. The noble Countess de Montfort returned to Bretagne with the same armament. Near Guernsey they fell in with the fleet of France, commanded by Don Louis of Spain, often already mentioned, and a brave leader as well on sea as on land. Both parties encountered with mutual animosity, the Countess de Montfort keeping the deck of her vessel with a drawn sword in her hand, like the knights and men-at-arms on both sides. The engagement was very fierce, being on the one side maintained by the crossbowmen of Genoa, and on the other by the English archers, both renowned for their skill in their weapons; but the fleets were parted by a storm, without the battle being decided for either party.

When Robert of Artois arrived in Bretagne with his forces, which were rather select than numerous, he made his first attack upon the strong city of Vannes, which he took by surprise. The success of the English in this enterprise induced their leaders to divide their forces. One party went to Hennebon, with the Countess de Montfort and Sir Walter Manny; another, under the Earls of Salisbury and Pembroke, laid siege to the city of Rennes, and Robert of Artois was left, with very inferior forces, in possession of Vannes, his late acquisition. Here he was suddenly surrounded by twelve thousand French, assembled for the purpose of overpowering him. The besiegers, being at the same time afraid that they might themselves be attacked by the English, who lay before Rennes, made a sudden and desperate attack on the city of Vannes, and took it by storm. Robert d'Artois was much wounded, and narrowly escaped to Hennebon. From thence he took shipping for England; but being detained upon the sea, his wounds rankled, and he died shortly after arriving in London. Thus perished that unfortunate exile, whose personal resentment and vindictive counsel had been so immediately the occasion of this bloody war. Even his death appeared to be the means of exasperating it. Edward III., who loved Robert d'Artois, and considered him as a martyr in his cause, swore he would not rest till he had revenged his death, and for that purpose he would lead an army in person into Bretagne. He kept his oath accordingly, and arrived in that province with considerable forces in October 1343.

Philip of Valois now saw the necessity of making a great exertion. He commissioned his son, John Duke of Normandy, to levy as strong a force as possible, and drive the English from Bretagne. Accordingly, this young prince raised an army, amounting to more than forty thousand men, greatly superior, of course, to that of the English which had been sent thither under Robert d'Artois, even when united with the force under Edward himself. A battle might have been expected between two such considerable armies; and such a crisis seemed, indeed, to be actually approaching. King Edward encamped his force, now assembled into one body, before the city of Vannes, and the Duke of Normandy approached the same town upon the other side, with a view to raise the siege: but both armies were in a state of such difficulty as prevented their acting with effect. The English could not prudently make any attempt upon Vannes in presence of the French host; while, on the other hand, the French army, though more numerous, dared not assault the English, secured as they were by their strong intrenchments. Thus the armies lay fronting each other, both sufficiently distressed for want of provisions. Little passed but skirmishing. At length the contending princes became inclined to listen to the arguments of two cardinals, sent by the Pope to mediate a pacification between France and England, if such were possible. These eminent churchmen laboured so effectually, that, in 1343, a truce was concluded between King Edward and the Duke of Normandy, in the name of his father. France was therefore, for the present, relieved from the presence of the English armies and their warlike monarch; but the quarrel was too much embittered to permit of a speedy settlement.

A.D. 1343.

It was not long before both Kings accused each other of breach of the agreement, and of actions inconsistent with the truce. King Philip of Valois gave particular occasion to the charge, by putting to death certain Breton lords who had embraced the party of De Montfort, and who had fallen into his hands during the war, as well as others whom he considered as intriguing with Edward, though they had hitherto preserved the external appearance of French subjects. Among these was Oliver de Clisson, a brave, powerful, and popular noble, the father of the celebrated constable of France, of the same name, who was afterwards so staunch an adherent of the opposite party. On the other hand, the French King complained that

A.D. 1344.

King Edward kept on foot his party in Bretagne by all manner of indirect intrigues. In short, both monarchs expressed themselves deeply offended with each other, and desirous of renewing the war as soon as convenient.

The English parliament, although the French war entailed on the nation a burdensome and useless expense, entered nevertheless warmly into the passions of Edward, advised him to prosecute the war with vigour, and granted him large subsidies to enable him to do so. The King, thus encouraged by his subjects, sent in 1344 a small army into Guienne, of great part of which province, it must be remembered, the English were still possessed; and also in the same year despatched reinforcements to the party of De Montfort in Bretagne, where very many of the Bretons themselves, highly incensed against the French for the cruel execution of several of their nobles, were in arms for the Countess de Montfort. The English troops sent to Guienne were placed under the command of the King's near kinsman, Henry of Lancaster, Earl of Derby. By the good management of this gallant chief, the English army took various towns in the south of France, and defeated the French army under the Count de l'Isle, an excellent general.

The circumstances of this last action were somewhat extraordinary. A strong castle in Gascony, called Auberoche, had been taken by the English, and three knights of their party were stationed there with a garrison, for the defence of the place.

A.D. 1344

The Count de l'Isle, who had hitherto been outshone in activity and adventure by the Earl of Derby, now thought of recovering his reputation by regaining this place of Auberoche. He conceived he should be able to achieve this by such a rapid concentration of his forces, as would enable him to carry the castle, before the Earl of Derby, who was lying at Bourdeaux, could entertain any suspicion of his purpose. He summoned therefore around him all the vassals within reach, who owned the authority of the King of France, and having thus assembled a considerable army, suddenly laid siege to Auberoche, where the small English garrison was totally unprovided with means of defence. The Frenchmen brought with them, to the attack of the place, four very powerful engines, which they employed day and night in casting such huge stones as broke down the battlements, and shattered the roofs of the castle so much, that the garrison were compelled to shelter themselves in the vaults and cellars. The besieged knights saw no chance of escape or relief, unless they could communicate their hard case to the Earl of Derby, then lying at Bourdeaux, and request him to advance to their deliverance.

One of their attendants undertook this perilous task, and, in the character of a Gascon peasant, attempted to pass through the camp of the enemy; he was discovered, however, and seized. The letter of the besieged knights to the Earl of Derby which the captive messenger bore, informed the besiegers of the straits in which the garrison was placed; and, in order to make the besieged aware that their messenger had been intercepted, the French cruelly put the poor fellow upon one of their engines, and cast him into the town, accompanied with the insulting taunt, " Ask your messenger, sirs, where he found the Earl of Derby, since he went out but last night, and is returned again so shortly."

Frank de la Halle, a gallant German, and a faithful follower of Edward III., who was one of those within the castle, answered boldly, " Sirs, though we be enclosed here, we shall issue when it pleases God; and as to the Earl of Derby, if you will let us send a message to him touching our condition, there is not one of you will keep the field till his coming."—" Nay," answered the besiegers, " this shall not serve your turn; it will be time enough for the Earl of Derby to know of your condition when the castle is rendered."— " That it shall never be!" answered Frank de la Halle; " we will rather die under its ruins."

All these proceedings before Auberoche were conveyed to the Earl of Derby by a spy, whom that nobleman had in the French camp. So soon as he received news of the distress of the besieged, he assembled his troops, and sent to the Earl of Pembroke, then at Bergerac with a still larger force, to join him upon his march towards Auberoche. In the mean time, he himself instantly set forth, accompanied by the Earl of Oxford, Sir Walter Manny, Lord Ferrars, Sir Richard Hastings, and other good knights, though having with

them few followers. They tarried for some hours
at a village called Lyborne, to abide for the Earl
of Pembroke, who did not appear. On the suc-
ceeding evening they left the village, and, riding
all night, were within two leagues of Auberoche
in the dawning. Here they lighted from their
horses, and made a halt till it was noon, still hoping for the Earl of Pembroke's junction. He came
not, however; and the English were now obliged
to consider whether they should venture to prosecute their enterprise with their own slender force.
They were only three hundred spears, and about
six hundred archers, while the army of the French
lying before Auberoche amounted to ten or twelve
thousand men. The determination was not easy,
for, while the gallant knights felt the shame of
abandoning their companions at Auberoche, it
seemed rash to go on at such a disadvantage. "In
the name of God," said Sir Walter Manny at
length, "let us direct our march upon Auberoche,
under cover of this wood, which we may skirt
without being descried, till we come upon the rear
of the French, where we are divided from them by
open ground, and then take the advantage of a
sudden and unexpected attack."

To this the valiant knights present readily agreed,
and the men-at-arms continued their march towards
Auberoche, till they reached a small valley, where
the Frenchmen lay encamped,—none of them thinking of an enemy, and most of them busied with
their supper. The English men-at-arms then issued from the wood having gained the rear of the

besiegers, displayed their banners and pennons, dashed their spurs into their horses, and rushed upon the enemy, crying their war-shout of "A Derby! a Derby!"

The sudden surprise compensated for the inferiority of numbers; and such French knights and men-at-arms as could prepare for battle on the spur of the moment, found themselves exposed to the shot of the English archers, who were placed ready for that service. The Comte de l'Isle was taken in his tent, with many others. The besieged knights, also, hearing the tumult, and seeing the English ensigns, instantly armed themselves, and, rushing out, plunged into the thickest of the battle, and augmented the confusion of the French, who sustained, though by very inadequate means, a complete discomfiture. Their general, the Comte de l'Isle, with nine earls and viscounts, and almost all the lords, knights, and squires of his army, remained captives; and there was scarce an English man-at-arms who had not two or three prisoners.

The next morning, the Earl of Pembroke appeared at the head of a strong body of English, and blamed the Earl of Derby for engaging the enemy without him, since he might be sure, that, being sent for, he would not fail to keep the appointment. The Earl of Derby answered gently, that they had already tarried many hours for their companions; and that, had he suspended the attack longer, they might have been discovered by the enemy; in which case, the French might have attained the advantage which had so fortunately fallen to the English.

Thus terminated the campaign under the Earl of Derby, during the year 1344. In spring, 1345, the Earl of Derby, now become Earl of Lancaster by his father's death, was reinforced from England, and resumed his career of conquest in Gascony; and, as well by taking several towns, as by skirmishes in the field, gained great honour for himself, and extended in that province the authority of England. The Duke of Normandy, at the head of the knights and chivalry of that duchy, continued the principal opponent of the English, and the war was carried on with great activity on both sides.

A.D. 1345.

It is impossible for us to give a minute description of these events, although the gallantry with which they were performed, has enabled the celebrated Froissart to decorate his pages with many splendid details of romantic chivalry. It will be more useful for you to obtain some idea of the description of troops that formed the armies by which these wars were carried on, and of the tactics upon which they acted.

You are already aware, that the strength of the armies in the fourteenth century consisted in cavalry, which was levied almost entirely upon feudal principles, with the exception of the mercenary troops, who must be considered separately.

The regular feudal horsemen consisted of the knights, of whom I have endeavoured to give you some idea, together with their squires, pages, and

personal attendants. The number of those who
waited upon each knight varied with circumstances;
in especial cases, according to the means that their
master had of maintaining them, as well as to his
fame in arms; but it generally amounted to about
five men for each lance, that is, as the retinue of
each knight. This chivalry was called out as vassals of the crown, of whom the leaders held their
lands, and their service was considered as rendered
in requital of their several estates; each powerful
crown vassal being attended of course by his subordinate dependents, who served him on the same
terms as he served the crown. Such was the system upon which the feudal cavalry were formed

But it must be recollected that every knight was
not necessarily possessed of land, which he held for
military service; on the contrary, very many were
elevated to that dignity, who either never had any
estates of their own, or who had spent, or otherwise
lost them. This must have been frequently the
case, since the dignity of knighthood could be conferred upon any one whom an individual knight
judged worthy of the honour. The order could,
therefore, be multiplied to an infinite number, without regard to any thing but the personal qualities
of those on whom it was conferred, and especially
to their skill in arms and military exercises. The
number of knights without either lands or substance, who sought adventures merely to essay
their courage, and push their fortunes in life, was
very great; and these "bold bachelors," as they
were called, were the flower of every feudal army.

They subsisted by the bounty, or *largesse*, as it was called, of the princes whom they served, which was one great source of expense to those who embarked in war; and the intrepidity with which they engaged in combat was increased in proportion, in order to attract the favour of their leader.

A successful war had also its peculiar advantages to those chivalrous adventurers. The knights, or nobles, who were overcome in battle, and compelled to yield themselves to the more fortunate among the victors, "rescue or no rescue," were obliged to purchase their liberty at such sum as might be agreed on. The conditions of these bargains were well understood, and the prisoner, according to his rank and wealth, adjusted with his captor the price of his enfranchisement. On this subject, so much generosity prevailed among the French and English in particular, that the victorious party frequently did not carry their prisoners off the field, but freely dismissed them, under the sole condition, that they should meet the captors afterwards, at a time and place fixed, and settle the terms of their ransom. To fail in such an appointment would have been, on the part of the captive knight, held most unworthy and dishonourable, and he would have exposed himself to the scorn of the ladies, minstrels, and heralds, to stand high in whose praise was the especial object of every true son of chivalry.

Besides these casual profits, which, when the war was successful, and the enemy wealthy, often rose to a great sum, the knights adventurers, in time of peace, wandered from court to court, and castle to castle, exhibiting their skill in tournaments, gaining the favour of the lords under whose patronage such martial exercises were displayed, and sometimes acquiring the love of heiresses, by whom their fortunes were established. In the mean time, rich prizes were often gained by the victors in these military exhibitions; while, at any rate, the expenses of the knights who attended them, as well as of their retinue, were defrayed with prodigality by the sovereign prince, or high noble, at whose court the entertainment was given. Thus, though without lands and revenues, hundreds and thousands of those sons of chivalry subsisted with ease and honour, during this romantic period. There were also numbers of knights, doubtless, who died in poverty and misery, and the end of an unsuccessful expedition was usually signalized by the total ruin of the knights-adventurers who had been engaged in it. Such were the cavalry, the very flower, of course, of the feudal armies.

The appointments of these knights consisted in a suit of armour, more or less perfect, which defended the whole person. Sometimes it was made of mail, that is, links of iron, forming a sort of network dress, which covered the person, and was almost impenetrable either to sword or lance. Latterly, the armour was composed of plates of iron, which protected the men-at-arms from head to heel. The offensive weapons of the knight were, a lance, twelve or fifteen feet long, a heavy sword, a dagger, and often a species of battle-axe, or a steel club, called a mace-at-arms. The horse, like the knight, was covered, either with a housing made of mail, or with armour of plate. When mounted, and charging in squadron, as the knight and his horse were almost invulnerable, so their attack was wellnigh irresistible. Sometimes it was thought necessary to employ the men-at-arms on foot, on which occasion they were commanded to put off their spurs, and cut their lances to the length of five or six feet, so as to make the weapon less unwieldy.

The men-at-arms were sometimes liable to be surprised. Upon a march, they seldom wore the weightier parts of their armour; and their heavy war-horse was rode, or led, beside them by a page, while the knight himself bestrode a hackney, to receive his armed horse fresh for the moment of battle. A sudden attack, therefore, was apt to discompose the men-at-arms before they could be fully prepared for action. If the war-horse was killed in battle, the knight was, in most instances, taken or slain, since he could not raise himself from the ground, without assistance from the squires or pages who attended for that purpose.

We are now to consider the state of their infantry, which, in comparison, was of a very inferior description.

We must remark one great distinction, however, in favour of the archery of England, a species of troops almost unknown to any other country, and possessing qualities which decided very many battles in favour of their own. You can easily conceive that the infantry of every nation must be divided into two kinds, calculated for two distinct services, to which their weapons are severally adapted; one of these distinct species of force must be armed with missiles for distant warfare, the other with weapons fitted to strike or thrust in a close encounter. Modern times indeed have, in a great measure, united them both, by adopting the musket and bayonet; the former for more distant, the latter for close combat. But at the period we speak of, no weapon existed possessing this double advantage. Of the troops then employed, the bowmen of England were the most formidable at a distance. They were selected from the yeomen of the country, men to whom the use of the weapon had been familiar from childhood; for the practice of archery was then encouraged by prizes and public competition in every village, in order to keep up the skill which the youth had acquired, and to extend the renown of England, as producing the best bowmen whom the world had ever seen.

The equipment and mode of exercise of these archers were calculated to maintain their superiority. Their dress was light and had few ligatures. Instead of the numerous strings which then attached the jacket to the hose, or trowsers, one stout *point*, as it was called, answered the necessary purpose, without impeding the motions of the wearer. In battle the sleeve of the right arm was left open to increase the archer's agility. Each of them carried a bow, and twelve arrows, or, as they

termed them, " the lives of twelve Scots," at his
girdle; their shafts had a light forked head, and
were carefully adjusted so as to fly true to the aim.
In using the weapon, the English archers observed
a practice unknown on the continent, drawing the
bow-string, not to the breast, but to the ear, which
gave a far greater command of a strong bow and
long shaft. Their arrows were, accordingly, a
cloth yard in length, and their bows carried to a
prodigious distance. Upon the battlements of a
castle, or walls of a town, the arrows fell with the
rapidity of hail, and such certainty of aim, as
scarcely permitted a defender to show himself; nor
were they less formidable when discharged against
a hostile column, whether of cavalry or infantry,
and whether in motion or stationary. The principal danger to which the archers were exposed was
that of a rapid and determined charge of cavalry.
To provide in some degree against this, each archer
used to carry a wooden stake, shod with iron at
both ends, the planting of which before him might,
in some measure, afford a cover from horse. They
had also swords. The stakes, however, were not
always in readiness, nor were they always found
effectual for the purpose, neither were their swords
an adequate protection against cavalry. At the
famous battle of Bannockburn, Bruce obtained that
decisive victory chiefly by a well-executed manœuvre for cutting to pieces the English archers,
by a body of horse reserved for that service. Two
or three other cases may be noticed, in which the
French obtained similar advantages over the archers.

by providing themselves with *pavisses*, that is, long targets, strong enough to protect them from shot But these cases are very few, in comparison to the numerous instances in which the long-bow proved superior both in France and Scotland.

The second division of the English infantry destined to fight hand to hand, was armed with *bills*, as they were called, weapons similar in shape to those knives with which husbandmen dress hedges, but placed upon longer handles. These two kinds of weapons were used by the English infantry, so exclusively, that their cry to arms used to be, " Bows and bills—bows and bills!" It is remarkable that both the national weapons were used by the contending parties in the battle of Hastings, where the Normans were armed with the long bow, and the Saxons with the gisarme, or bill. The armies of the English, in later days, had troops armed with both, as intended not only for distant but close combat.

The bill which they used in close fight was a formidable weapon, though clumsy in action, since it required to be wielded with both hands, and therefore prevented those who used it from forming a compact body. It was certainly unequal, in a fair field, to the lances of the Scots, nor does it seem to have given to those who bore it, any permanent or assured superiority over the same force in the French army.

This may, however, be said with truth, that neither the bowmen nor billmen of England were, generally speaking, exposed to the same oppres sion to which the peasants of France were subjected, and that, possessing a more independent character as individuals, they were less liable to lose heart in danger, and more eager to sustain their national reputation. Upon the whole, however, the efforts of the infantry were so little relied upon at that period, that little was trusted to them in action, except in the case of the English archers. The men-at-arms on both sides might be considered as upon an equality; and the infantry who fought hand to hand were so much so, that, in so far as regards that class of soldiers, it was accidental circumstances only which could decide the event of a field betwixt France and England.

To oppose the archery of their national antagonists, the French had no better resource than hiring, from Genoa and elsewhere, Italians and other strangers, well skilled in the use of the cross-bow, a species of weapon accounted so murderously fatal, that it was at one time prohibited by an edict of the Church as unchristian. To defend a fortress, or the walls of a town, where the shooter was in some degree sheltered by a parapet, the cross-bow was indeed a terrible instrument, though even there it was often found inferior to the English long-bow; still more was this the case in an open field, where an English archer might shoot five, or perhaps ten arrows, while the difficulty of charging these steel-bows, which required to be bent by the slow operation of a windlass, hardly permitted the cross-bowman to send forth a single bolt. Of this you will find several instances in the sequel.

The ordinary infantry of France, levied among the lowest drudges among her peasantry, added much to the numbers, but little to the military strength, and a great deal to the unwieldy confusion, of their great armies. These poor men felt that they were little trusted to, and cannot be supposed to have displayed much zeal in behalf of masters by whom they were contemned and oppressed. They wore almost no defensive armour, if we except tanned hides, and were irregularly armed with swords, spears, or clubs, as offensive weapons. No kind of discipline was taught them, and when attacked by the men-at-arms, they seem frequently to have made no more effectual defence than might have been expected from a flock of sheep.

I may here mention, that gunpowder was discovered about this period; but it was not till a much later period that it was generally used or understood in war. One author pretends that Edward III. had field-pieces at the battle of Cressy; but, had it been so, it seems probable that so remarkable a circumstance would have been more particularly noticed. Such awkward and unwieldy cannon as the age possessed were chiefly used in sieges. They were clumsy to transport, slow to load, and often burst when discharged. So that, as already hinted, it was long ere the invention began to produce that alteration in warfare, which it finally accomplished to so great an extent.

Such being the general state of the French and English armies, so far as they consisted of national troops, I have now to remind you, that the armies of both were often augmented by the mercenary soldiers of the period,—men who had learned, among the tumults of the age, the desperate trade of war, and who, without acknowledging any nation or king of their own, were desirous to afford the benefit of their discipline and experience to those who were most willing to pay for their assistance. These bands were composed of adventurers of different nations, commanded by approved soldiers, who were sometimes recommended by their birth and rank, often by their superior activity and rapacity, but in all cases by their valour and success. These leaders followed upon a greater scale the course of individual knights, and hoped, not by their own prowess alone, but by the assistance of the soldiers whom they levied and commanded, to rise to wealth and consequence. These bands were the terror and scourge of the peasantry, whom they oppressed without mercy, since, when they were not in the actual pay of some prince, they subsisted themselves by force at the expense of the natives of the country in which they resided or the time.

The Kings of England, and especially of France, set themselves at times seriously to the task of extirpating these debauched bands of ruffian soldiery, who, having no home or country of their own, were a general plague to other nations. But the purpose of extirpation was never effectually followed out; for the sovereigns were every now and then taught by necessity the convenience of being able to collect for a certain expenditure of treasure a body of experienced soldiers, as brave and better armed than any whom they could levy in their own dominions, and thus were freed from the necessity of depending on the humour of a fickle and overgrown crown vassal, who might be pleased with an opportunity of distressing and thwarting his liege lord, and enabled to rely upon that of a mercenary leader, whose faithful adherence might be calculated upon so long as his pay was duly furnished. Thus the same plague which was complained of during the reigns of Stephen and John of England, and the contemporary sovereigns of France, revived in its wildest extent, during the calamitous period which we are now treating of

CHAPTER XVII.

Edward III. loses several of his adherents in the Low Countries, as the Brewer Artavelde, and the Counts of Hainault and Montfort—his Interest is espoused by Godfrey of Harcourt, a discarded Favourite of the King of France—by the advice of Harcourt, an Invasion of Gascony is resolved on, and takes place—Philip assembles an army at St Denis, and marches to the defence of Rouen, which is threatened by the English—Manœuvres of Edward, by which he accomplishes a passage from the left to the right bank of the Seine—after two days' march, followed by the French army, he crosses the Somme, and takes up battle-ground in the Forest of Cressy—the French come up—Battle of Cressy.

[1343—1346.]

At the end of the preceding chapter, we gave a brief account of the manner in which troops were trained and armed during the thirteenth and fourteenth centuries. We must now return to the proper subject of this little work, which is intended to convey some general idea of French history, especially as it bears upon, and is connected with, that of Britain.

I must first observe, that the plans by which Edward III. endeavoured to establish himself on the throne of France, and to revenge the affront which he had received from Philip of Valois, were rather more frequently changed than accorded with that prince's reputed sagacity. In 1343, he again returned to a project in which both his grandfather and he had already failed; namely, that of attacking France upon the eastern frontier, by means of the Brabanters, Flemings, and Germans. But, on the present occasion, he did not appeal to the nobles or princes of Flanders, but to the inhabitants of the great towns, in which he followed a policy adopted at one time by Philip the Fair, although his successors had exchanged it for the counter-plan of supporting the earls and nobles of the Low Countries against the insurgent citizens of the towns.

A.D. 1343.

We have already observed, that Edward was in close correspondence with Jacob van Artavelde, a brewer of great wealth and importance, who appeared for a time to have the command of all the common people of the great towns of Flanders. Through means of his influence with this demagogue, Edward had formed the plan of advancing his own son, also named Edward, afterwards the celebrated Black Prince, to the dignity of Earl of Flanders, in preference to the natural lord, Louis who was attached to the French interest. Th proposal, however, was so offensive to the more moderate burgesses to whom it was communicated, that Artavelde, who had lately reigned like a prince among them, was now looked upon with as much abhorrence as ever he had been held in estimation

At length, the displeasure of the citizens against him rose so high, that, as this once powerful demagogue rode into Ghent, accompanied by a small guard of Welshmen, who had been appointed to attend him by Edward III., he was encountered by such evil looks and menaces, that he was compelled to take refuge from popular indignation in a house, which the Welshmen for a space defended. But this place of refuge being afterwards forced by the multitude, they were themselves the assassins of their former favourite; and with him perished Edward's hope of establishing his son as Earl of Flanders.

Edward sustained another loss about the same time in the person of his brother-in-law, the Count of Hainault, a brave young man, who was slain in an attempt to subdue the revolted natives of Friesland. Sir John of Hainault, uncle to the slain Prince, became, after his death, unfriendly to Edward, to whom he had been hitherto attached, but, as he thought, without receiving adequate requital. He therefore left the service of the English King for that of Philip of France.

About the same period also, John de Montfort escaped from a French prison, or was set at liberty by Philip in consequence of the previous truce, and once more took the field in Bretagne, with the assistance of an English auxiliary force, under the Earl of Northampton. They laid siege to Quimperlé, where the Count of Montfort completed his career of misfortune, by dying of a fever before the town.

A.D. 1345.

GODFREY OF HARCOURT.

Upon the whole, therefore, these successive losses of powerful friends diminished the various means by which King Edward had hoped to make an impression upon France, either on the eastern or western frontier.

In this same eventful year, 1345, however, Edward III. acquired another counsellor, a deserter from the enemy, by whose advice he again altered, in a great measure, the direction of his attacks upon France. This was a powerful nobleman of Normandy, named Godfrey of Harcourt, Lord of Saint Sauveur le Vicompte, and brother to John, Earl of Harcourt. Sir Godfrey himself had once stood as high in the favour of Philip of Valois, as any nobleman of his kingdom. But upon the occasion of a quarrel betwixt him and Sir Robert Bertram, Marshal of France, the King took the part of the latter so earnestly, that if he could have got Sir Godfrey into his power there is little doubt that he would have dealt with him as with the Breton Lord de Clisson, whom, on small suspicion, he had caused to be executed for alleged adherence to the English interest. Sir Godfrey of Harcourt fled in good time to England, and, like Robert of Artois before him, employed his address and eloquence, both which he possessed in perfection, to animate the King of England to make Sir Godfrey's own country of Normandy the principal scene of his attacks upon France. " It is," said Godfrey of Harcourt, " one of the most plentiful provinces in the kingdom; it has not witnessed war for two centuries, and is occupied by

A.D. 1345

great and wealthy towns, unprotected by any adequate fortifications. The nobility of Normandy are," he continued, " now absent from the country, having accompanied Philip's eldest son, John, who has conducted them southward to carry on the war with Gascony." The exile urged that Normandy was an ancient inheritance of the English, which they might now recover with little trouble, and which, if subdued, would be a conquest glorious to King Edward, particularly useful from its vicinity to England, and an event not altogether displeasing to the Normans themselves.

Encouraged by this advice, Edward III. put himself at the head of a considerable army, which he pretended was designed for prosecuting the war in Gascony. But, instead of holding this course, the King, when embarked, steered straight to the coast of Normandy, and landed at the town of La Hogue. No sooner was the King of France informed of this attempt, against which he had made no preparation, than he hastened to collect the whole force of his kingdom, together with those of his allies, John of Luxembourg, the old King of Bohemia, with his son Charles, Emperor-elect of Germany, the Duke of Lorraine, John of Hainault, once the King of England's ally, Louis, Earl of Flanders, and James, titular King of Majorca. The titles of some of these princes were more considerable than their power, but still, by their assistance, and that of his own liegemen and great vassals, Philip found himself at the head of a powerful and gallant army,

A.D. 1346.

which emboldened him to swear resolutely that the King of England should not return to his own country without battle, in which he should be sufficiently punished for the slaughter, depredation, and extreme violence, which he was now exercising in the kingdom of France. The greater part of Philip's army was assembled at St Denis, close to Paris; but the King himself, assuming the command of such forces as could be got presently in readiness, moved down the Seine to defend Rouen, the capital of Normandy, which was threatened by the English.

In the mean time, Edward III. divided his strong army into three bodies; the first of which was commanded by himself; the second by the Earl of Warwick; and the third by Sir Godfrey of Harcourt, whose advice the King used, as principal marshal of his army during all this expedition, of which indeed he had been the main author and adviser. The English, as Sir Godfrey had prophesied, found the cities of Normandy at once wealthy and ill-defended, so that they made very great spoil with little danger, while the loss to the unfortunate inhabitants was, as usual in such cases, much greater than the riches acquired by the invaders. The city of Caen, full of merchandise and wealth of every kind, was carried by storm, after so obstinate a resistance, that Edward, in resentment, would have burned the place to the ground, had not Sir Godfrey of Harcourt's intercession deterred him from this violence.

It may be mentioned, that while Normandy was

sustaining this severe treatment from the land forces in the interior, the English fleet was as busily employed plundering, destroying, and burning the seaport towns on the coast, with the shipping which they contained. In this manner the English Monarch ascended the left bank of the river Seine, with the purpose of assaulting Rouen, the capital of Normandy. This, however, was prevented by the march of Philip of Valois to its relief, before noticed. The river Seine now divided the two armies; and, all the bridges being broken down, neither host durst pass the river for the purpose of attacking their enemy, lest in the act of doing so they should be taken at advantage by that which held the opposite bank. The French King, in particular, was more reconciled to postpone a general battle, being conscious of possessing a great superiority of numbers, from which he entertained a well-judged hope that Edward's army, prevented from crossing the river, might be enclosed in the country on the opposite side, and compelled to fight at disadvantage.

In the mean time, the citizens of Paris were in the utmost consternation, dreading the near approach of the English army, and afraid of the terrors of military execution, attendant on the march of Edward, who was by no means famed for clemency. King Philip with difficulty persuaded them that the measure which he had taken, of marching down the right bank of the Seine, which had the appearance of leaving Paris open to the enemy, if the English should ascend the opposite bank, was, in fact, that which was best adapted to cover his metropolis.

It soon, however, became plain, that Edward had no design against the French capital; for that King, having made a sudden movement upon Poissy, repaired the bridge there, which had been but imperfectly demolished, and, by an able military manœuvre, crossed the Seine, and moved eastward towards Flanders. He thus extricated himself from the difficulty in which Philip conceived him to be involved.

When the English Monarch had attained the right bank of the Seine, the fires raised by his soldiery, in their destructive progress, alarmed the capital once more; but the English, after defying the King of France to instant battle, departed towards Beauvois, of which town they burnt the suburbs. In this manner eluding the French army, King Edward pursued his course with all diligence towards Flanders, closely followed by King Philip and his army.

But after a day or two's march, the English King seemed once more entangled in the toils drawn round him by his enemy. The march of the English was here interrupted by the deep river Somme, impassable at all points, and on which every bridge had been destroyed. To have awaited the advance of the numerous French army, with an impassable river in his front, would have been a perilous adventure. The King of England was therefore extremely desirous to find the means of passing the deep Somme, although a noble French lord, called Gondomar de Fay, was stationed on the opposite bank, at the head of the gentlemen of Artois and Picardy, in order to defend the passage, which must be at best a dangerous one, with a superior army in the rear, and over a river so near to the sea as to be affected by the tide. Having made enquiry among the French prisoners concerning the means of crossing, and offered liberty for himself and thirty of his companions, to any one who should point out a practicable ford, King Edward received from one of his captives the following agreeable intelligence. "Know, sir, that during the ebb-tide, which happens twice in twelve hours, the river Somme is so low that it may be passed with security, either by horse or foot, at a ford to which I can guide you. At this place the bottom is hard and firm, and being composed of chalk, and similar materials, it is called Blanchetaque" (that is, *white water*).

Overjoyed at this news, Edward drew his army to the ford, where, as the flood tide was still making, he was compelled to wait for an hour or two. In the mean time, Sir Gondomar de Fay, made aware of the purpose of the English, drew up his men, who amounted to near twelve thousand, on the opposite side of the river, resolved to dispute the passage. But the moment had no sooner arrived when the ford was practicable, than Edward, having commanded his marshals to enter the river, called aloud, "Let those who love me follow me," and plunged in among the foremost, his army following in good order. Notwithstanding a valiant resistance on the part of the French, who defended the opposite bank, they were compelled to give way, after losing two thousand men-at-arms, and the greater part of their infantry, who had no means of escape from the English cavalry, so soon as the passage was completed.

This was a very delicate and important manœuvre on the part of the English, for the main army of Philip followed so close, that part of King Edward's rear-guard suffered from the vanguard of the French, before they could cross the river. Philip himself soon afterwards came up, and having been full of hope either that the English would not discover the ford at Blanchetaque, or that it might be effectually defended against them by Sir Gondomar de Fay, he was proportionally vexed at finding how the English Monarch had again extricated himself from the risk of being compelled to fight at disadvantage, and exclaimed, though unjustly, against Sir Gondomar de Fay, as guilty of treason and disloyalty, in failing to maintain his ground.

By the advice of his best leaders, the French King determined not to follow the English by the ford, lest they should turn back and attack him in the passage; but, drawing off his army to Abbeville, he judged it better to secure the bridge over the Somme at that town, and after spending a day there to refresh his troops, and give such forces as followed in his rear time to come up and join him, to advance in quest of the English. Accordingly, Philip employed the 25th of August in these manœuvres

In the mean time, King Edward, being now on ground fitted for engaging the enemy, declared his purpose, that he would pursue his retreat no further, but fight with Philip of Valois, whatever the odds of numbers might be. "This county of Ponthieu was the just heritage of Queen Eleanor, my mother," said he; "I now challenge it as my own; and may God defend the right!"

The place where he made this declaration was open ground, called the Forest of Cressy, a name which has been made memorable by the events of the following day. The army of the English was here drawn up, arranged in three divisions, to await the advance of the French.

In the first was Edward, Prince of Wales, now in his sixteenth year, but of strength and courage far beyond his age, and whose brief career has made historians observe, that few characters have put more feats of heroism into the compass of so few years. Many veteran warriors were placed under the command of the young prince, who was thus ranked foremost in the battle; but Lord Warwick, and Sir John Chandos, were specially intrusted by his father with the task of directing and defending him in any difficulty. His division amounted to eight thousand men-at-arms, four thousand archers, and six thousand Welshmen.

The second division consisted of eight hundred men-at-arms, two thousand four hundred archers, and four thousand bill-men.

The third, and last of the English divisions was commanded by the King in person, and consisted of seven hundred men-at-arms, six thousand archers, and four thousand three hundred bill-men. The full amount of the English army was therefore about thirty-six thousand men.

These three divisions were drawn up in the order which they were to preserve in battle, and then appointed to take refreshment, and go to sleep on the grass, upon their arms. The night was warm, and rendered this interval of repose acceptable and refreshing to troops, fatigued with long marches and spare diet. Their spirits were gay and cheerful; and though they were conscious of considerable inferiority in numbers to their adversaries, that reflection, far from inducing them to doubt of the issue of the day, inclined them only to pay more scrupulous attention to the command of their officers, by whose guidance they hoped to gain it. The presence of their experienced monarch, and his valiant son, filled the host with hope and confidence.

The next day was the memorable 26th of August, 1346. Early in the morning the English army arose in the same order in which they had lain down to rest the evening before.

The French forces were some time in coming up. During this interval, to increase the enthusiasm of his soldiers, Edward conferred the honour of knighthood on the Prince of Wales, and a large band of noble youths, companions of the heir-apparent, who were expected so to behave in the conflict as to *win their spurs;* that is, to show themselves worthy of the distinction they had received, by their admission into the order of chivalry, of which the spurs were an emblem.

On the same morning, King Philip, mustering his army at sunrise, led them forth from the town of Abbeville, where they had passed the night, and, with more haste than caution, advanced towards the English, a distance of between three and four leagues.

A. D. 1346.
Aug. 26.

Many circumstances contributed to increase King Philip's confidence, and impress upon his army feelings which amounted to presumption. They had for several weeks been superior to their enemy in the field; and, since the crossing of the Seine, as well as the subsequent passage of the Somme at Blanchetaque, it had been the object of the English to avoid that engagement which was now fast approaching. The French cavalry had also received a considerable reinforcement by the arrival of Amadeus, Earl of Savoy, who had joined Philip at Abbeville the day before, with a thousand lances, a great addition to his previous superiority These circumstances inspired both officers and soldiers with an overweening confidence, perhaps natural to men who conceived that they were in chase of a flying enemy.

The movements of this great army were therefore hurried and precipitate, like those of men who advanced to a pursuit rather than a battle. Yet all did not partake the sanguine hopes which dictated these hasty movements. The advice of a veteran German warrior, sent to reconnoitre the English army, strongly recommended to King Philip to halt the advance of his own forces, and put off the battle till next morning. "The English," he said, "have reposed in a position which they have deliberately adopted, and doubtless will not abandon, without a desperate defence. Your men are tired with their long morning's march from Abbeville, confused with the haste of their advance, and must meet, at great disadvantage, a well-prepared enemy, refreshed by food and repose."

The King of France listened to this experienced counsel, and expressed his desire to follow it, by halting his army for the day, and postponing the battle till the morrow. But the evil genius of France had decreed otherwise. The troops who formed the vanguard of the French host halted indeed at the word of command, but those who came behind hurried onward, with the idle bravado that "they would make no stop till they were as far forward as the foremost." In this way they exhausted their spirits, expended their strength, and confused their ranks, many brandishing their swords with idle exclamations of "Attack, take, and slay!" before they were even in sight of the enemy. To stop men in this state of excitation was impossible.

King Philip, thus hurried forward to battle by the want of discipline of his own troops, divided his army into three bodies. The first was under the command of the King of Bohemia, seconded by Charles of Luxembourg, his son, Emperor-elect of Germany, and of Charles, Earl of Alençon, the brother of King Philip, a brave, but fiery and rash young cavalier. The Genoese cross-bowmen, fifteen thousand in number, were all placed in this first division. The French accounted them a match for the English archers, and trusted that their superior discharge in the commencement of the action would clear the field of these formidable forces. They had also more than twenty-nine thousand men to support their bowmen.

The second division was commanded by King Philip himself, with his broad banner displayed, surrounded by six thousand men-at-arms, and forty thousand foot. The blind old King of Bohemia was afterwards posted into this second division, as well as James, the titular King of Majorca.

Lastly, the rear division of the French was led by the Earl of Savoy, with five thousand lances and twenty thousand foot.

These large bodies appear to have been unequally divided, probably owing to the state of confusion into which the French army was undoubtedly thrown by their too hasty advance, which rendered it difficult to transmit and execute orders.

On the approach of the Genoese towards the English position, these strangers, who formed the vanguard of the French army, gave signs of fatigue, from marching three long leagues with their weighty cross-bows. When the word was given to " begin the battle, in the name of God and St Denis!" the Italians answered by remonstrances, saying, they had more occasion for rest than to fight that day. This moved the resentment of Alençon, the commander of the division, who said with contempt, " A man has much help from these fellows, who thus fail him at the pinch!" The order for attack was therefore repeated, and obeyed.

Some singular appearances in the heavens now seemed to announce the great and bloody conflict which was about to take place upon the earth. A heavy thunder-cloud darkened the sun like an eclipse, and before the storm burst, a vast number of crows and ravens came driving before the tempest, and swept over both armies. A short, but severe thunder-storm, with much lightning and heavy rain, suspended for half an hour the joining of the battle, until the weather became fair, and the sun began once more to shine out, darting his rays on the backs of the English, and in the eyes of the French.

The Genoese, now approaching towards the Prince of Wales's division, made a great leap and cry, thinking to daunt the English by the symptoms of instant attack; but King Edward's archers, who were drawn up with their ranks crossed after the fashion of a *herse*, or harrow, so that the shot of the one might support the others (like that of the combined squares of musketry in modern warfare), remained firm and steady. The Genoese, a second time, advanced forward, leapt and cried, without making more impression upon the English than before; a third time they advanced, shouted and leapt, and then began to use their cross-bows. But the English, who seemed only to wait for the actual commencement of hostilities, stepped each of them one pace forward, and shot their arrows so closely together, that it seemed as if it snowed

The volleys of the Genoese bolts were returned
with this incessant storm of arrows, and with so
much interest, that the Italians became unable to
keep their ground. Their bow-strings also had
been wetted by the late storm, while those of the
English had been secured in cases which they carried
for the purpose. Finally, there were eight or
ten arrows returned, for every cross-bow shaft discharged.
All these circumstances of advantage
rendered the Genoese unable to withstand the English
archers, so that that large body of Italians
lost heart, and, cutting their strings, or throwing
away their bows (as an excuse for not continuing
the conflict), they rushed back in confusion upon
the rest of the vanguard, and especially upon the
men-at-arms, by whom they were to have been
supported. The confusion thus occasioned in the
French army became inextricable, as the recoil of
the cross-bowmen prevented the regular advance
of the knights and squires, upon whom the ultimate
fate of the day must necessarily depend,
especially after the retreat of the Genoese. The
King of France added to the confusion, by calling
on the cavalry to advance to the charge, without
any regard to the cross-bowmen, who, now a confused
multitude of fugitives, lay straight in the way
of their advance. "Slay me these poltroons," said
he, " since thus they do but trouble us;" and the
French men-at-arms advanced at full gallop on the
unfortunate Italians, many of whom were thus
trodden down and slain by their auxiliaries, while,
at the same time, the ranks of the cavalry were

disordered by riding over their own bowmen before they could reach the enemy.

In the mean time, the English archers kept pouring their shafts, without an instant's intermission, as well upon the Genoese who fled, as the French men-at-arms who were endeavouring to advance, and augmented the dreadful confusion which took place. Many of the bravest French knights lay stretched on the plain, who might have been made captive with ease; but King Edward had strictly forbidden the taking of any prisoners during the action, lest the desire of securing them should be a temptation to his soldiers to quit their ranks. The grooms, therefore, and mere camp-followers of the English, had the task of despatching the fallen with their knives; and by these ignoble hands much noble and knightly blood was shed.

Yet, notwithstanding the loss attending this horrible confusion, the courage of Alençon, and the native bravery of the French cavaliers, impelled them still forward. A part of them extricated themselves at length from the unfortunate Genoese, and pushed on along the line of English archers, by which they suffered great loss, until at length they arrived on their right flank, where the Prince of Wales was placed, at the head of his men-at-arms. By these, the French were so roughly encountered, that the greater part of them were beaten down and slain. But this victory was hardly won, before three other squadrons of French and Germans rushed on with such fury in the same direction, that they burst an opening for themselves through the archers, who had but imperfect means of repelling horse, and dashed furiously up to the place where the gallant prince was stationed. The Earl of Warwick now became alarmed; for he concluded that the standards of the French King and his numerous army were following close upon the new comers. In this belief, Warwick and Chandos sent to King Edward, requesting succour for his valiant son, when the following dialogue took place between the King and the messengers.

"Is my son," said Edward, "dead, wounded, or felled to the ground?"

"Not so, thank God," answered the messengers; "but he needs assistance."

"Nay, then," said King Edward, "he has no aid from me; let him bear himself like a man, and this day show himself worthy of the knighthood conferred on him; in this battle he must win his own spurs."

In the mean time, a strong detachment of men-at-arms, despatched by the Earls of Arundel and Northampton, the commanders of the second division, had relieved Prince Edward from his temporary embarrassment. And now the English archers opening in the centre, suffered their cavalry to rush forward through the interval, and encounter the French men-at-arms, who were in total confusion. This was augmented by the fierce attack of the English; and the most experienced on the opposite side began to despair of the day. The King of France himself fought with the greatest valour, was repeatedly wounded and dismounted, and would have died probably on the field, had not Sir John of Hainault led him off by force. Not more than sixty of his gallant army remained in attendance upon their sovereign, and with these he reached, after nightfall, the castle of Broye. When the warder demanded what or who he was, "I am," said the King, "the fortune of France;"—a secret rebuke, perhaps, to those who termed him "the Happy," an epithet not very suitable to his present condition, and, as his own example showed, apt to prove inapplicable if conferred before death.

The King of Majorca is generally said to have been among the fallen, and the slaughter among princes, counts, nobles, and men of rank, was without example. But the most remarkable death, among those of so many princes, was that of John, King of Bohemia, a monarch almost blind with age, and not very well qualified, therefore, to mix personally in the fight. When all seemed lost, the old man enquired after his son Charles, who was nowhere visible, having, in fact, been compelled to fly from the field. The father receiving no satisfaction concerning his son from the knights who attended on him, he said to them, "Sirs, ye are my knights and good liegemen, will ye conduct me so far forward into the battle, that I may strike one good stroke with my sword?"

To satisfy this wish, which his followers looked upon as the words of despair, four faithful knights agreed to share their master's fate, rather than leave him to perish alone. These devoted attendants tied the old king's bridle-reins to their own, and rushed with him into the middle of the fight, where, striking more good blows than one, they were all slain, and found there the next day, as they had fallen, with their horses' reins tied together.

Thus ended this celebrated battle. There lay upon the field of Cressy two kings, eleven high princes, eighty bannerets, one thousand two hundred knights, and more than thirty thousand private soldiers.

The meeting of Edward and his son took place by torchlight, after the battle was over. "Well have you won your spurs!" said the brave King; "persevere in the career which you have opened, and you will become the brightest honour of the noble kingdom of which you are the worthy heir."

The battle of Cressy was one of the greatest victories ever gained by a King of England, and Edward prepared to avail himself of it, in a manner which should produce some permanent advantage.

CHAPTER XVIII.

Edward resolves to secure a permanent footing in France, by making himself Master of Calais—Siege of Calais—War in Bretagne—Siege of Roche-d'Arien—Anxiety of the two Monarchs, Edward and Philip, to obtain the Alliance of the Flemings—The People of Flanders favourable to Edward, and their Earl to Philip—Attempt of Philip to raise the Siege of Calais—it fails, and the Citizens are compelled to treat for a Surrender—Noble Conduct of Eustace de Saint Pierre, and five other Burgesses, who, in order to save their Fellow-townsmen, deliver themselves up to Edward—they are ordered for Execution by him, but saved by the intercession of his Queen, Philippa—Measures of Edward for securing possession of Calais—Sir Emeric of Pavia, Seneschal of the Castle of Calais for the English King, treats with Sir Geoffrey Charny to betray the place to the French for a sum of money—his Treachery discovered, whereupon he makes his peace with Edward, by undertaking to betray Sir Geoffrey, and on that Knight coming to receive possession of the Castle, Sir Emeric takes payment of the money agreed upon, and delivers Sir Geoffrey to an Ambuscade of the English under Sir Walter Manny, by whom the French Party are defeated, and their Leader, Sir Geoffrey taken Prisoner—Edward's treatment of the Prisoners—Pestilence rages in France and England—Submis-

sion of *Godfrey of Harcourt to the French King—Death of Philip VI.*

[1346—1350.]

The result which Edward promised himself from his great victory, was, in fact, the opportunity of carrying into effectual execution the plan of Godfrey of Harcourt, by obtaining a firm footing in Normandy. Spoil and havoc had hitherto seemed his only object; but it was his secret plan to attain some permanent possession in the province, as near to England as possible, to enable him to attempt future conquests in France. For this purpose, he resolved to avail himself of his victory, which he knew must long disable Philip from taking the field, and lay siege to Calais, a seaport rich and strongly fortified, being immediately opposite to the coast of England, from which it is only between twenty and thirty miles distant. It was clear that, if the English could obtain possession of this place, the flat and swampy country around Calais would permit them easily to fortify it; and its vicinity to England, and the superiority of her naval power, would always afford means of relieving it when besieged. King Edward, therefore, sat down before Calais with his large army, shortly after the battle of Cressy, and proceeded, by every means in his power, to hasten the siege.

Philip of France, in the mean time, did all he could to obtain the means of retrieving the disaster of Cressy. He summoned from Gascony his son, the Duke of Normandy who was engaged there with a considerable body of forces, partly in the siege of Aiguillon, partly in making head against the Earl of Lancaster, formerly Earl of Derby, who had found him employment for two campaigns. The retreat of the Duke of Normandy, in conformity with the orders of Philip, left the west of France much at the command of this noble Earl, whose soldiers were so much sated with spoil, that they hardly valued the richest merchandise, but were only desirous of gold, silver, or such feathers as were then worn by soldiers in their helmets.

While Philip, in this emergency of his bad fortune, thus abandoned a part of his dominions to save the rest, he endeavoured, by every argument in his power, and particularly by advancing large sums of money, to prevail upon the Scottish nation, and their king, David II., to declare war against England, by which means he hoped that Edward might be disturbed in his siege of Calais The Scottish king and nation did, accordingly, unfortunately take arms, and began a war which was terminated by the battle of Neville's Cross, near Durham, in which $\;^{\text{A. D. 1346}}_{\text{Oct. 17.}}$ they sustained a formidable defeat, and their king, David, was made prisoner.

The siege of Calais still continued, the French making many desperate attempts to relieve it, and particularly by sending in provisions by sea. The low and swampy situation of the grounds around the town exposed the besiegers to great loss by sickness and disease; and the garrison of Calais did not omit to make many sallies, which were partially successful.

Mean time, the war in Bretagne still raged betwixt the contending parties of Blois and Montfort. A noble knight named Sir Thomas Dagworth was created by Edward general of the English auxiliary forces in that province, and carried over considerable succours to the valiant Countess of Montfort, who still maintained the war there in the name of her son.

Charles de Blois, who claimed this duchy by the decision of the King of France, assembled among his partisans in Bretagne a very considerable force, amounting to no less than sixteen hundred men-at-arms, with a proportional number of cross-bows and infantry, and some formidable military engines; with this force he besieged a fortress, called Roche-d'Arien, which had lately been taken by the English. The captain of the garrison, whose wife was at the time indisposed, was so alarmed at the effect of the engines, that he offered to deliver up the castle upon easy terms, which Charles de Blois was ill-advised enough to refuse. In the mean time, Sir Thomas Dagworth formed the resolution of relieving the garrison of Roche-d'Arien. He united his own forces with those of the Countess of Montfort, who were commanded by a good knight, called Tanneguy de Chatel. In their first attempt on the French, who lay before Roche-d'Arien, the English and Bretons were defeated; but having, by the encouragement of Sir Thomas Dagworth and of a Breton knight, called Garnier de Cadoudal, resolved to renew the enterprise, they made a second attack on the ensuing evening, when the victory of the French might be supposed to render them secure and unguarded. In this unexpected attempt their success was complete. The French were surprised and totally defeated, and their general, Charles de Blois, became prisoner to his female antagonist, Jane de Montfort.

A similar heroine arose, however, in the family of Charles de Blois. His wife, a lady of a lofty spirit, undertook to maintain the war, which would otherwise have terminated on her husband's captivity.

In the mean time, the two contending Monarchs were not idle. King Philip, who had already held a parliament, in which he prevailed upon his peers and liege vassals to lend him their utmost assistance, was employed in levying a strong army, with which he proposed to compel Edward to raise the siege of Calais. He used his utmost efforts to recover from ancient receivers and taxgatherers the sums which they had not accounted for. Heavy assessments were also imposed upon the clergy as well as upon the laity, and great rigour was manifested in the mode of recovering payment. Philip even demanded from the monks of St Denis a crucifix of massive gold, being a treasure bestowed by the devotion of his predecessors. To this, however, the monks replied that "the crucifix could not be taken away, or converted to a secular use, without inevitable danger to the souls of all parties concerned;" with

A.D. 1347

which answer, even in the urgency of his necessity,
Philip was obliged to remain satisfied.

The friendship of the Flemings was of equal importance to both kings at this momentous crisis; in which country the affections of the prince and of the people remained divided as before. The free towns and their citizens were strongly inclined to England, and had settled that their young lord should wed the daughter of Edward III., the beautiful Lady Isabel of England. But the young Earl himself objected to this match, and was inclined to the alliance of France, the rather that his father, a faithful confederate and vassal of Philip of Valois, had fallen in his quarrel at the battle of Cressy. The rude Flemings, incensed to find their prince averse to the policy which they recommended, laid violent hands on his person, and assured him he should not obtain his liberty till he consented to ally himself with England, and marry the Princess Isabel. The young Earl, finding himself so roughly handled by his subjects, resolved to dissemble his sentiments, and carried his acquiescence so far as to go to King Edward's camp before Calais, with a party of Flemish citizens, who seemed to act as his tutors, and whose will he in no shape contradicted. He was well received by Edward, who even condescended to apologise for the death of his father, as an accident out of his power to prevent. Thus the young Earl found himself in high favour with the English Monarch, and paid his addresses to the Princess Isabel, with the same attention as if he had been serious in his courtship. In private, however, he meditated his flight, and being indulged with permission to follow the sport of hawking, he seized the opportunity, while apparently engaged in it, to make his escape by the speed of his horse, and took refuge at the court of France, where his presence was cordially welcomed by King Philip.

While these things were passing, the inhabitants of Calais were reduced to the last extremity. They despatched a messenger by sea with letters to King Philip, saying, that his good people of Calais, having eaten their horses, dogs, and rats, had nothing left to subsist upon unless they fed upon each other; wherefore they conjured their King to succour them, otherwise the town must be certainly lost. The vessel bearing these letters was taken by the English, and King Edward forwarded the missives to the French King, after having perused their contents, and superscribed them with a taunting indorsation, asking, "Why he came not to rescue his people of Calais, who were so distressed for his sake?" Philip needed no incentive either from friend or enemy, having assembled an army of a hundred thousand men, with the sole purpose of relieving Calais.

On the other hand, King Edward, considering the extreme importance of the place, and the trouble, expense, and loss, which it had cost him to bring it to its present reduced state, was determined that no effort of the King of France should avail for its relief. For this purpose he strongly fortified the approaches to Calais on every point, so as to make it impossible for King Philip to draw near the place, or annoy the besiegers, either by an advance along the sea-shore or by the high-road. These were the only two roads practicable to armed forces, as all the rest of the grounds in the vicinity of Calais were swampy marshes, where troops could not act.

Against the approach along the sea-shore Edward had placed his ships, well supplied with artillery, and he had besides strongly fortified the shore. Similar defences were constructed on the causeway which approached the town by the bridge of Neuillet.

When the King of France, therefore, with his immense host, approached the neighbourhood of Calais, he had the mortification to find that he could not, without the extremity of imprudence, attempt to enter the town either by the highway or by the shore, and to pass through the marshes was altogether impossible; after displaying therefore his great army at a place called Sangate, in sight of Calais and its besiegers, King Philip found himself wholly unable to enter the place, and was compelled to withdraw without fighting. He endeavoured to rouse the pride of Edward by a letter, defying him to leave his fortifications, and fight in a fair field. Edward replied that " he took no counsel from an adversary; that he had been before Calais for more than a year, and had reduced the place to a state of extremity; that he would not quit the advantage which he had gained; and if Philip wished a passage into the town, he might seek it as he best could, since he was to expect no assistance from him."

The hopes of the people of Calais had been at first strongly excited, when they beheld from their towers the numerous forces of France advancing to their relief. The first day, therefore, they intimated their confidence of assistance by decorating their walls with banners, and for the same purpose lighted large bonfires, and sounded all their martial instruments of music, attended with loud shouts. On the second night, the bonfires were fewer, and the shouts less cheerful, than before. On the third night, the towers showed a decaying fire—emblem of expiring hope—and the acclamations of mirth and joy were changed into screams and groans, which seemed designed to attract pity. On the following morning, all the banners on the principal towers were lowered, save the banner of France, which still floated from its summit.

But when the inhabitants of Calais beheld at length the pennons of King Philip's host retiring from their view, they knew all hopes of those succours, which they had waited for so anxiously and vainly, were at an end. They had suffered such extremities, that human nature could endure no longer; and, to intimate that resistance was at an end, they lowered the banner of France, and displayed that of England in its place. But they had to learn that their obstinacy had offended King Edward more than either their gallantry or their reluctant submission could atone for. He gave them presently to understand, that he would not receive their surrender, unless they yielded implicitly to his mercy, without any capitulation either for their lives or property. When this severity was objected to even by his own commanders, Edward would agree to show no further favour than to the following extent. He demanded that six of the chief burgesses of the town should come before him bareheaded, barefooted, and in their shirts, having halters around their necks, bearing the keys of the town and castle of Calais, which were to be humbly surrendered to him. These six men were to submit to the King's pleasure, how severe soever that might be, without reservation even of life; and in consideration of their doing so, the stern conqueror reluctantly promised that the rest of the citizens of Calais should have mercy.

These conditions were sent to the town, and read before the assembled citizens. The tidings were followed by a general lamentation, which, considering the difficulty of finding men willing to take upon themselves this strange submission, was not to be wondered at. After some deliberation, a burgess, the most substantial in the city, addressed the assembly. His name, Eustace de Saint Pierre, ought never to be forgotten while disinterested patriotism is revered among mankind. "He that shall contribute to save this fair town from sack and spoil," said this gallant man, "though at the price of his own blood, shall doubtless deserve well of God and of his country. I will be one who will offer my head to the King of England, as a ransom for the town of Calais." The greater part of the assembly were moved by this speech to tears and exclamations of gratitude. Five other burgesses caught emulation from the noble devotion of Eustace de Saint Pierre, and offered to partake with him the honourable peril which he had incurred. They quickly put themselves into the humiliating attire required by Edward, but which, assumed in such a cause, was more honourable than the robes of the Garter, which that King had lately instituted. In their shirts, barefooted, and with halters round their necks, they were conducted before Edward, to whom they submitted themselves for disposal, as the stipulated ransom for the pardon of their fellow-citizens. The King, looking on them with indignation, upbraided them with the losses he had sustained through their obstinacy, and commanded them to be presently beheaded. Sir Walter Manny, and the bravest English nobles and warriors, interfered to prevent the execution, and even the Prince of Wales interceded for their lives in vain.

The Queen Philippa was the last resource of these unfortunate men. She had recently joined her husband's camp, in circumstances equally flattering to Edward as a monarch, and interesting to him as a husband. It was during her regency in England that the great victory of Neville's Cross had been obtained; and it was under her auspices that David II. of Scotland was made prisoner. The Queen was also at this time great with child, and thus in every respect entitled to the highest regard of her royal husband. When she saw that Edward would be moved with no less entreaty than her own, she rose hastily from her seat, and kneeled before the King, saying, with many tears, "Ah! my lord and husband, have I not a right to ask a boon of you, having come over the sea, through so many dangers, that I might wait upon you? therefore, let me now pray you, in honour of our Blessed Redeemer, and for love of me, to take pity upon these six prisoners!"

Edward looked doubtfully upon the Queen, and seemed to hesitate for a space, but said at length, "Ah, madam, I could well wish that you had been elsewhere this day; yet how can I deny any boon which you ask of me? Take these men, and dispose of them as you will."

The gracious Queen, rejoiced at having prevailed in her suit, and having changed the dishonourable attire of the burgesses for new clothing, gave each of them six nobles for immediate use, and caused them to be safely conveyed through the English host, and set at liberty.

Edward III. had no sooner obtained possession of Calais, than he studied to secure it by fortifications and otherwise, but particularly endeavoured, by internal changes among its inhabitants, to render it in future an important and permanent possession of the crown of England. For this purpose, he dispossessed the inhabitants of Calais (who were, indeed, much reduced in numbers) of their houses and property within the town, and conferred their possessions upon Englishmen born. The new inhabitants whom he established in the town were substantial citizens from London, and a great number of countrymen from the neighbouring county of Kent, to whom he assigned the lands and tenements of the French. Calais became from that period, until the reign of Philip and Mary, in all respects a colony of England. The King also fortified the castle and the town with additional works. Lastly, before he set sail to return to England, Edward agreed to a truce with France, which lasted from 1347, until the year 1355, though not without infractions on both sides.

We must not here end the history of Calais, without adverting to some circumstances which happened shortly after its capture, and are highly illustrative of the manners of the time.

In supplying the place with a new garrison, Edward had not omitted to choose valiant officers, and such as he thought men worthy of trust. These were the Lord John Montgomery, as governor of the town, and, as seneschal of the castle, which commanded the place, a Lombard knight, named Emeric of Pavia. This last officer was a favourite of Edward, in whose court he had been educated from childhood; but he was infected with the vice of avarice, to which his countrymen were esteemed to be generally addicted. At the same time when Edward left Calais under such custody, a wise and valiant French lord, called Sir Geoffrey de Charny, acted as lieutenant for the French King, to defend his frontiers, near Saint Omer, and watch the garrison of the new English acquisition This officer, who was high in his master's confidence, knew the failing of the Lombard governor, and tempted him, by offering the sum of twenty thousand gold crowns, to deliver up to him the castle of Calais. To this treacherous proposition, Emeric of Pavia acceded, and took a solemn oath to discharge faithfully his part of the bargain. This negotiation reached the ears of King Edward, who sent for the Lombard to come to see him in England, and, when Sir Emeric arrived there, took a private opportunity to charge him with having sold to the French the castle of Calais, the dearest thing he had on earth, excepting his wife and children. Emeric confessed the accusation, but returned a mercantile answer, that his bargain with Sir Geoffrey de Charny might as yet easily be broken, since he had received no part of the stipulated price. Edward, who had some regard, as we have said, for this venal knight, forgave him the treason which he had meditated, on condition that he should go on with his bargain, and inform him of the time that he and Sir Geoffrey de Charny should finally fix upon for the surrender. Edward also gave his avaricious favourite permission to get as much money as he could from Sir Geoffrey de Charny, provided he betrayed every particular of the negotiation to the King himself, and kept the whole matter a secret from others.

Sir Emeric, thus secured against the consequences of the treason, and resolved once more to be true to his indulgent master, returned to Calais, and, renewing his intercourse with Sir Geoffrey de

Charny, fixed on the last night of December, 1349 as the term for executing their secret treaty fo. the surrender of the castle. King Edward, thus enabled to counteract the French stratagem, embarked very secretly with eight hundred choice men-at-arms, and a thousand archers, with whom he landed privately, and introduced them into the castle of Calais. He then called to him the celebrated Sir Walter Manny, and said, " Sir Knight, I mean to grace you with the honour of this night's enterprise, and I and my son will fight under your banner."

In the mean time, Sir Geoffrey de Charny, contriver of this enterprise, arrived at Neuillet bridge, on the causeway, or high-road to Calais, with a part of his force, and there waited till the rest joined him. He then communicated with Emeric of Pavia, by messengers sent to the citadel; and, learning that the time for his admission into the castle was approaching, he despatched twelve knights, and a hundred men-at-arms, having with them the money agreed upon, while he himself halted nigh to the nearest city-gate with the rest of his company. He left also a small rear-guard on the bridge at Neuillet. The captain of the French advanced guard moved on towards the castle, and met with the double traitor, Emeric, at the postern of the fortress, which he kept open, as if to admit the French. They delivered to him the stipulated sum in French crowns. Sir Emeric took the money, and cast it into a chest, saying, " We have other work to do than to count money at present

You shall enter the donjon, gentlemen, and then
you are masters of the castle." But the French
had no sooner entered at the postern of the castle,
thus opened to them, than they were assailed in
front, flank, and rear, by the English, who lay
ready for them within the castle, and exclaimed,
" Manny! Manny! To the rescue! What! thought
a handful of Frenchmen to take the castle of
Calais!" The French men-at-arms, surprised and
outnumbered, rendered themselves prisoners, and
were thrust into the donjon, not as conquerors,
but as captives, while the victors prepared to sally
from the gates upon Sir Geoffrey de Charny and
his party, the rear of whom held their post at the
bridge of Neuillet, while the main body had advanced to the Boulogne gate of the town, expecting
to be speedily called to the support of their ad-
vanced-guard, who they calculated ought to be by
this time in possession of the castle.

These were, however, at a loss to account for
the delay of the expected surrender, and their
commander was exclaiming impatiently, " Unless
this Lombard admit us hastily, we are like to
starve here with cold."—" Oh, sir," said a French
knight of his company, " you must remember that
the Lombards are a shrewd and suspicious people.
I warrant me, Sir Emeric of Pavia is counting his
crowns, and looking that they be all of just weight."
As Sir Geoffrey and his party spoke thus among
themselves, the Boulogne gate of Calais, to which
they had approached, suddenly opened, and a body
of men-at-arms issued forth in good order; most of

them were dismounted, and they were attended by three hundred archers. The French, from this apparition, and the cry of "Manny, to the rescue!" instantly knew that they were betrayed; but, as the causeway on which they stood was narrow, Sir Geoffrey de Charny exclaimed aloud, "Gentlemen, if we turn our backs, we are certainly lost; dismount speedily, and cut your spears to the length of five feet, for fighting on foot." The English, hearing these words, replied, "Well said, by Saint George! shame on them that shall first turn their backs!" Edward, who was himself engaged in this skirmish, though without any marks of royal distinction, despatched six banners and three hundred archers on horseback, who, by a circuitous route, reached the bridge of Neuillet, where the French had left a rear-guard, as already noticed.

At this last place the battle waxed very hot; but the Frenchmen were taken at great disadvantage, and, after a stout resistance, compelled to retreat. In the mean time a furious contest was continued upon the causeway nearer to the town, between the troops of Sir Geoffrey de Charny and those under Manny. King Edward was distinguished amid the crowd of combatants by the exclamations of, "Ha, Saint George! Ha, Saint Edward!" with which he accompanied every stroke of his two-handed sword, seeking to match himself with the stoutest antagonist whom the affray afforded. He had the luck to encounter Sir Eustace de Ribeaumont, one of the strongest men and best knights who then lived. This distinguished French champion gave the English Monarch so stout a meeting, that he more than once nearly forced him upon his knees. Nor was it until the increasing numbers of the English, who sallied from the town to the assistance of their friends, rendered longer defence on the French part unavailing, that Ribeaumont resigned his weapon to the antagonist whom he only knew as a brave warrior, and said the fatal words, " Sir Knight, I surrender myself—rescue, or no rescue!" The French lost in this skirmish the greater part of the men whom Sir Geoffrey de Charny had brought towards Calais, except some who had not alighted from their horses, and had therefore the means of escape; the rest were either slain or made prisoners.

King Edward caused his principal officers and prisoners to be feasted at supper that same night, in a great hall, where he placed himself at the head of a royal table. Here the King sat alone and in state, while the Prince his son, and the peers of England, served during the first course; but after this sacrifice to ceremony, the guests were arranged without farther distinction at the same board. Edward walked up and down, bareheaded, excepting a circle of gold, and a chaplet of pearls of great value, around his brows, and passed in this manner round the table, and conversed freely with his captives. On approaching Sir Geoffrey de Charny, the contriver of the enterprise, he said, with some signs of displeasure, " I owe you but little thanks,

Sir Knight, who would have stolen from me by night what I won in broad day. You are a better bargain-maker than I, when you would have purchased Calais for twenty thousand crowns; but, God be praised, you have missed your aim." The Lord of Charny, who was much wounded, remained silent and somewhat abashed, and Edward passed on to the other guests, to whom he spoke with much condescension and politeness. But it was upon Sir Eustace de Ribeaumont that Edward conferred the highest praises, styling him the most valiant and courageous knight in that skirmish. " Nor did I ever," said the King, " find a man who gave me so much to do, body to body, as you have done this night. Wherefore, I adjudge to you this chaplet, as the prize of the tournament," taking off the string of pearls which he wore. " I pray you to wear it for my sake at all festivals, and declare unto the ladies that it was given to you by Edward of England, as a testimony of your valour. I discharge you also of any ransom, and you are free to depart to-morrow, if such be your pleasure."

In this strange anecdote, you may recognise some proceedings, which, had such taken place in our days, on the part of a great general and great monarch, would have necessarily been considered imprudent and inconsiderate. There was no great wisdom certainly in trusting to the double treachery of Emeric of Pavia, and there was great rashness in a monarch like Edward venturing his person, without any distinction of his rank, in the nocturnal confusion of so desperate a skirmish

To encounter such dangers, however, was the
proudest boast of chivalry; and a monarch, however
wise and sagacious, was expected to court the
most desperate risks of war, if he desired the
praise of an accomplished knight, which was then
held the highest that a man could aspire to, how
eminent soever his hereditary rank. It is not less
worth your notice, how generously Edward III.
rewarded the French knight who had struck him
down in battle, although the same monarch could
shortly before hardly be induced to pardon the six
burgesses of Calais, whose sole offence was, the
honourable discharge of their duty to their King
and country, and the defence of their town. This
is one instance among many, that it was reckoned
presumption on the part of citizens or peasants to
meddle with martial affairs, which were accounted
the proper business of the nobility and gentry, and
their followers.

It is also remarkable, that the attempt upon
Calais might have been made a legitimate pretext
for breaking off the truce, on the part of the King
of England. But as Geoffrey de Charny pretended
to no authority from the French King, and as
Philip disclaimed the attempt, Edward III. was
well disposed to pass it over.

The evils of these continued wars, though carried
on with great increase to the glory of individuals,
were attended with so much misery to both kingdoms,
that they probably never endured a greater
state of wretchedness. In France, a pestilential
disorder of a dangerous kind completed what had

been commenced by want and bad nourishment.
The populace died in great numbers, and those who
remained entertained a natural horror of the feudal
oppressors under whom they suffered such unpitied
misery. This pestilence swept over not only the
greater part of Christendom, but Africa, and Asia
itself, and reached England, where it was equally
fatal. It fell most heavily on the poorer sort of
people; and of the inferior clergy so many died,
that very many churches were without either parson or curate to serve the cure. Besides this disastrous scourge, the King of England, although his
parliament had been repeatedly liberal in voting
him supplies of money, was afflicted by the embarrassment of his finances. It was at a very extravagant cost that he had been able to support these
wars of France, and the subsidies granted to him
by his English subjects were speedily exhausted in
the expenses which attended the prosecution of
hostilities in a foreign country, and the pay of so
many auxiliary troops. The large spoil made by the
English soldiers contributed as usual to debauch
the morals of the people, and accustom them to
extravagance and unbounded expense.

These national evils had at least one good effect;
they restrained the Kings of France and England
from renewing the war. The attempt, therefore,
upon Calais passed over without notice.

It does not appear, however, that the treacherous
seneschal, Emeric of Pavia, ever recovered the
entire good opinion of the King. He was deprived
of the government of the castle the very day after

the skirmish; and, although he remained in the
service of the English King, he never appears to
have regained his confidence. He was retained in
his active service, however, gained possession, by
stratagem, of the fortress of Guines, near to Calais,
and attempted also to surprise Saint Omer. In
this last enterprise, Sir Emeric was defeated and
made prisoner by his old acquaintance, Sir Geoffrey
de Charny, who availed himself of the opportunity
to be revenged of his former treachery. He caused
the Lombard to be put to death with all the dis-
honours of degradation, commanding his spurs to
be hacked from his heels, as one unworthy of the
honour of knighthood, and his body to be torn to
pieces by wild horses drawing in different directions; a cruel, yet not undeserved punishment, for
the perfidious part he had acted at the attempt
upon Calais.

But this last event took place after some others
that were of greater importance. One of these
was the submission made by Godfrey of Harcourt,
the counsellor of Edward III., to his native kinsman
and king, Philip of France. The penitent threw
himself at that monarch's feet, with a towel twisted
round his neck, in the form of a halter, confessing
the remorse which he felt for having been a principal cause of the defeat of Cressy, and regretting
that he should have added to the number of those
French princes of the blood-royal who had so often
contributed to the misfortunes of their native country. Philip, though subject to violent passion, was
placable upon submission, and forgave a penitent

against whom he had several real subjects of offence. Their reconciliation did not, however, last long.

Shortly afterwards, the King of France united the county of Dauphiny to the crown, for the sum of one hundred thousand florins, paid to Hubert II., its feudal sovereign, as the price of cession in favour of Charles, the grandson of Philip. The Dauphin himself retired from the world, and adopted the ecclesiastical habit; and Charles, who married Joanna, daughter of the Duke of Bourbon, was the first French prince who bore the title of Dauphin, afterwards selected as that of the first-born male heir to the crown of France. Charles is often termed Duke of Normandy, the appanage which his father John possessed until he succeeded to the crown. In January, 1350, Philip himself married a second wife, the Princess Blanche, sister of the King of Navarre, then only eighteen years of age, and who had been destined to be the partner of his son and successor; but he did not long survive this union, having died in the   A.D. 1350. month of August following, in the twenty-third year of his reign, and fifty-ninth of his age.

Philip of Valois was hated by the nobility, on account of the frequent encroachments which he made on their privileges, and for the readiness with which he subjected many of their number to capital punishment. He obtained, at the commencement of his reign, the title of the Fortunate, because, although three princes stood between him and the throne at his birth, he had nevertheless the good luck to survive them all, and obtain possession of it; but, as happened to other princes, the long course of unsuccessful war in which he was engaged, and the miseries undergone during his reign, would have better justified the epithet of "the Unfortunate."

CHAPTER XIX.

Accession of John the Good—Truce with England violated, but renewed—Intrigues of Charles King of Navarre—Charles assassinates the Constable of France, and extorts his pardon from the King—Edward and his son, the Black Prince, invade France, and ravage the Country—the Black Prince winters at Bourdeaux—King John assembles a large army, marches into Poitou, and comes up with the English encamped at Maupertuis, within two leagues of Poitiers—Battle of Poitiers—King John taken Prisoner—his Reception by the Black Prince—Return of the Prince, with his Prisoner, to England.

[1350–1356.]

JOHN, DUKE OF NORMANDY, ascended the throne on the death of his father, Philip of Valois. He had attained the mature age of thirty-one, had commanded armies with reputation, had acquired character both for courage and conduct, and was, in every respect, a more hopeful Prince than his predecessor.

Yet King John of France, though distinguished by the flattering title of the Good, early adopted a course of severity, which occasioned him much unpopularity. At a solemn festival at Paris, immediately after his coronation, he caused to be arrested Rodolph de Brienne, Count of Eu and of Gnines, and Constable of France, who was accused of wishing to put the English Monarch in possession of his county of Guines, adjacent to the town of Calais. The unfortunate Constable was arrested, and beheaded, in presence of the lords of the council, after three days' confinement, and without any form of trial; an execution which greatly awakened the fears and suspicions of the nobility, respecting the new King.

In the year 1349, the English commander in Bretagne, Sir Thomas Dagworth, fell into an ambuscade, said to consist of banditti, by whom he was slain, in violation of the truce. In resentment of this slaughter, Henry Plantagenet, already celebrated under the titles of Lancaster and Derby, to which that of Earl of Lincoln was now added, was sent as Edward's lieutenant-general into Bretagne, with an army which his reputation soon augmented to thirty thousand men. In the mean time, in contempt of the truce which still subsisted, constant skirmishes were fought between the French and English, which hovered between the character of hostile engagements, and of the tournaments which that age considered merely as martial recreations. In these stormy times, the various commanders of garrisons made war upon each other, as they saw occasion or opportunity, without the kings' positively either authorising or resenting their quarrels; and in this manner much blood was spilt, of which neither prince was willing to acknowledge the blame. The Pope, Innocent XI., again used his intercession to prolong the truce, which seemed of such uncertain character, and succeeded in his endeavours in 1353, although he was unable to bring the kingdoms to such a solid peace as His Holiness desired.

About this time, King John and his court were extremely disturbed by the intrigues occasioned by his young kinsman, Charles, King of Navarre. This young Prince, nearly connected with the French crown, his mother being a daughter of Louis X., called Hutin, possessed at once the most splendid and the most diabolical qualities. He was handsome, courageous, affable, liberal, and popular in his address, and a person of great talents and ingenuity. Unfortunately, he added to these gorgeous qualities a turn for intrigue and chicane, together with an ambition altogether insatiable, and a disposition capable of carrying through the worst actions by the worst means. From this latter part of his character, he received from the French the name of Charles the Bad, or Charles the Wicked, which he appears abundantly to have deserved, since even the strong tie of his own interest could not always restrain his love of mischief.

On the arrival of this monarch at the court of John, he set up various pretensions to favour, both with the King and people of France, and rendered himself so agreeable at court, that he carried his point of marrying Joan, the daughter of the French Monarch. He demanded certain places in Normandy; and when the King, to elude his pertinacity, conferred that county upon Charles de la Cerda, his constable and favourite, A.D. 1351.

the King of Navarre did not hesitate to assassinate
that unfortunate officer, in his castle called De
l'Aigle, in Normandy. Having committed this
atrocity, he afterwards boldly avowed the deed;
put himself at the head of troops, and affected independence; treated with the English for their
assistance; leagued together all the fiery and dis-
affected spirits of the court, that is to say, great
part of the young nobility who frequented it, in
opposition to the crown; and threatened to create
such confusion, that King John felt himself under
the necessity of treating with this dangerous young
man, instead of bringing him to justice for his
crimes. Charles of Navarre, however, refused to
lay aside his arms, or come to court, unless upon
stipulation for an absolute pardon for the death of
the Constable, great cessions in land, a large payment of money, and, above all, complete security
that whatever terms were granted, should be kept
with him.

King John saw himself, by the necessity of his
affairs, obliged to subscribe to these demands,
which were rather dictated than preferred by his
refractory vassal. He was even compelled to deliver his second son to Charles of Navarre, as a
hostage, that the promises made to the latter should
be faithfully kept. After this, it was in vain that
John desired to conceal his weakness under a pomp-
ous display, designed to show that the pardon of
Navarre was not granted in virtue of a previous
stipulation, but the result of the King's own free
will.

In March 1355, this high offender came to Paris in person, as had been previously agreed upon, and appeared before parliament, where the King was seated on the tribunal. Here Charles of Navarre made a formal speech, acknowledging his errors, and asking forgiveness, with some affectation of humility. The Duke of Bourbon, then Constable of France, placed his hands upon those of the royal criminal, in symbol of arrest, and led him into another apartment, as if to execution. The Queens of France (of whom there were at that time three) threw themselves at the feet of the Monarch, to implore pardon for one so nearly connected with his family, and the King appeared reluctantly to grant what he dared not have refused, for fear of retaliation on the prince, his son. It is probable that the whole ceremony had no effect, except that of incensing the King of Navarre, and irritating his love of mischief, which he afterwards repeatedly indulged, to the great prejudice of the King and kingdom of France.

A.D. 1355.

In the mean time, King Edward, fully expecting that this discord between King John and Charles of Navarre would break into an open flame, made preparations to take advantage of it. For this purpose, he constituted the Black Prince, who obtained that celebrated name from the constant colour of his armour, his lieutenant in Gascony and Aquitaine, and sent him over with a considerable army, which, by the number of troops there levied, was augmented to about sixty thousand men. With this large force the young Edward marched into the country of Toulouse, taking several towns, which he burnt, wasted, and destroyed. But Charles of Navarre becoming for the present reconciled with the King of France, the Prince of Wales returned to Bourdeaux, after these extensive ravages.

His father King Edward was, on his part, no less active in the desolation of France. While the Black Prince laid waste the southern provinces of that country with fire and sword, the father landed at Calais, and marched from thence towards Saint Omer, where King John lay at the head of a considerable army. The remembrance of Cressy perhaps made the King of France decline an engagement; so that King Edward, unable to bring the French to action, returned to his own country to advise with his Parliament, and make head against the Scottish nation, who, notwithstanding all their losses, were again in arms. It has been reasonably suggested, that injured pride and wounded feelings, the recollection of the dishonour sustained at Cressy, and the hope of avenging the disgrace of that day, were more powerful with John of France, than any reasons of sound policy, in inducing him to refuse the offers preferred by Rome for establishing peace between the countries. The scenes of blood and devastation which France every where presented, the ravages of the pestilence, and the total silence of law and justice throughout a kingdom which strangers and robbers had in a manner partitioned amongst themselves, made the country at that time in every respect unfit to maintain a war with a powerful and active enemy. It was, however, the fate of King John to rush without reflection upon dangers yet greater, and losses more disastrous, than those which had befallen his unfortunate father. A period now approaches much celebrated in English history.

The Prince of Wales, who had spent the winter in recruiting his little army at Bourdeaux, resolved the next year to sally forth, and lay waste the country of the enemy, as he had done the preceding summer. King John, on the other hand, having determined to intercept his persevering enemy, assembled a brilliant army, in number about 50,000 men, of which there were twenty thousand men-at-arms, headed by the King himself and his four sons, and most of the princes of the blood, with a large proportion of the nobility and gentry of France, few of whom chose to stay at home, when called to attend the royal standard in such an emergency. Scotland sent him an auxiliary force of two thousand men-at-arms. With this overpowering army, the King of France marched into Poitou, and came upon the English army so suddenly, as to leave its commander no choice of retreat. The Black Prince, therefore, determined to fortify himself in the best manner he could, and to wait the enemy's attack.

His whole force did not amount to more than 2000 men-at-arms, 4000 archers, and 2000 light infantry, scarcely the eighth part of that which was arrayed against him. The place which he selected for his encampment was called the field of

Maupertuis, near Beaumont, and within two leagues of the town of Poitiers, a strong position, where the advantages of the ground were such as in some measure compensated his numerical inferiority.

This memorable field formed the summit of a gentle declivity, planted with vineyards, which could only be approached by one road of no great breadth, flanked by thickets and hedges. To add to the strength of the ground, the English had laboured hard at fortifying it, and covered their ranks with trenches, in addition to the trees, bushes, and vineyards, by which it was naturally defended. Amidst these natural and artificial defences, and only accessible by this narrow and difficult pass, the English troops were drawn up on the side of the gentle acclivity, with the admirable foresight and judgment which, from his early days, had distinguished their princely commander.

Sir Eustace de Ribeaumont, and three other knights, were despatched to make a reconnoissance of the English position, and on their return made this report to the King:—" Sir, we have seen the enemy. By our guess, they amount to two thousand men-at-arms, four thousand archers, and fifteen hundred or two thousand other men; which troops appear to us to form but one division. They are strongly posted, wisely ordered, and their position is wellnigh inaccessible. In order to attack them, there is but one passage, where four horsemen may ride abreast, which leads to the centre of their line. The hedges that flank this passage are lined with archers, and the English main body itself consists of dismounted men-at-arms, before whom a large body of archers are arranged in the form of a *herse*, or harrow. By this difficult passage alone can you approach the English position. Consider therefore, what is best to be done."

King John determined, that in such difficult circumstances, the attack should be made on foot. He commanded, therefore, his men-at-arms to dismount, cast off their spurs, and cut their spears to the length of five feet, in order to do battle as infantry. Three hundred men-at-arms alone were commanded to remain mounted, in order that their charge might begin the combat, break the archery, and make way for the columns of infantry; and in this order King John resolved to undertake the attack.

An attempt, however, was made to save the approaching effusion of blood, by two churchmen, the Cardinal Talleyrand de Perigord, and the Cardinal Capoccio, who visited both the French and English armies, to incline them to peace. The Prince of Wales, conscious of the difficulty of his situation, and of his great inferiority of forces, was not unwilling to listen to honourable terms; but as the King of France insisted that Edward and one hundred of his principal lords should yield themselves prisoners, the Prince indignantly rejected this condition as dishonourable, and an end was put to the negotiation.

But before the battle took place, one or two circumstances happened, highly characteristic of the spirit of the times.

It chanced that the celebrated Sir John Chandos was, on the morning before the action, reconnoitring the French host, while John de Clermont, a marshal of the French army, performed the same duty on the other side. These two knights bore the same device, which was the Virgin Mary, surrounded by sunbeams. This was in those days a great offence; and it was accordingly challenged by Clermont with these words:—" How long is it, Chandos, since you have taken it on you to bear my device?"

"It is mine own," said Chandos; "at least it is mine as well as yours."

"I deny that," said Clermont; "but you act after the fashion of you Englishmen, who have no ingenuity to devise your own appointments, but readily steal the invention of others."

"Let us prove which has the right in the battle to-morrow," answered Chandos, "since to-day is truce, on account of the cardinals' negotiation." They parted thus upon terms of mutual defiance.

Early on the following morning (Monday the 19th of September, 1356), the valiant young Prince of Wales reviewed the position of his troops, and briefly said to them, "Sirs, be not abashed for the number of our enemies; for victory is not in the multitude of people, but where God pleases to grant it. If we survive this day's conflict, our honour will be in proportion to the odds against which we fight; if we die this day, there are men enough in England to revenge our fall."

As the Prince thus addressed his people, the Lord Audley came forward, and besought a boon of him. "My lord," he said, "I have been the true servant of your father and of your house; and out of respect for both, I have taken a vow long since, that when I should be in any battle where the king your father, or any of his sons, should command, I would myself begin the battle, or die upon the field. May it please you now to permit me to pass to the vanguard, and accomplish my vow?"

The Prince willingly granted his desire, saying, "Sir James, God give you grace so to bear yourself, that you shall be acknowledged the best and foremost knight of all, this day!"

The Prince then proceeded somewhat to change the order of his army. When reconnoitred by De Ribeaumont, he had shown only one division. But when about to fight, he divided his little army into three, drawn up close in the rear of each other, on the sloping and defensible ground we have described. He also placed, apart, a body of men-at-arms, under the Captal de Buche, designed to fetch a compass round the hill, unobserved, and fall on the rear of the French when they should commence the attack.

The French accordingly began the battle with the three hundred select men-at-arms, whom they had caused to remain on horseback, for the service of dispersing the archers, and forcing a passage

for the rest of the army. These had no sooner
entered between the hedges, however, than the
archers, by whom they were lined, commenced
their fatal discharge, and the horses of the men-
at-arms recoiled and turned restive, disordering
their own ranks, and rendering it impossible for
their masters to perform the orders given to them.
Sir James Audley, with four squires of undaunted
valour, fought in the front of the battle, and stopped not to take prisoners, but went straight forward against all opposition.

It was in vain that a great body of dismounted
men-at-arms entered the fatal pass, under two of the
French marshals, to relieve the mounted spearmen.
One of these leaders was slain, the other made prisoner; and their troops, driven back, were thrown in
confusion upon the second line, commanded by the
Dauphin. At the same time, the strong body of English men-at-arms, who had been reserved for that
service, with a corresponding number of archers,
burst unexpectedly from the ambuscade in which
they had been till now concealed. This was commanded, as already mentioned, by the valiant Gascon knight, called the Captal de Buche, a faithful
vassal of England. He attacked the French column
on the flank and rear, and compelled it to fly. The
Scottish auxiliaries shared the fate of their allies.
The victory being now on the side of England,
the Prince commanded his men-at-arms to take
horse, seeing the moment was come to advance.
They mounted, and prepared to charge accordingly, the Prince himself giving the word, "Advance

banners, in the name of God and Saint George!"
Upon seeing the approach of this strong body,
those French lords who commanded the second
division, and had charge of the three younger
princes of France, retreated from the battle, in
order, as they afterwards alleged, to place these
royal persons in safety. The army of the French
was now in such confusion, that the third division
was exposed to the full fury of the English assault,
by the retreat of the second line, and the person
of King John, who commanded it, was placed in
the greatest danger; his nobles, who fought around
him, were almost all slain or taken, and the victors, who disputed with each other the glory and
advantage of taking so great a prince alive, called
out, " Yield you, sir, or you die!" The gallant
monarch disdained the safety which was to be
found by complying with these invitations, and
continued manfully to defend himself with his
battle-axe. "If," says Froissart, "the knights of
King John had fought as resolutely as he did himself, the event of the day might have been different."

Finding himself left almost alone, and overpowered by numbers, the unfortunate King expressed a
wish to surrender to his cousin, the Prince of Wales;
but as this was impossible—for the Prince was in
a distant part of the field—King John gave his
gauntlet in token of surrender to Sir Denis Morbeque, a Frenchman by birth, but who, exiled from
France for a homicide there committed, was in the
Black Prince's service. From this gentleman King
John was soon after taken forcibly by several

knights of England and Gascony, who disputed the prize with so much violence, that the captive Monarch was only delivered from the tumult, and even the personal danger which it involved, by the Earl of Warwick and Lord Cobham, sent by the Prince of Wales to save him amid the general disorder. Philip of France, youngest son of King John, remained captive with his father. He behaved so resolutely on that fatal day, that he was said to have then acquired the epithet of the Hardy, by which he was afterwards distinguished.

The Prince of Wales, whose courtesy was at least equal to his bravery, caused a banquet to be spread in his pavilion, where he entertained the captive Monarch, with his great nobles, while he himself refused to sit down at the table, as not worthy of so great an honour as to eat with the King of France. He bid his royal captive, at the same time, make no heavy cheer for his misfortunes, though the fate of battle had been otherwise than he would have desired. "You shall find my father," said he, "willing to display towards you all honour and friendship, and you shall, if you will, become such friends together as you have never hitherto been. Consider," he added, with well-meant flattery, "though you have lost the field, you have attained the praise of being the bravest knight who has this day fought upon your side" The unfortunate King was much affected by the courtesy of his victor, from which he experienced whatever consolation his condition admitted of.

The Prince of Wales was not less anxious to

reward his friends, than by his generous conduct to soften the misfortunes of his enemies. Lord Audley, who had commenced the battle of Poitiers, had continued, as long as the action lasted, still pressing forward, without stopping to make prisoners, until at length he was nearly slain upon the spot; and he was the first object of the Prince's gratitude. Upon this noble knight the Prince bestowed, with his highest commendations, a free gift of five hundred merks of yearly revenue, which Sir James Audley received with suitable expressions of gratitude.

When he returned to his own pavilion, the noble knight sent for his brother, and some other friends, and made them bear witness that he transferred to his four faithful squires the gift which the Prince had given him, since it had been by their means and steady support through the whole battle, that he had been able to render the services which the Prince had valued so highly.

On the second day after the battle, the Black Prince marched towards Poitiers, into which a distinguished French warrior, named the Lord of Roye, had thrown himself, with a considerable body of men, which he was leading to join the French army, but which came too late for that service. Moderate, however, in his wishes to improve his victory, and chiefly desirous to secure his important prisoner, King John of France, the Prince declined entering into any considerable enterprise at this time, and passed steadily on his retreat to-

wards Bourdeaux. His march was so slow, that
he was at liberty to attend to the business of his
army, and the details in which individuals were interested.

Among other information, the Black Prince
learned the generous manner in which Lord Audley had disposed, among his four esquires, of the
splendid gift which his bounty had conferred upon
him. He sent for him therefore to his presence,
and requested to know wherefore he had parted
with the gift of his sovereign? and whether his
conduct arose from the present not being acceptable to him. Sir James Audley confessed that he
had presented to his esquires the gift which his
highness's bounty had conferred; but he alleged,
that the fidelity of those esquires had been the
means of his being able to execute the vow which
he had made; and that, by their constant attendance through the bloody day, they had repeatedly
saved his life at the imminent risk of their own.
"Wherefore," said the noble Lord, "it was well my
part to transfer to them that bounty which your
highness designed for me, especially since, renoun-
cing in their behalf this royal gift, I have still, God
be praised! revenues sufficient to maintain my place
in your highness's service. But if this should of-
fend your highness, I am right willing that it shall
be ordered according to your pleasure."

The Black Prince joyfully accepted an apology
so congenial to his feelings. He highly approved of
Lord Audley's generosity to his esquires, but made a

point of pressing upon him an additional gift of four hundred pounds yearly, which he required him to retain for his own use and behoof.

It was also, apparently, on this march, that the Black Prince decided the important question, who was to be considered as the immediate captor of King John of France. With the same generosity and justice which usually marked the conduct of this gallant Prince, Edward adjudged the glory and profit of this action to the poor French exile, Sir Denis of Morbeque, to whom King John had given his gauntlet in token of surrender, rather than to the powerful knights and barons, who disputed with him the advantages of so important a capture. I have already stated, elsewhere, that the ransom of a captive belonged to the person by whom he was taken prisoner. But the person of King John fell under an exception, which adjudged, that prisoners, whose ransom was rated at ten thousand crowns or upwards, should not belong to individuals, but to the general of the army. The Prince, therefore, finally closed this affair, by secretly transferring to Denis Morbeque the sum at which King John's ransom was rated.

After spending upwards of six months at Bourdeaux, the Black Prince proceeded to England with his prisoner, and made a solemn entrance into London, where the citizens *April, 1357.* received him with a gorgeous display of their power and wealth. In the procession which traversed the city on the occasion, King John of France appeared in royal array, mounted upon a beautiful white

courser, while the Prince of Wales, avoiding the
triumphant display of a victor, rode beside his
captive upon a little black palfrey of an ordinary
appearance. In modern times, this might be considered as an affectation of humility, and a more
pointed personal triumph, than if the Prince had
shown less apparent deference. But we are not to
judge of the feelings of a rude age from those of a
civilized one. In Edward's time, it was no uncom-
mon display of the victor to show conquered
princes to the people, loaded with irons, as in the
triumphs of the ancient Romans: and the very
opposite conduct of the conqueror of Poitiers was
considered as a mark of moderation and humility
on his part, and received as such by the vanquished
monarch, and all who witnessed it.

CHAPTER XX.

Consequences to France of the Battle of Poitiers—Disputes between the Dauphin and the States-General—Suppression of an Insurrection under Sir Godfrey Harcourt, who had again revolted to the English—Siege of Rennes—Truce concluded—Capture of the Castle of Evreux by Sir William Granville—Escape of Charles of Navarre from Prison—he organizes the Faction of the Navarrois—Insolence of Marcel, Provost of Paris—Insurrection of the Peasantry, called Jacquerie—Partial Success of the Regent against the English—Treaty for the ransom of King John—the states of France refuse to sanction this treaty, and Edward again invades France—Siege of Rheims—Peace of Bretigny—Death of King John, and Accession of the Dauphin Charles.

[1356—1364.]

THE battle of Poitiers was even more disastrous in its consequences to France than that of Cressy. For, as the combat had A.D. 1356. been chiefly fought on foot, and almost wholly by dismounted men-at-arms, a much larger portion of the French nobility had been slain than at Cressy, and the kingdom was, in a great measure, deprived of those on whose courage its protection was supposed chiefly to depend. The three sons of King John, who were naturally looked to as heirs of the

crown, were too young to be capable of retrieving
so dreadful a misfortune as the defeat of Poitiers.
The King had left no regent, or other legal representative;
a deficiency which his son Charles, who
bore the title of Dauphin and Duke of Normandy,
endeavoured to supply, by summoning a meeting
of the Estates of the kingdom, naturally
hoping that, in a period so calamitous, he
should find them disposed to act unanimously
for obtaining the release of King John, and
restoring good order in the kingdom of France.

<small>17th Oct. 1356.</small>

Unhappily, however, the members of this national
body were more strongly inclined to avail
themselves of so favourable an opportunity for
depressing the royal power, and raising their own,
than to combine in a joint effort for extricating the
nation from its difficulties.

One principal cause of the general discontent
and disorder, was the intrigues and conspiracies of
the King of Navarre, who at this period might be
justly termed the Evil Genius of France. It is
here for an instant necessary to resume his history
between 1354 and the battle of Poitiers. We
have mentioned, that, at the former period, by the
solemn farce of a condemnation and pardon, a reconciliation
had been patched up betwixt him and
King John. Charles of Navarre felt more resentment
at the harsh manner of his trial than gratitude
for the easy terms of his pardon. He seems also
to have been deeply imbued with that love of mischief
for mischief's sake, which is in some a symptom
of a tendency to insanity. He organised new

conspiracies, into which he seduced even the heir of the crown, whom he persuaded that he was not sufficiently intrusted with power by his father. John, however, detected the plot of this wicked Prince, and having a full explanation with the Dauphin, prevailed on him to desert the pernicious faction with which he had engaged. The King, by the Dauphin's personal assistance, next seized upon the person of the King of Navarre, and threw him into prison, where he remained till after the battle of Poitiers. The Count of Harcourt, brother of Sir Godfrey, was executed, among other adherents of the King of Navarre, upon the apprehension of their leader.

A.D. 1356.

But when the field of Poitiers was lost, it was not the least amidst the various calamities of that disastrous period, that the spirit of Charles of Navarre influenced the deliberations of the States-General, although his person was confined in the castle of Creve-Cœur. The States made it soon evident that they were less bent on the restoration of the King to his subjects, than upon the degradation of the crown, and engrossing the sovereign power within their own body. They divided themselves into separate committees, for executing various branches of the public service hitherto transacted by the King's ministers, and transmitted several lofty demands to the Dauphin, requiring the punishment of certain officers of state, of whom they complained, a general change of the King's ministry, the deliverance from prison of the King of Navarre, and the subjection of the Dauphin's government to the control of a committee of thirty-six of the members of the States-General, in which it was proposed to vest the powers of their whole body.

The Dauphin Charles, embarrassed by the engrossing and grasping spirit displayed by the assembly from which he had expected assistance, endeavoured to evade demands which he could not have granted without great hazard to the crown of which he was heir, and disrespect towards his father, who, although a prisoner in England, was still its owner. He dissolved the States, in spite of the remonstrances of the citizens of Paris, who, headed by Marcel, the provost of the merchants, and Ronsac, the sheriff, declared violently in favour of the assembly of representatives, and insisted upon their being reinstated in their authority.

While these intestine divisions were proceeding with violence in the metropolis, war was laying waste the more distant provinces of the kingdom of France. The celebrated Duke of Lancaster was in arms in Normandy, and in his company Sir Godfrey of Harcourt, whose name we have frequently had occasion to allude to. He had, as we have already mentioned, submitted to King John, after the battle of Cressy; but, incensed by the death of his brother, John, Count of Harcourt, he had again revolted to the English interest, and, having joined the Duke of Lancaster, was appointed his lieutenant.

One slender ray of light alone remained. Ere the States were dissolved, they had granted some

DEATH OF GODFREY DE HARCOURT.

supplies, enabling the Duke of Normandy to levy a small army to suppress this internal enemy in the province where he claimed an especial personal interest. By the judicious use of these supplies, a valiant French knight, Sir Robert de Clermont, with about three hundred men-at-arms, and a sufficient body of infantry, was enabled to march against Sir Godfrey de Harcourt, whom he speedily met with. The troops which that eminent malecontent commanded, were chiefly revolted Frenchmen, like himself, but of no great reputation in arms. Part of his troops consisted of a body of archers, who operated with little effect on the French men-at-arms, who covered themselves under their bucklers, and when the quivers of their enemy were expended, advanced to close quarters. The men of Sir Godfrey de Harcourt then shrunk from the attack; but their General continued fighting with courage worthy his reputation. Seeing, however, that escape was impossible, he took his resolution to die like a man. Being slightly lame, he placed himself so as, by the inequality of the ground, to supply in some degree the deficiency of his limbs, and wielding an axe of great weight (for he was very strong in the arms), he dealt such furious blows, that for a time no one dared to approach him. At length, after he had thus valiantly defended himself against all who attacked him on foot, two French knights mounting their horses, charged him at the gallop, and bore him to the earth with their spears, where he was slain by the

infantry who crowded around him. Thus died
Sir Godfrey de Harcourt, paying at length the
penalty frequently incurred by those who have been
the means of plunging their country into the evils
of civil war. This battle was fought near Coutan-
ces, about November, 1356.

Shortly afterwards, the Duke of Lancaster, in
revenge of the death of Sir Godfrey de Harcourt,
besieged Rennes very closely, pressed it hard, and
threatened, by the taking of that city, to complete
the separation of Bretagne from the French kingdom. Charles of Blois, who continued his efforts
to obtain the sovereignty of Bretagne, urged the
Dauphin strongly to assist him with soldiers; but
the Dauphin had other work upon his hands, for
the dissolution of the States-General had then
thrown every thing into disorder.

A truce was, however, made, at the earnest intercession of two cardinals of the church. It
afforded a moment's breathing time to the unhappy
kingdom of France, and obliged the Duke of Lancaster to raise the siege of Rennes, which was on
the point of surrender. But the evils of France
were so great that this partial relief was scarcely
felt. In fact, the confusion and general discontent
in that kingdom broke out in so many and such
dreadful forms, that, to understand them, it is
necessary to consider them separately; and, without minutely attending to the order in which the
events happened, we may observe, that they were,
each and all, the portentous consequences of general

confusion and discord, of the absence and captivity of the King, the mutiny of the common people, and the disposition of all ranks to violence and spoil.

The first great evil was the progress of war with the English, which, although not violently pursued by King Edward, was yet followed up by his captains in Bretagne, Normandy, and Gascony. The manner in which such enterprises were carried on may be well illustrated by the successful attack of William of Granville upon the strong town and castle of Evreux. This nobleman dwelt about two leagues from that town, and often visited it. He was privately attached to Philip of Navarre, younger brother of Charles the Bad, who served with the English host, commanded by the Duke of Lancaster. But the Lord of Granville had never openly borne arms in the quarrel; no suspicion attached to him, therefore, at Evreux, and he had the means of making a strong party among the burgesses. He came by degrees to use the open ground before the castle-gate as a place for his ordinary promenade; and as the governor sometimes went abroad for refreshment, and entered into conversation with him, they fell into a sort of familiarity.

One day, having every thing prepared to support his attempt, William of Granville began to tell an idle story to the governor concerning a pretended attack upon England by the joint forces of the King of Denmark and the King of Ireland, who, for that purpose, had, he said, taken the sea with a numerous host. When the Frenchman demanded from whence he had this intelligence, William of Granville replied, that a knight of Flanders had sent the news to him, and with it a set of chessmen, the most beautiful he had ever seen. This excited the governor's curiosity, who was a great admirer of the game of chess, and desired to see them. William of Granville, accordingly, sent for the chessmen, and proposed that they should play a game together. The board and men were brought; and the governor was so imprudent as to admit the knight within the entrance of the fortress. He was privately armed with a shirt of mail concealed under his upper clothing, and held in his hand a small battle-axe, and thus, while apparently intent on his game, stood prepared to take advantage of such opportunity as should present itself. In the mean time, his valet warned the conspirators, burgesses of the place, to hold themselves in instant readiness. In the course of the game, William of Granville seized an opportunity to dash out the governor's brains with his battle-axe, and winding a bugle horn which he carried with him for the purpose, the burgesses ran to his assistance, and found him bestriding the body of his victim, and defending the gate, which he had occupied, against such of the garrison as hastily took the alarm. The insurgents speedily seconded him, and made themselves masters of Evreux, which became a headquarter of the faction of the English, or Navarrese, in Normandy.

Such was the nature of the exploits which were then achieved in every corner of France, in which

FACTION OF THE NAVARRESE. 117

good faith and personal fidelity seem to have been little observed by either party.

It was not, however, so much the national war between the French and English which brought so much harm upon the former nation, as the violent factions among the French themselves, which were about this time considerably augmented in number, and no less so in rancour.

I have told you more than once of the peculiar and dangerous character of Charles King of Navarre. It was another of the misfortunes of France that this person, of so faithless a disposition, joined to qualities so showy and so popular, should have escaped, at this moment of the greatest confusion, from the castle of Creve-cœur, in which he had been confined by King John for his former intrigues. The liberated prisoner was received with great joy, not only at Amiens, and other cities, but in Paris itself, where Marcel, the provost of the merchants, became his principal adherent.

Being an accomplished orator, Charles of Navarre harangued the Parisians in public, and with great effect on their credulity; he seemed to declare himself for a republic, or rather an aristocracy, instead of a monarchy, by supporting the claims of the States, in opposition to those which were preferred for the Crown on the part of the Dauphin and others. Those who adhered to the party of Charles, or in general to that of the States, obtained the name of Navarrese. Philip of Navarre, however, though the brother of Charles, remained in the English camp; nor could he ever be prevailed on to declare in favour of a republic, in which, he said, there could never be order, honour, or stability, but a constant succession of shame and confusion.

Mean time, the Dauphin was under the necessity of again assembling the States-General, in order to obtain, through their means, the power of imposing taxes, and levying money for the support of the war. The provost of the merchants thwarted the Dauphin in all his projects; for, like the King of Navarre, his patron, he mortally hated the Dauphin. Marcel, in particular, mixed in all the King of Navarre's proceedings, and caused the people, who followed him in great numbers, to assume blue hats, as a mark of their adherence to his party. The slightest offence given to any of these armed burgesses called the whole party forth; and it became absolutely impossible to maintain good order even in the capital itself, far less to make any exertion, by levying money or otherwise, in behalf of the King, who was still a captive in England. The Dauphin endeavoured to temporize, and strove, by every means in his power, to keep up the spirits of the royal party. He had in some measure succeeded, when an accident again threw all into irretrievable confusion.

An ordinary citizen, named Macé, had murdered Jean Baillet, the Treasurer of France, and taken refuge in a neighbouring church. The Dauphin sent two mareschals, one of France, and one of Champagne, with orders to take the criminal into custody, and lead him to instant execution. The

Bishop of Paris exclaimed against this act of necessary justice, as a violation of the sanctuary of the church, and the provost of the merchants called his followers into the streets, and marched with the whole mob of Paris directly to the lodgings of the Dauphin, in what was then called the Palace of Justice. Entering furiously, and without reverence, into the presence of the Dauphin, Marcel seized upon the two mareschals, and put them to death, so close to the Prince, that he was covered with their blood. " How now, sirs," said the Dauphin, apprehensive of farther violence, " would you shed the blood-royal of France?" Marcel answered in the negative; and, to show his good intentions, he snatched rudely from the Dauphin's head the embroidered hat or hood which he wore, and clapped on him in its place the blue hat, which was the sign of the Navarrese faction. He himself, to complete his insolence, wore during the rest of the day the hat of the Prince, which was of a withered rose colour. The bodies of the murdered mareschals were dragged through the streets, and the King of Navarre, who had avoided being present in the city during the insurrection, endeavoured to take advantage of the incident, so as to further his own plans, by the most extravagant demands, which he founded upon it. The Dauphin, however, was received as regent by the States, to whom the Navarrese had proposed to dethrone the King, and dispossess the Dauphin. Thus fortified at least with nominal authority, the Dauphin withdrew from the metropolis and its turbulent citizens to the counties of Picardy and Champagne, where he assembled the states of those provinces, and received such succours and obedience as they had the means of yielding to him. All France was thus shaken to its centre by internal discord, and its disasters seemed past the possibility of increase, when two circumstances, both of a most alarming kind, carried the general misery to a height hitherto unknown, and even blunted the feelings of the public to the wretchedness which they had hitherto undergone.

We have already mentioned the bands of mercenary leaders, who acknowledged no officer or superior but those who promised to procure them the greatest share of plunder. These troops, or at least their leaders, were generally English; and although they made no great distinction of political principle, they were chiefly followers of the Navarre party, as that which promised them the widest privilege of plunder. By means of these Companions, as they were called, Charles of Navarre proposed to carry into effect his dream of a republic, or rather a species of oligarchy, in which, doubtless, he proposed that he himself should act the principal part. For this purpose, he drew to his party as many of the leaders of the Companions as he possibly could, and prepared by their means to lay waste the kingdom of France.

Neither was the Dauphin backward in his attempts to reduce the kingdom to subjection; for, as we shall presently see, a second great and overpowering calamity, namely, the insurrection of the peasantry, was in its consequences the means of strengthening and increasing the army which he assembled. This *Jacquerie*, or war of the peasants, so called, because the gentry gave to them the contemptuous name of *Jacques Bonhomme*, or Goodman James, was the most dreadful scourge which had yet ravaged France; it is impossible to conceive, and it would be indecent and disgusting to attempt to describe its horrors. It arose from the series of oppression, scorn, and injury, which the peasants, or cultivators of the soil, had so long sustained at the hands of the nobility and gentry. These last saw in the peasantry creatures whom they deemed of an inferior species to themselves, and whose property and persons they held alike at their disposal. What little protection the common people had received from the crown was now at an end, by the King's captivity, and the general confusion throughout the kingdom. In these sad days, each noble or knight became the uncontrolled feudal tyrant of the estate which belonged to him; and most of them were induced, by the intoxication attending the possession of arbitrary power, to make a harsh and tyrannical use of their privileges, each practising on his vassals the most unlimited oppression. The effects of such absolute power terminated in the grossest abuses, and at length drove to utter despair the peasantry, who were themselves starving, while, as an insult to their misery, they saw their lords revelling in the excess of luxury and ill-timed extravagance. After witnessing the evils of the country proceed from bad to worse, the peasantry at length became des perate, and seizing such rustic arms as pitchforks, scythes, clubs, and reaping-hooks, they rose with fury, and joined together in large bodies, resolving to destroy all the nobility and gentry in the kingdom.

This insurrection took place in several provinces; and, as is usually the case in a war of such a description, where an oppressed and ignorant people burst suddenly from their bondage, and revel in every license which ignorance and revenge can suggest to them, they burnt or pulled down the houses of the nobility, stormed their castles by main force, misused their wives and daughters, put them to various modes of death, equally cruel and protracted, and in short behaved like fierce bandogs, suddenly unloosed from their chain, and equally incapable of judgment and of humanity. There was one instance, and not a solitary one, where this furious rabble roasted a noble, whose castle they had stormed, alive on a spit, and compelled his wife and children to partake of his flesh. We willingly leave these horrors in oblivion, only remarking, that it is a double curse of slavery and oppression, that for a time it renders its victims, after they succeed in breaking their bonds, incapable of thinking or acting like human beings.

The horrors of this servile war had this good effect, that they impelled all men to join in putting a stop to so aggravated an evil. The nobility, however, who made the use of arms their sole profession, soon united together for mutual defence, and, completely armed as they were, found no difficulty in defeating the frantic peasants, though with the most unequal numbers.

An instance is given by Froissart of an interesting nature. The Duchess of Normandy, the Duchess of Orleans, and nearly three hundred other ladies of quality, young damsels, and children of the nobility, had taken refuge in the town of Meaux, where they hoped to be defended against the fury of the Jacquerie. Here they were beset by about nine or ten thousand of the insurgents; and it became too apparent that the rabble of the town were to take part with the peasantry, and admit them into the place without opposition. The Count of Foix and the Captal of Buche, chanced to pass near the town where the ladies were enclosed by such numbers, and heard an account of their imminent peril, and of the multitude of savage clowns by whom they were surrounded. The knights were of different political principles. The Earl was French both in birth and opinions; the Captal of Buche, so called from a district in Gascony, of which he was governor, was distinguished by his valour in the service of Edward III., being the same who led the successful ambuscade at the battle of Poitiers. Both, without regarding their difference in other particulars, were alike disposed to show themselves good knights, and put their persons in jeopardy for the safety of so many noble ladies, who were destined to death and infamy by a furious rabble. The armed attendants of the knights might be sixty lances, probably making, with all their retainers, about three or four hundred men.

At the head of this very inferior force, the Count of Foix, and the Captal of Buche, rode straight to Meaux, where the ladies were still protected in a citadel, or fortified quarter of the town, although the inhabitants had admitted the ruffian mob into the market-place and streets of the city. The two valiant knights arrived just in time to prevent the females from falling into the cruel hands of their outrageous enemies. They lowered their lances, and rushed into the market-place, then full of the disorderly rabble, who were ill able to endure an attack so furious. They were borne out of the town at the spear's point, broken, beaten down, and pursued for miles. Historians assure us, that seven thousand of the peasants were slain, which is not impossible, considering that their antagonists were so fully armed as almost to be invulnerable, while their opponents were entirely defenceless. The knights returned in triumph, and burnt a part of the town of Meaux, to revenge themselves on the inhabitants who had admitted the peasants within the walls. The warriors who (though personal and national enemies) had acted with so much gallantry in behalf of the distressed females, were applauded, and generally imitated. Other battles, like that of Meaux, took place in France, in different places, and the Jacquerie, which had raged so horribly, was finally suppressed.

As I have before hinted, the horrors of this in-

surrection of the peasantry obliged the nobles to
unite themselves together, and rendered them more
obedient to the command of their natural chiefs.
Their campaign, it may be believed, was a bloody
one, since they gave no quarter, but hanged, upon the
next tree, such insurgents as fell into their hands.
Though a sharp remedy, it proved a sure one, and
this rebellion was at length stifled in the blood of
the unfortunate peasants. The Dauphin-regent
was thus enabled to place himself at the head
of an army of thirty thousand men, raised for the
purpose of subjecting the Jacquerie, but at the
head of which he speedily took an opportunity to
blockade the rebellious city of Paris, of which he
earnestly desired to render himself master. He
hoped for success, the rather that he had a party
also within the town secretly attached to him,
though not strong enough openly to contend with
the faction led by the provost of the merchants.

The King of Navarre, on the other side, brought
together a strong body of the bands of Companions
of whom I have before spoken, and encamped at
St Denis, in order to take such opportunity as
might offer to support the Provost Marcel, and the
Parisians of the Navarre faction. The Provost,
in the mean time, became satisfied that matters
could not remain long in this uncertainty, and resolved to admit the King of Navarre and his forces
into the city, in order to enable him to continue a
resistance to the Dauphin, to which he began to
feel his own influence was not equal. He communicated therefore, to the chiefs lying at St Denis,

the scheme he had formed, and directed them to approach the gates of St Antoine and St Honoré, at twelve o'clock the ensuing night, with a choice body of forces, whom he proposed to admit into Paris.

It happened, however, that two citizens, heads of the opposite, or regent's party, called John and Simon Maillart, having some suspicion of what was going on, apprehended the Provost about midnight, at the gate of St Antoine, having the keys of the city in his hands. They instantly charged him with treachery, and slew him on the spot. Thus died Marcel; and his party, having been detected in so disloyal an enterprise, fell into public discredit, and was dispersed. The immediate effect of these events was, that the Dauphin, on the one part, entered Paris in triumph, and the King of Navarre, on the other, declared war formally against the whole kingdom of France.

This defiance he carried into execution, by means of the bands of Companions, who, as we have intimated, were in possession of many strong places in different parts of France, from whence they made unexpected sallies and long marches, by which they took castles which were thought in absolute security, and pillaged defenceless villages when they least thought of danger. The prisoners whom these adventurers made on such occasions, were ransomed for large sums of money; and those who could not, or would not, pay these exactions, were put to death without mercy.

Providence, however, had not entirely deserted

France, and even out of the extremity of disorder and confusion, divine wisdom wrought means of recovery. It was observed, that the English commanders began gradually to lose the superior good fortune which had attended their banners.

Sir Eustace d'Ambreticourt, one of the bravest of the commanders of the Companions, in the service of England, held at least twelve good fortresses under his command, in different parts of the country, and had at his disposal upwards of seven hundred combatants. He was nevertheless defeated and made prisoner, chiefly by means of another leader of a free company like his own, called Broquart of Fenestrages, who, on this occasion, was engaged on the part of the French. In other places also, the Dauphin had partial successes, which gradually restored the spirits of the French faction.

Still they suffered severely by this mode of warfare, as appears from the expedition of another celebrated Captain of Companions, called Sir Robert Knolles. This leader was an Englishman born, of low birth and mean estimation; but he distinguished himself by his military talents as a leader of a Free Company. He passed from Bretagne to the river Loire, wasting, burning, and ravaging the country, with the avowed purpose of marching to Avignon, where the Pope then resided, and forcing the Holy Father and his cardinals to ransom themselves at a high price. The presence of a considerable French army induced him to alter this intention. He offered them battle, which they declined, and gave them the slip, when they expected to have surrounded him. Sir Robert Knolles acquired by this expedition, and other plundering excursions, the wealth of an earl, and many lands, which he surrendered to King Edward, stipulating only for his own free pardon. But we may here quit the account of these occurrences, with the general observation, that the existence of these independent companies of adventurers long continued one of the most rankling grievances of the age. In the mean time, the restoration of peace between the nations did not advance, although France suffered so much, and England gained so little, by the continuance of the war

The unfortunate King John of France, of whom we have lately had occasion to speak but little, appears, after his defeat and captivity at Poitiers, to have been in a great measure forgotten by his subjects, although the duty of vassals to pay the ransom of their lord when prisoner, was one of the most sacred obligations of chivalry. Finding himself abandoned to his own exertions, he endeavoured to accommodate his differences with Edward. By an agreement entered into with this prince, King John engaged to surrender Aquitaine, Gascony, Calais, and other fiefs, which Edward and his successors were to hold free of homage, or feudal fealty of any kind. The King of France became farther bound to pay four millions of gold crowns in ransom for himself and the other prisoners taken at Poitiers. King Edward, on the other hand, in consideration of this treaty, agreed to renounce all claim to the title of King of France, as well as all possessions in Normandy and the other provinces, not expressly ceded to him by the present articles.

Such were the terms on which King John would have been satisfied to close the war, and to obtain his liberty. King Edward gave his assent to them, as comprehending all he expected to gain by the events of the war, for he must have abandoned all hope of conquering France. But the consent of the States-General was essential to the validity of the treaty. This great body, representing the French nation, positively refused to accede to terms by which so great a portion of the kingdom should be surrendered to the English. The consequence was, that the preparations for war were resumed with great animosity on both sides. The King of England, on his part, renewed his preparations, and assembled an army of no less than a hundred thousand men. A truce had been made, which was prolonged till midsummer 1359, so that it was the end of the harvest ere Edward III., with this large army, arrived at Calais.

In the mean time, the news that Edward was about to renew the war with a view of absolute conquest, had no small influence on the Navarrese party, and even on Charles himself, who became sensible of a sudden, that any success on Edward's part would bring upon him, in the person of the King of England, a competitor more formidable than he had yet found in the lawful regent. He, therefore, to the surprise of all men, renounced, at least for a time, the factious principles which had hitherto guided him in his intercourse with the Dauphin, and made a peace with that prince upon very reasonable and equitable conditions. Philip, the brother of the King of Navarre, continued to act under the influence of England, and declared, that in making so ill-timed a peace, his brother Charles must have been acting under the influence of witchcraft; indeed, the adoption of moderate or pacific views was, on his part, widely out of character.

Edward III., in the mean time, commenced his march, and, traversing in great order the provinces of Artois and Picardy, he laid siege to the ancient city of Rheims, and it was said that he designed to have himself crowned there, according to the ancient custom of the Kings of France. But the city was gallantly defended. The Archbishop encouraged the citizens to stand on their defence, and many noblemen with their followers were also in the place. During this siege, which lasted for three months, the King of Navarre relapsed afresh into his usual perverse politics, and, on some slight pretext, again broke out into war with the Dauphin; but whatever advantage Edward received from the conduct of this versatile Prince, he lost by the rebellion of the Flemings, whom the intrigues of France again diverted to the interest of that country.

In 1360, Edward found himself obliged to abandon the siege of Rheims, and drew off his army towards the capital of France—a species of insult, or menace, repeatedly used by the English during these wars, but with little real effect. The Dauphin-regent occupied the capital at the head of a numerous army; but, as on the one hand that Prince declined to put the fate of the country upon the dubious issue of another battle, which might in its event have resembled that of Cressy or Poitiers, so, on the other hand, the King of England was too prudent to attempt the assault of a large city garrisoned by a numerous army. King Edward therefore thought it expedient to retreat towards Bretagne to recruit his forces, while the Regent and his council, deeply affected by the scene of desolation which France presented on all sides, saw the necessity of submitting to sue for a peace, however disadvantageous. The King of England was still averse to relinquish his high pretensions to the crown of France, and it is said that an intervening thunder-storm, or hurricane, which he considered as a special sign of the displeasure of Heaven against those princes who should prolong the war, first bent his stubborn spirit to accept of peace.

But in fact the successes of Edward had been bought at a price which even the wealth of England could not pay; and besides exhausting his finances, the events of the late campaign had plainly shown him what he could, and what he could not do. He could march through France without opposition, but this was not subjecting it to his sovereignty; and a solitary city like Rheims was, if determined on resistance, sufficient to arrest his progress. The issue of the Scottish wars had probably taught this great warrior the difference between overrunning a country and subjugating it; and the readiness with which a poor and small nation vindicated its independence, might teach him the impossibility of subduing France, so much more populous and wealthy than Scotland—if, like her, she was determined to defend her liberty—and that such was her resolution, the siege of Rheims made manifest. The conqueror was therefore taught to prefer the possession of Gascony in complete sovereignty, out of which in time a permanent possession might be formed, to a protracted war, in the vain hope that any subsequent victory could do more than those of Cressy or Poitiers.

Edward, therefore, instead of persevering in his attempt to conquer the kingdom of France, determined to remain for the present satisfied with possessing Gascony, that portion of it which was ceded to him in full sovereignty. He should thus, he hoped, secure one compact and permanent possession, while he had free access to invade France by means of Calais, and was thus ready to avail himself of such opportunities of farther conquest as might arise.

Still farther to secure his dominions in Gascony, the King of England erected them into a principality, created the Black Prince his lieutenant and representative there, confident that, by the courage and wisdom which his son had so often displayed, he could not in any way provide so well for their government and safety.

The articles of peace were, of course, favourable

to England, to whom the King of France relinquished, in full superiority, the province of Gascony, with various other dependencies in Aquitaine; and in the north of France, the town of Calais and earldom of Guines. On his side, King Edward renounced all title to the crown and kingdom of France, and all claims to Normandy, Touraine, Anjou, and Maine.

Upon these conditions the peace of Bretigny was concluded, a peace most acceptable to the subjects of both crowns, though not agreeable in all respects to either of the kings themselves. A.D. 1360. Oct. 24. Difficulties arose concerning the surrender of some part of the territory and castles yielded to the English; and the high-spirited noblemen who there held fiefs, did not understand being transferred, like a flock of sheep, from the allegiance of one sovereign to another. Many Gascon knights refused to exchange the sovereignty of France for that of England. France, they said, might herself dispense with their faith and homage, but she had no right to substitute a strange king in her place. These difficulties suspended the benefits expected from the peace. The Dukes of Anjou and Berri, with the Dukes of Orleans and of Bourbon, still remained hostages in England, for payment of the ransom stipulated for the prisoners of Poitiers. These princes obtained, on their solicitation, permission to pass to Calais, under pretence that they might be able to furnish the means of concluding the disputed points of the treaty. Instead of doing so, the Duke of Anjou took the opportunity of abusing this indulgence, and made his escape into France.

King John had been set at liberty when he first came to an understanding with Edward, and had returned to France accordingly. But he was deeply hurt and offended at what he considered the dishonourable conduct of his son, and took the generous resolution of restoring to the English their full security for the ransom, by surrendering his own person once more into their hands. To such of his counsellors as would have cautioned him against this step, he firmly replied, that " if faith and loyalty were banished from the rest of the world, they ought still to remain enshrined in the hearts of kings."

The generous feeling expressed in this noble sentiment, seems to show that John of France deserved better fortune than that which had followed him during his whole life, and now accompanied him to the grave. A very short time after his return to England, John was seized with an indisposition, of which he died in the Savoy; and his son Charles, who had undergone so many difficulties as regent, now mounted the throne in the capacity of king, carrying with him to that eminence all the experience which many years of difficulty and misfortune had enabled him to attain, and which has procured for him in French annals the well-deserved epithet of the Wise.

A.D. 1364.
April 8.

CHAPTER XXI.

War in Normandy—Battle of Cocherel—War in Bretagne, between the adherents of De Montfort and De Blois.—Battle of Aurai—Financial Difficulties of King Charles—Sumptuary Laws—Free Companions—Charles's Plan of removing them from France—their leader Du Guesclin marches upon Avignon, and exacts a Fine from the Pope—he next engages in a war against Don Pedro the Cruel, King of Castile, and drives him from his Kingdom—Pedro solicits assistance from the Black Prince, and is by him reinstated in his Dominions—Du Guesclin, having been taken Prisoner, is ransomed—Tax upon Chimneys, called Fouage, imposed in Gascony by the Black Prince, to defray the expenses of his Castilian Expedition—Unpopularity of this Tax.

[1364—1370.]

CHARLES the Fifth, the fifty-first monarch of France, took up the affairs of his government in an involved and confused state. The dispute concerning Bretagne was not yet determined, and disturbances continued in Normandy between the Navarrese and the French partisans, the last of which parties was headed in a great measure by a valiant Breton knight, called Bertrand du Guesclin, to whose courage France owed much during the present reign. The Navarrese, on the other hand, were commanded by the Captal of Buche, already mentioned in this narrative. These two heroic leaders joined battle near Cocherel, in Normandy, with equal valour and skill, and the action is more particularly taken notice of on account of the merit of the leaders, and because fortune was on the side of the French, being the first action since Cressy in which that nation had been victorious. The Navarrese were completely defeated, and their stout commander, the Captal of Buche, fell into the hands of the conquerors. He was received with great distinction by King Charles, who would have bestowed upon him an earldom, had the Black Prince permitted the Captal to accept of it.

This was a fortunate commencement of King Charles's reign; but it was not without its reverse in Bretagne. The King had sent the aid of a thousand lances to Lord Charles de Blois, in order to strengthen his party in Bretagne, while Edward had despatched Sir John Chandos with an equal number, to support the cause of John de Montfort, and of his heroic mother, remarkable for her defence of Hennebon. These inveterate enemies, De Blois and De Montfort, finally encountered each other near the town of Aurai. Friends on both sides endeavoured to accommodate the matter betwixt the contending nobles, but in vain; each declaring himself resolved to peril their long-depending and long-disputed claims upon the event of that day. They approached each other with slowness and caution, calculated to give an idea of the desperate resolution which each had adopted, to fight this long-protracted quarrel concerning the sovereignty of Bretagne, for the last time, and to the last extremity.

Chandos, who had the chief command of the army of the Count de Montfort, divided his forces into three battalions, allotting to Sir Hugh Calverley, an English knight of great renown, the command of the rear-guard, or rather the reserve. This valiant champion, who was a man of distinguished courage, remonstrated against this arrangement, as it was his wish to fight in the front of the battle. The Lord Chandos explained his order of battle, and assured Sir Hugh that if he declined to lead the reserve, he must conduct it himself, and submitted to him which in that case was most proper. Sir Hugh was overcome with this gentleness and deference on the part of a leader so distinguished as Chandos, and saying, " he was sure that Chandos would put him on no duty inconsistent with his honour," acquiesced in the post allotted to him.

A little before the hour of prime, the two armies approached each other. The French came on in fair array, "in such close order," says Froissart, " that, had one thrown an apple among the battalion, it must have lighted upon a helmet or a head-piece." They were also covered with strong and large targets, to parry the shot of the English archers. Accordingly, advancing among the bowmen, without having endured the usual damage from their arrows, the French laid about among them, with the axes which they had prepared for close fight. The archers, on the other hand, being strong and active men, threw themselves among the French, and casting down their bows, and wrenching the axes from the hands of their enemies, made a defence with singular though unavailing fury. The leaders on all sides fought most valiantly, and Chandos, with an axe in his hand, set an example to all the field. Sir Hugh Calverley well supported the place intrusted to him, and by bringing up his reserve with undaunted valour, and in a moment of extreme need, vindicated the judgment of Lord Chandos in assigning to him so important a command, and finally decided the fate of the day. Lord Charles de Blois was slain on the field, for whom his adversary, De Montfort, shed many tears, generously lamenting the fate of a gallant enemy. Two of his sons, and Bertrand du Guesclin, were also made prisoners. Thus deprived of their principal leaders, the Blois party was totally discomfited.

This battle ended the hostilities of Bretagne, which had now lasted for so many years; but the faction of Edward III., who had so long supported the war, derived little advantage from its conclusion. It had been decided by the peace of Bretigny, that the King of England should lay no claim to the superiority of Bretagne, in whatever manner the dispute between De Montfort and Charles de Blois might be terminated. The duchy alone was adjudged, by the event of this battle of Aurai, to the young Count de Montfort, who obtained, for his behaviour in the action, the envied title of the Valiant. The King of

Sept. 1364.

France received the young victor, to do homage as Duke of Bretagne, while he settled large and liberal appointments upon the lady of the deceased Charles de Blois.

The difficulty of finding the means of bearing the various expenses of the kingdom embarrassed King Charles greatly, and drove him to means of raising funds, which, in the nature of things, could not be very popular. This was a general resumption of those gifts which the King and his predecessors had made, as well to the great vassals of the crown, as to inferior subjects. In the course of this delicate task, Charles, by his wisdom and oratory, made such an impression upon his uncle, Philip of Orleans, as to prevail on that high prince of the blood to resign all that he possessed by the favour of his father, brothers, and nephew, saying, " that although he conceived he had a legitimate right to the donations of the crown, yet he resigned them all at the pleasure of the King, his nephew, knowing that the service of the state rendered them necessary to him." Moved by so eminent and generous an example, given by a prince so near to the throne, others, taking the same course of submission, acquiesced also in the revocation of such crown gifts as they held, which the King partly accepted, and partly returned to the persons by whom they had been abandoned to his pleasure. These last were so sensible of the extremity to which the crown was reduced, that perhaps a measure of state necessarily obnoxious in itself, and severe upon individuals, was never carried into execution with so little unpopularity to the sovereign.

The King also made many laws against luxury in entertainments, festivals, and apparel; and by strictly acting up to his own regulations, produced a considerable reform in the expenses of the great, which were a constant source of envy and odium to the poor. He was regular and steady in the execution of justice, and, so far as he could, active in enforcing the judgments which he pronounced; but the state of the country, overrun by bands of soldiers, who acknowledged no sovereign, rendered his efforts to restore order for a long time, and in many instances, unavailing.

These associations of military adventurers, which, when they reached to a certain extent of numbers, were called the "Great Companies," continued an abiding, and apparently incurable, national evil. The King of France found himself, from the state of his finances, totally unprepared to clear the country of these land-pirates, as they might be properly termed. In his distress, he applied to Edward III., who, by an article in the treaty of Bretigny, had bound himself to lend his assistance, if required, in relieving France of these military locusts. Edward, thus cited to fulfil his engagement, sent forth a proclamation, commanding these companies to lay down their arms, and evacuate the territory of France. Some few obeyed, but the others treated his proclamation with contempt, saying they held no land of him, owed him no allegiance, and would not disband their forces at the bidding of any king upon earth. The fiery Edward resolved instantly to march against them with an army; but Charles, not desirous to afford a pretext for the re-entrance of English troops into France, returned for answer, that he disapproved of the mode of proceeding proposed by his brother of England, and meant to rid himself of the Great Companies by another expedient. The King of England indignantly replied, " that in that case he must trust to his own strength, for he could expect no assistance from him."

King Charles, justly called the Wise, had, in fact, devised an expedient for ridding France of the wasting plague occasioned by these companies, without the hazardous experiment either of engaging in war with them, or of seeking relief from an army of English, commanded by the Black Prince, or his father.

His purpose was to hold out to these adventurers a more distant field of war, which should afford them a prospect of the wealth which they coveted, while their departure would relieve France of their burdensome presence. A large body was accordingly prevailed upon to prosecute their trade of arms in the Italian wars, where their commander, Hawkwood, an Englishman, originally of low rank, rose to wealth and eminence.

But the King of France pursued the same policy on a larger scale. Bertrand du Guesclin, renowned for his valour, and personally acquainted with the leading chiefs of the Companies, was instructed to deal with them, for the purpose of engaging them in a distant expedition. He was at this time a prisoner to Sir John Chandos, having been taken, as we mentioned, at the battle of Aurai.

But the King of France, the Pope, and other Princes, who saw the necessity of Guesclin's agency in this plan, mediated betwixt him and Chandos, made personal contributions to pay the heavy ransom at which his freedom was rated, and thus restored him to liberty. The influence of this renowned warrior engaged thirty-five of the principal chiefs of the Companies, in what was at first represented to be an expedition against the Moors in Spain, and in so far a species of crusade. He induced them to join in such an enterprise the more readily that he himself proposed to accompany them, and accepted the chief command. The King of France readily gave his consent and approbation to this species of crusade, and presented those concerned in it with two hundred thousand francs to assist them in their march, caring but little, it well may be supposed, whither their road might lead them, provided it carried them out of the realm of France. The Companies assembled according to their agreement at Chalons upon the river Marne, and from thence took a route towards Avignon, then the habitation of the Pope. His Holiness, much alarmed at the approach of an army so composed, sent a cardinal to meet them, to demand what troops they were, and with what purpose they came. Du Guesclin answered with gravity, that they were sinful men who had taken the cross against the infidels, and were marching against the Moors, and that they approached the footstool of the Pope to request absolution for their sins, and a sum of two hundred thousand florins, by way of alms, to enable them to proceed upon their pious undertaking. The absolution was promised by the cardinal without any delay or scruple; but there went more words to payment of the money. The Pope would fain have satisfied these sturdy beggars with one hundred thousand florins, raised by a tax upon the inhabitants of Avignon; but this did not suit Du Guesclin's policy. "We came not," said he, "to pillage the poor, but to receive alms from the rich; the full subsidy must be paid by the Pope and his college of cardinals, who have plenty of money, and the taxes must be remitted to the poor inhabitants of Avignon." The Pope was under the necessity of complying with this unceremonious request, liberally adding to the subsidy the pardon about which these robbers affected to be solicitous.

Bertrand du Guesclin, and such captains of the Companions as he trusted with his secret purpose, had an expedition in view very different from that of an attack upon the infidels. There reigned at this time in Castile, one of the principal Christian kingdoms of Spain, Don Pedro, called, for his inhumanity and tyranny, the Cruel. He had murdered his beautiful and youthful bride, a near relation of the King of France, and, besides innumerable other cruelties, had threatened the life of two or three brethren by the father's side, and particularly one of them, Henry Count of Transtamar, who stood high in the esteem of the world, and was supposed to head the numerous party of Castilians whom Pedro's cruelties had rendered malecontent. The Castilian monarch had also in several ways offended the church, whereby he had incurred a sentence of excommunication, and it appeared to the Pope, it seems, highly fitting and convenient that this motley army, formed out of the refuse of all nations, should be the executors of his holy purpose.

Without embarrassing ourselves with the minute particulars of the expedition, it is sufficient to say that Bertrand du Guesclin and his army easily dispossessed Pedro of the crown which his vices had rendered very insecure, and compelled him to fly to Corunna.

Reduced to this extremity, Pedro took the resolution of going from Corunna to Gascony in person, and soliciting as a suppliant the formidable alliance of the Black Prince of Wales, whose residence was fixed at Bourdeaux, from which capital he governed, as his father's lieutenant, all those beautiful provinces which had been ceded to England at the peace of Bretigny.

Pedro's story was that of a lawful but unfortunate monarch, dethroned and driven from his dominions by his bastard brother, and he therefore made a confident appeal for the support of all those of his own rank, in re-instating him. His desolate condition naturally moved the heart of the noble

Edward, who deemed it his duty as a true knight to extend his powerful protection to a distressed monarch craving succour at his hands.

There was, however, to be considered the deficiency of numbers, and the necessity of being at great expense, if the Black Prince should embrace the cause of the fugitive. All this was pointed out to him by his faithful counsellors, who urged him to consider the crimes of Don Pedro, and also the great charges which must necessarily be encountered, if he would needs succour him. They implored the Prince of Wales that he would at least wait until he saw what cost his father was willing to bestow upon such an expedition; and they failed not to show him, what he afterwards felt to be true by bitter experience, that should he, by assisting Don Pedro, lay himself under the necessity of taxing the inhabitants of Gascony, he must lay his account with losing their regard and allegiance. These arguments weighed nothing with the Black Prince, impressed as he was with the justice of Don Pedro's cause, and lending an ear as he did to the treacherous promises of that tyrant, who readily engaged to find treasure, provisions, and whatever was demanded. Edward assembled, therefore, a large body of feudal forces, and took the dangerous resolution of increasing it by bands of Companions, whom he received into his army. As large pay was necessarily promised to these men, many of whom belonged to Companies which had aided Du Guesclin in the conquest of Castile, and assisted to dethrone the King Don

Pedro, and were now equally ready to become active in his restoration, they were soon assembled in great numbers. Prince Edward set forth with a very considerable army, with which he crossed the Pyrenean mountains, and advanced on the river Ebro, to a town called Najara, or Navarette. Here Henry, chosen King of Castile, met Edward at the head of an army still larger than that of the Prince, consisting partly of Spaniards, partly of those Free Companions whom Du Guesclin had brought into Spain, and who still continued under his command, to the number of four thousand men-at-arms. The battle was exceedingly furious, and fought with great bravery on each side. But the conduct and valour of the Black Prince were decidedly conspicuous; and after a victory as complete as any which he had yet won, Edward found no difficulty in restoring his ally Pedro to a throne, of which his crimes rendered him unworthy. It was the natural and just doom of Providence, that the Prince should be the first sufferer by the ingratitude of the wolfish tyrant whom he had assisted, without sufficient reference to the justice of his cause.

The payment of necessary sums of money, the furnishing of wholesome provisions, in sufficient quantities, all which had been liberally promised before the expedition, were now, since the victory of Navarette, entirely neglected by the ungrateful tyrant; and the Black Prince was at once disturbed by the murmurs of his unpaid soldiers, and distressed by the maladies which began to sweep them off in numbers. The heat of the country, to which the English constitution was not accustomed, and the use of strange and unwholesome food, not only made his men sicken and die, but sowed the seeds of an incurable disease in the frame of the gallant Prince himself. He therefore returned to Bourdeaux with disappointed hopes, a diminished army, an exhausted exchequer, and a broken constitution; and it is observed by historians, that the support of the tyrant Pedro must have been unpleasing in the sight of Providence, since it was followed by so marked a change of fortune in so eminent a person as the Prince of Wales.

Some advantages, however, Prince Edward derived from the expedition across the Pyrenees, and he accounted it not the least of them, that he had in his possession as prisoner the renowned Bertrand Du Guesclin, of whose courage and address it was thought the Black Prince condescended to be somewhat jealous. It is certain, that the presence of this renowned knight was accounted of such importance, that when it was desired first to engage him in the Spanish wars, the King of France, the Pope, and Henry of Transtamar, were, as we have already stated, glad to subscribe for his ransom a sum amounting to one hundred thousand francs, for at such a rate was he valued. On his second capture, when he surrendered at Navarette to Sir John Chandos, the knight by whom he was formerly taken, it is said the Black Prince formed a determination that so formidable a leader should not again be admitted to ransom

But the wily Frenchman attained his purpose in the following manner:—Being in presence of the Prince at Bourdeaux, and answering some incidental questions concerning his captivity, Du Guesclin observed, it could not be unpleasing to him, since it was attended with so much glory. Edward naturally asked, in what that glory consisted? Du Guesclin replied, that the world affirmed that the Black Prince was afraid to deliver him from prison, on account of his reputation in chivalry; "too honourable a circumstance," he said, "for a poor knight like myself."

The Prince was naturally piqued at a speech which ascribed to him a sentiment of ignoble jealousy, and was perhaps the more displeased that he was sensible of the truth of his remark. "It is not for fear of your chivalry, sir knight, that I keep you captive," said he, in reply; "and to show you it is not, you shall have your liberty, if you can pay for your ransom one hundred thousand francs."

"Willingly, my lord," replied Sir Bertrand; "and I thank your highness for the honour of rating me so high." By recurrence to the French King, the Duke of Anjou, Henry of Transtamar, and other friends, a warrior so renowned as Du Guesclin speedily obtained his liberty, and was again restored to the wars.

I have mentioned that the Prince of Wales had imprudently embarrassed his finances by this expensive campaign in Spain; and he was now equally unfortunate in the mode which he adopted for retrieving them. This was by a tax upon chimneys called by the French, *fouage*, which, amounting to a franc upon each chimney, would, it was supposed, in five years, discharge the Prince's debts, as it afforded an income of above a million of francs yearly. But the tax was new to the Gascons, who showed a general disinclination to submit to the imposition. "When we belonged to France," they said, "we were never grieved with such assessments; nor will we now submit to them. When we vowed fidelity to Prince Edward, he swore on his part to protect our privileges; and we will not abide by our oath, unless he keeps what he has sworn to us." The greatest of the Gascon barons, who had been previously engaged against their will in the expedition to Castile, caught eagerly at this new subject of offence, and combined, so soon as the opportunity should be fitting, to free themselves from the dominion of England.

The mere pressure of an unpopular tax, though that upon the chimneys seems to have been felt as a severe grievance, will hardly of itself account for a defection which proved so general. But the lieutenancy of the Black Prince had been showy and extravagant; a fault which seldom fails to provoke, on the part of the public, dissatisfaction and displeasure. Besides, amid the high qualities which few princes could boast in more perfection, the Black Prince showed flashes of his father's haughty and severe temper, which were at times unpleasant to the proud barons of Gascony, although they were obliged to endure them at the moment. They were galled especially by the bitter reflection that they were governed in some measure by the right of conquest, and that, though Frenchmen by birth, and principal contributors to the very victory of Poitiers which sealed the fate of their country, they were still a part of the great French nation, while subjected to an English governor, who was undoubtedly somewhat partial to his countrymen. The influence of patriotism was felt more and more in Gascony as new grievances arose, and many pretexts for discontent were found which would never have suggested themselves, had it not been for the influence of national feeling and national rivalry. A crisis therefore approached, which threatened the dominion of England in France, and seemed likely to destroy all the influence which Edward III. and his son had acquired in the latter country by such an enormous expenditure of blood and treasure.

CHAPTER XXII.

Don Pedro of Castile taken prisoner, and assassinated by his brother Henry—Charles of France fosters the disaffections in Gascony, and at last, claiming the rights of Lord Paramount, summons the Black Prince to Paris, to answer the complaints of the discontented Gascons—Mutual Preparations for War—The Earl of Pembroke wastes Poitou—he is enclosed by the French in the village of Puyrenon, and rescued by Sir John Chandos—Ineffectual attempt of Chandos to recover Saint Salvin, which had been betrayed by a Monk to the French—Skirmish at the Bridge of Lussac, in which Chandos is slain—Edward III. sends an Army under his Son, John of Gaunt, to Calais—The Duke of Burgundy, son of the King of France, marches to oppose him with a much larger force, but, not being able to draw the English from a strong position, returns to Paris—Predatory expedition of Sir Robert Knolles—Adventure of a Knight in Knolles's army, who, in performance of a Vow, strikes his spear against the gate of Paris, but, in his return through the suburbs, is killed by a Butcher.

[1369—1370.]

Two persons of great power and importance watched with anxiety the progress of discontent in Gascony, and the various embarrassments, which, like clouds arising upon the disk of a setting sun, overshadowed the latter days of the Black Prince.

One of these, though himself no sovereign prince, possessed in the time in which he lived, enough of warlike fame and personal importance to place him upon a level with great potentates. This was Bertrand du Guesclin, so often before mentioned, who, from having been a knight of no great power in Gascony, had raised himself by his military fame to the rank of a great general, the ally of kings, and disposer of crowns. This warrior, having seen the change of government which he accomplished in Castile altogether reversed by the victory at Navarette, had, after obtaining his freedom, renewed his intercourse with Henry of Transtamar, and combined measures to seize the first opportunity of accomplishing a counter revolution. The war between the two brothers, Pedro and Henry, for the crown of Castile, was again renewed, so soon as the decayed state of Edward's health, and the embarrassment of his finances became public, and was speedily brought to a decision, by the advice and assistance of Du Guesclin.

Henry took arms with a very considerable force, and joining battle with Don Pedro, who defended himself with the most desperate valour, defeated that tyrant, and compelled him to fly into the castle of Montiel, where he was instantly blockaded. The castle, though strong, was not victualled for defence; so that Don Pedro and his company, which did not exceed twelve men, were compelled to attempt a passage, by night, through the army of the besiegers. They were unsuccessful, and were made prisoners; and so bitter was the hatred between the brothers, that Henry of Transtamar hastened in person to the lodging of the French knight who had taken Pedro prisoner, and as he entered, called out furiously, " Where is that Jewish bastard, who dares call himself King of Castile?"—" Here I am," answered Pedro, who had no sense of fear any more than humanity, "'Tis thou thyself art a bastard, and I the lawful son of Don Alphonso." The two brothers then engaged in mortal struggle; and Pedro, having forced Henry backward over a bench, unsheathed his poniard, and would have slain him on the spot, had not one of Henry's squires seized Pedro by the leg, and turned him undermost, giving him the disadvantage in the struggle. Henry then availed himself of the opportunity, and despatched Pedro with his dagger; a woful instance how ambition and rivalry can dissolve the nearest ties of kindred and relationship. Thus was one great work of the Prince of Wales totally reversed and undone; and, unhappily for him, the dethronement and death of Don Pedro by no means freed him from the evils which he had brought upon himself, by espousing the cause of that tyrant.

We have said that another person besides Bertrand du Guesclin watched the progress of the discontents which agitated the English provinces in France, with the intention of profiting by them as opportunity should present itself. This was Charles V. of France, called the Wise, and whose wisdom turned itself so much to the accumulation of riches, that he was also entitled the Wealthy

He had nursed his revenue, and exerted his wisdom, with the lawful and meritorious purpose of rendering himself fit to overthrow the English power in France, that power from which his predecessors and himself had suffered so severely. The mode, however, in which he finally found it advisable to avow this intention, was in singular contradiction to his father's noble maxim, that if good faith were banished from the earth, it should at least be found in the breast of kings. If it was possible for a Prince to be bound down by the direct words of a treaty, King Charles was obliged by that of Bretigny to abstain from disputing the unlimited title of England to the province of Gascony, without any badge of feudal dependence. Yet, though bound so strictly by this treaty, the King of France determined to encourage the discontented Gascon lords by assuming once more the title of Lord Paramount of that country, and by receiving an appeal to his parliament of Paris from those who claimed justice at his hands against the proceedings of the Black Prince. In vindication of his assuming a power disowned by the peace of Bretigny, the French pretended that Edward had not so absolutely renounced the title of King of France, as he was bound by the same treaty to do. The fact, however, was, that the opportunity was tempting; and Charles made use of it.

When the French King saw the moment favourable for declaring himself, he sent a clerk and a knight, both men of gravity and eminence, to intimate to the Prince of Wales the course which he intended to pursue. These messengers found the Prince at his court in Bourdeaux, and, kneeling before him, craved permission to deliver their message in presence of his council. "Speak on, sirs," said the Prince, little suspecting the nature of their message. The clerk then read a summons in the name of Charles, directed to his nephew the Prince of Wales, setting forth, that various prelates, barons, knights, &c. of Gascony, had complained to the King of France of grievances sustained at the hands of the said Prince of Wales, through evil counsel, and therefore commanding him to appear in person in the city of Paris, and present himself before the King of France and his peers, to make answer to the petitions which complained of injury at his hands.

Jan. 1369.

The Prince of Wales heard with no little astonishment a summons founded on the right of homage, which was expressly renounced by France at the treaty of Bretigny. His eyes sparkled with indignation, as looking fiercely upon the French messengers, he thus replied, "Is it even so? Does our fair uncle desire to see us at Paris? Gladly will we go thither; but I assure you, sirs, it shall be with basnet on our head, and sixty thousand men in our company." Perceiving his resentment, the messengers dropt on their knees, and reminded him, that for their part, they only did the message of him who sent them. The Prince, however, left them in indignation; and they were counselled by the English lords then present to depart as fast as they could, least their safety should be endangered

In fact, when the news of the departure of the envoys reached the Prince, he sent after and arrested them, as being, he said, the messengers of his own discontented subjects of Gascony rather than of the King of France. They suffered, however, nothing eventually; but the Prince retained his purpose of making instant war against France; while the French King, on the other hand, strengthened himself, as was usual at that period, by hiring a certain number of the Free Companions. Being secure also, of the assistance of the numerous malecontents in the Gascon provinces, he laid aside all thoughts of peace, and prepared for a war against England, under auspices more fortunate than those under which France had lately fought.

Charles, in again renewing the contest, had the infinite advantage of the general assent of his people, who, fired with the reviving hope of national glory and independence, pledged themselves to support him in the quarrel with their lives and fortunes. The peace, which had now lasted a considerable time, had also greatly diminished the forces at the command of Edward III. and his son the Black Prince. The Free Companies, which might be considered as something corresponding to a standing army of the period, had been, owing to the want of money, dismissed from the pay of England, and in a great measure disbanded, or sent to find employment elsewhere. The feudal troops and archery of England herself, whom it would have been difficult or impossible to detain in Gascony or France for any length of time, after the war was at an end, had returned to their native country, and it would require new efforts and new expenditure of treasure to recall them to the field when their services should become necessary.

On the other hand, the kingdom of France was replenished with a young generation, who had neither experienced the terrors of the former English victories, nor felt any thing save the desire to be avenged of their invaders. Charles himself might, indeed, remember the disasters of Cressy and Poitiers; but he had at the same time the satisfaction to know that Edward III. was now in an advanced old age, embarrassed, too, by the discontent of his subjects, who were unwilling to submit to further assessments for the support of foreign war, and by the increasing indisposition of the Black Prince, whose body could no longer execute the dictates of his dauntless mind, and who had, moreover, to lament the loss of so many brave men, cut off in Spain, less by war than by wasting disease. On the whole, therefore, the King of France was prepared, with good hopes of a successful result, once more to revive the bloody war which had so long wasted his kingdom. Nor did the commencement of the struggle deceive his expectations.

Yet the spirit of Prince Edward flinched not under the infirmity of his body. He purposed, as we have already hinted, to take the field in person, and advance to Paris, at the head of a numerous army. His father had again influence enough with his parliament to obtain large subsidies, and levied

a considerable army, which he despatched to the
assistance of the Prince of Wales, under the command of the Earl of Cambridge, his brother, and
the gallant John Hastings, Earl of Pembroke, his
brother-in-law. The Black Prince received also
a powerful reinforcement from the Free Companies, who, as their trade was war, were naturally
determined in their choice of a side, by their reliance on the military qualities of the commander-in-chief, for skill, valour, generosity, and success,
and certainly there was no man alive who could in
these respects be termed the equal of the Prince
of Wales. Sir Hugh Calverley, whose deeds at
the battle of Aurai have been already noticed, was
devotedly attached to his native prince; and, by his
interest among the Free Companions, he collected,
in Spain and elsewhere, six thousand lances of this
description, whom the Prince, perhaps hastily, sent
instantly forward, to make war on the territories
of such of the great Gascon barons as had set an
example in revolting against the *fouage*, or tax upon
chimneys, and, as Prince Edward supposed, had
busied themselves in exciting King Charles to summon him before the Parliament of Paris.

But although the Prince was thus far armed
against the impending evil, the schemes of Charles
for undermining the English power in France
were so skilfully laid, that they took effect with
considerable success. The province of Pontbieu
was seized upon without much opposition, an acquisition rendered easy by the intrigues carried on
by the friends of France in that district. The

Dukes of Anjou and Berri, brothers of the king, each at the head of a considerable army, the one levied in Auvergne, the other in Toulouse, were ready to invade the provinces of Gascony and Poitou; and for some time it was difficult to say which party obtained the ascendency, so many were the feats of valour, skirmishes, and captures of castles, and so various was the success attending each of them.

In another species of warfare the King of France had perhaps a more decided advantage. This was in the original character of the dispute, the justice of which was warmly debated by the gownsmen and churchmen on both sides. In this, King Edward revived his old claim to the kingdom of France, founded upon his denying the validity of the Salic law; an antiquated plea, renounced by himself at the peace of Bretigny, and which he would certainly have done better to have abandoned for ever, and limited his claim to the rights of sovereignty in Poitou and Guienne, which had been acknowledged with all formality by the King of France himself, and by the estates of his kingdom. In the former case, Edward III. claimed the succession in right of his mother, which had never been acknowledged by the law of France. On the contrary, in preferring a claim of sovereignty to Gascony, and its dependencies only, King Edward would only have founded upon the terms of an existing treaty, solicited by Charles himself, while regent, and by the estates of his kingdom. Edward III., however, chose to enlarge, as much as possible, the title on which he founded, being conscious that men would regard it less with reference to its justice and validity, than to their own passions and partialities. Be that as it may, the clergy of France were generally decidedly favourable to the cause of their native sovereign; and there can be no doubt that the manner in which they recommended and enforced upon the public, the right of Charles, in the different provinces possessed by the English, had a great effect in producing the general disposition to revolt from the English to the French monarch, which was every where manifested. It was with sharper weapons, however, than words, that the cause of either king was to be finally determined, and accordingly, blood flowed freely on both sides, in every county of France where the English had any footing.

What appeared in particular to intimate the doom of heaven against the cause of England, was the death of some of those remarkable persons by whose assistance the Black Prince had often gained his victories, but who now were, by various, and some of them insignificant actions, compared to the reputations of those to whom they happened, altogether removed from the scene, when their services would have been most advantageous to their great commander.

One of the most remarkable persons, and equally distinguished by valour and talents, was Lord James Audley, Seneschal of Poitou, who fell sick and died, while the war was at the hottest. This was the son of that Lord James Audley, whose conduct at the battle of Poitiers was so remarkable. His father was now too old for the wars, and had retired into England, where he died in 1386. The death of Lord James Audley, the younger, greatly grieved the Prince of Wales, who replaced him as Seneschal in Poitou by the celebrated Sir John Chandos.

As this brave leader was an active partisan in that kind of warfare which distinguished the period, he proposed to the young Earl of Pembroke to join with him in an expedition, at the head of a very considerable force, against Louis of Sancerre, Mareschal of France. But the Earl of Pembroke declined to join Chandos in the enterprise proposed to him, listening to the paltry insinuations of some flatterers, who persuaded him he would have little share of personal glory if he went out under the command of Chandos, who would engross the whole renown of any joint expedition in which they might be engaged. Sir John Chandos, piqued at Pembroke's refusal to join him, dismissed great part of his troops, and retired with the rest to the city of Poitiers.

No sooner had Chandos thus retired into quarters, than the Earl of Pembroke, with a force of at least two hundred spears, took the field, with the purpose of winning glory upon his own account, and wasting the lands of those nobles who were hostile to England. As soon as the French lords who held these garrisons heard that this nobleman had declined the company of Lord Chandos, and was come abroad on his own adventure, they resolved to gather their forces, and attack him suddenly, as his youth and imprudence had already shown him liable to be surprised in such expeditions. They collected, therefore, an overpowering force, and attacked the Earl of Pembroke and his men at unawares, near a village called Puyrenon, slaying a number of men-at-arms, and forcing the rest to take refuge in a churchyard, which surrounded a building formerly belonging to the Knights Templars. The French knights, commanded by the Mareschal de Sancerre, said among themselves, jestingly, "They have got into a churchyard, it is but fair to give them time to choose out and dig their graves; and after we have taken dinner, we will visit them, and see how they suit them." But the Mareschal himself commanded an instant attack. The assault was made, but with little success on the part of the French, who were repulsed by the English Earl and his party. Still, as the French drew off, they promised themselves better fortune the next day, for the walls of the Temple-house were but thin, and might be easily broken through; and, at all events, the party within were ill appointed both in food and ammunition.

The Earl of Pembroke, who had now reason bitterly to lament his foolish jealousy of Lord Chandos, despatched an esquire, with orders to issue by a postern-gate, and tell the Seneschal of Poitou the danger in which he was placed, adding, that he might yet receive succour from him if he marched speedily, since he hoped to defend his post until noon next day. The esquire went on his errand accordingly.

Early next morning the French attacked the English position anew, and persevered from dawn till nine in the morning when the assailants began to collect among the neighbouring peasants pickaxes and mattocks for the purpose of undermining the walls. This mode of attack being that which the English most dreaded, the Earl of Pembroke called a second esquire, desiring him to take the Earl's best horse, and convey to his good friend, Lord Chandos, the news of the jeopardy in which they stood, conjuring him by a token to come to his deliverance. The token was a valuable ring, which Chandos had formerly given to the young Earl. The messenger escaped by a postern, and went off at full gallop. It chanced that the esquire first despatched had missed his way, so that he did not reach Poitiers till nine o'clock. When he did arrive, he delivered the Earl of Pembroke's message to Chandos, requiring his assistance. The good knight received it but coldly, as he still resented the young Earl's having declined to join him, though repeatedly invited. He answered indifferently, "there was but little time to hear mass;" a religious ceremony which Catholics then laid much stress upon. When the mass was over, dinner was announced as ready, and the first course was hardly served, when the second esquire arrived, and delivered the Earl of Pembroke's later and more pressing message, requesting assistance. Lord Chandos was still sullen; "to deliver him is impossible," he said, "if he is in such a strait as you speak of. Let us sit down to dinner—the meat will be cold else."

But this dogged and ungracious humour was not natural to the noble Chandos. The first thought of his mind having been given to resentment, the next reverted to more exalted sentiments. As the second course was served, he raised his head, which he had held depressed upon his bosom, and said to the knights and squires around him, " Hear me, sirs; the Earl of Pembroke is a noble person, and of high lineage, son-in-law to our natural lord, the King of England. Foul shame were it to see him lost, if I may help it; wherefore I will go to his assistance, with the grace of God. Make ready, sirs, for Puyrenon!" All rushed to arms; and Lord Chandos, at the head of two hundred spears, made towards the village with such speed, that they had good hope of surprising the French who besieged it. But the Mareschal de Sancerre heard of the approach of Chandos, by spies, and took the resolution of drawing off his troops, and securing such prisoners and booty as they had made at the first onset, which last comprehended all the treasure and baggage of the Earl of Pembroke. The Earl and his knights, on their part, also retired from the Temple-house with such horses as they had left, some mounted two on one horse, and others walking on foot. When they met with John Chandos, the Earl and he embraced, with tears; and Chandos greatly reflected upon himself that he had not moved on the first summons, when he might have reached Puyrenon time enough to surprise Sancerre and his forces, who had now retired to a place of safety.

This anecdote, besides illustrating the manners of the times, shows also the sort of disputes and rivalry which began to take place between the younger English nobility and those who stood high among the more ancient chivalry, and which doubtless existed on many other, although less memorable, occasions than the affair of Puyrenon, where such considerable injury was sustained, by the rashness and presumption of Pembroke, while the opportunity of retaliation was lost, through the sullen resentment of Chandos.

But England was not only to view the services of this distinguished warrior interrupted and traversed, but also to see them for ever ended, and that in a trivial encounter.

The assault upon the Earl of Pembroke in Puyrenon took place in 1370; and about the end of that year, a certain monk, belonging to a convent in Saint Salvin, a town in Poitou, contrived, out of spite to his superior the abbot, to betray him and the convent, as well as the town itself, into the hands of Sir Louis Saint Julien, and an adventurer, called Carlonet the Breton, leaders of the French party, who garrisoned it for that crown. Lord Chandos made several attempts to recover this place; for, although of no great consequence, he accounted it a diminution of his reputation to have it lost in that manner. But the vigilance of Sir Louis of Saint Julien frustrated all his attempts.

A.D. 1370.

Persevering in his purpose, Sir John, in his character of Seneschal of Poitou, sent to several knights of that country to meet him in the city of Poitiers, on the evening of the 30th of December, with the purpose of surprising Saint Salvin. The Poitevin knights, who loved and respected Chandos, obeyed his summons, met him accordingly, and their united numbers made up three hundred spears. With this retinue, he marched to the little town of Saint Salvin, and descended into the fosse, which he prepared to pass upon the ice, as the frost was then severe. The warder of the castle at this moment blew his horn; and the sound, so unusual at this late moment, made the English knights conclude that they were discovered. They drew back, therefore, out of the moat in which they lay in ambush, without persisting in an attempt, which, if discovered, as they supposed, must of course have been rendered impracticable. The watch horn, however, had no reference to the attack on Saint Salvin, but was designed by the person who blew it to intimate to the fortress the arrival of Carlonet the Breton at the opposite gate, who came to require Sir Louis of Saint Julien to go abroad with him that night, in search of adventures, as was the practice of the time. If, therefore, Chandos could have concealed himself for any time, however short, these two knights must have sallied from Saint Salvin, which, in their absence, would have been an easy prey But the evil fate of this renowned warrior was too strong for his better genius. He retreated to a

village about three leagues from Saint Salvin,
where the Poitevin lords, understanding the service of the time to be ended, were dismissed to
their homes. Mean time, Sir John Chandos declared it his intention to stay, during the next day,
being 31st December, in the town where he now
was. Sir Thomas Percy, who was in his company,
then asked his permission, since he did not stir
abroad himself, to go forth to meet adventures on
his own account. Chandos granted his request,
and was thus left with a retinue amounting only to
forty or fifty spears.

Historians notice, with singular minuteness, the
various steps by which this great warrior approached the fatal close of his life.

Sir Thomas Percy had not long left the town
when intelligence reached Chandos that Sir Louis
and Carlonet were certainly abroad in the country.
Now, although they were almost the personal
enemies of Chandos, yet at first he intimated no
desire to go in quest of them. He remained for
some time in the village, talking with his men,
while they warmed themselves at the fire, until, as
if upon a sudden reflection, he changed his purpose,
and declared his intention to take horse, and
return to Poitiers. He had not advanced far along
the side of the river when he heard the neighing
of horses; these were the steeds of the French
squadron, whose situation, had it been understood
by the opposite party, was, in fact, a very dangerous one. Sir Louis Saint Julien and Carlonet
had, by mere accident, fallen into the rear of Sir

Thomas Percy's party, and they were themselves followed, though without knowing it, by that of Lord Chandos. In this awkward situation, with one enemy in front, and another in the rear, the French knights took the resolution to possess themselves of the Bridge of Lussac, where they dismounted, gave their horses to their pages, and stood on their defence, afraid that they might be attacked in front and rear at once. But they were thus far fortunate that Sir Thomas Percy was not aware of the presence of the party of Chandos, and did not, therefore, know the difficulty in which the French were placed.

Chandos, who was the first of the English that arrived, saluted his enemies in this manner:—" Ha! Sir Louis Saint Julien, and Carlonet, you make no fair war, riding about by night, and taking towns and captives. I have long desired to see you. I am John Chandos—look upon me well; we shall presently see whether you or I are the best men!" As he spoke these words, he opened the visor of his helmet, which he forgot again to close, and, throwing himself from horseback, advanced, with his axe in his hand, to charge the Frenchmen, who were also dismounted. But in the very act of joining with his enemy, Chandos's foot slipped, and he fell down upon the bridge, which was steep in its ascent, and covered with hoar-frost. A French esquire took the advantage, as he was rising, and thrust a rapier through his eye into his forehead. This was the more easy, because Chandos, who was blind of an eye on that side, could not see the thrust in time to parry it, and also because his visor was open. The blow penetrated to the brain, and the valiant leader never spoke another word. The fight continued fierce around his body; for the French were determined to avail themselves of their superiority of numbers, and of the great advantage they had obtained, while the English were desirous to revenge the death of Chandos. The squire who had dealt the fatal thrust was mortally wounded in his turn; but, nevertheless, the numbers of the French must have gained the victory, had it not been that their pages and squires, terrified at seeing the banner, and beholding the advance of the formidable Chandos, had fled from their masters at the very first onset, carrying their horses off with them. Sir Thomas Percy could without difficulty have turned the scale, had he not gone too far forward to be recalled by the noise of the conflict with Chandos. But, to complete the mistakes and changeful accidents of this extraordinary night, another large body of the English party appeared, advancing at a round trot, with lances displayed and streamers waving in the wind. The Frenchmen, alarmed at this unexpected apparition, and unable to escape for want of horses, thought it better to surrender themselves prisoners to the companions of Chandos, whom they had wellnigh discomfited, than to abide the mercy of these new comers. They surrendered, accordingly; and thus the skirmish which, from beginning to end, seemed a blind work of fortune, terminated in a manner totally unlike its commencement.

The death of Lord Chandos was deeply regretted, not only by the English and Gascons, but by the French themselves, who respected him as the person most likely to have brought about a good understanding between the Kings of France and England, and a steady peace between the kingdoms. After his death, a considerable decay of wisdom, spirit, and conduct, might be observed on the side of the English, and the removal of so great a general from the field of battle could in no respect be made up or compensated.

It is true, that, before the event which we have narrated here, in order to conclude the subject of Lord Chandos, Edward III. had endeavoured to strengthen himself in France, by despatching to Calais, his son, commonly called John of Gaunt, with five hundred men-at arms, and a gallant force of archers, with whom the Count of Namur united himself as an auxiliary of England.

The King of France, on the other hand, hearing that an army, commanded by a son of England, had entered Calais, and made frequent incursions into the country around, despatched, to oppose him, the Duke of Burgundy, who was the ablest of his brothers, with a force, which, compared with that of the invaders, was more than seven to one. He imposed, however, upon this Prince, strict commands, that he should on no account venture upon an engagement, for the recollections of former battles lost in spite of the greatest inequality of numbers, rendered such a risk extremely unadvisable. Thus restrained by the royal command, the Duke of Burgundy took post in the vicinity of

Calais, between Saint Omer and Tournehan, while the Duke of Lancaster, on the opposite side, occupied a very strong position, fortified with hedges, ditches, and enclosures, which rendered those who lay there unassailable; so that the armies faced each other, while little passed that was remarkable, except a few skirmishes.

In the estimation of those times, the character of the Duke of Burgundy suffered considerably in the eyes of the public, by shunning an encounter with so inferior an army; yet it was precisely by the French attacking an inferior number of English, in a post of extraordinary strength, that Edward III. and the Black Prince had gained their immortal trophies. The Duke of Burgundy was, notwithstanding, so much hurt by his situation, that he applied to the King, his brother, requesting either to be allowed to give battle to the English, or to retire from a position in which his reputation suffered.

Charles preferred the alternative which should put the country in the least peril. He therefore commanded the Duke of Burgundy to raise his camp, and come to him at Paris. The French Prince effected this manœuvre so cautiously, that the first intimation which the English had of their enemy's retreat, was the fires which consumed the tents and huts which they had lately occupied. The Duke of Lancaster, on the retreat of the great French army, determined to march into the interior, and advancing from Calais to the eastward, inflicted severe marks of his dis-

A.D. 1369.

pleasure upon the villages and cultivated country, subjecting to especial rigour those which had shown themselves unfriendly to England.

As the Duke returned to Calais, after a wasteful tour, little that was interesting took place, although the following turn of fortune may be worth mentioning:—Hugh de Chastillon, a captain of the crossbows of France, commanded the French garrison of Abbeville. This gentleman took horse, with ten or twelve attendants, resolved, seeing the Duke of Lancaster was tending that way, to view with his own eyes, the preparations made to receive him. Now, while he was on this service, Sir Nicolas Louvaine, an Englishman, was reconnoitring in the same direction. He had been a seneschal of the King of England in that country, was well acquainted with all its fastnesses and bypaths, and had insinuated himself into a ruinous village hard by the gates of Abbeville, where no ambuscade could be suspected. This Sir Nicolas had been made prisoner the year before by the same Chastillon, and he felt as an injury the high sum of ten thousand crowns, which he had been obliged to pay as his ransom. It was to his infinite joy, therefore, that he saw, in the person of a cavalier who advanced carelessly, and ill prepared for battle (for his page was riding his war-horse, and carrying his helmet), his late captor, Sir Hugh of Chastillon. "Come on," said Louvaine to his party, being twenty men-at-arms, "yonder is our prey, whom I would rather possess, than all the world beside!" He rushed then suddenly on Chas-

tillon, with his lance in rest, calling aloud, " Yield
ye, or die!"—" To whom must I yield?" said
the captain of the crossbows, astonished to find
himself overpowered, when he supposed himself
most in security.—" To your old acquaintance
Louvaine, who requires from you the ten thousand
crowns which you exacted as his ransom." Accordingly it became Chastillon's turn to rescue
himself upon the terms which Louvaine prescribed.

Such accidents as these might impoverish or
enrich the military men to whom they happened,
but the general effect of the war on both countries
was that of exhausting them both of men and
money. Still the French, relying on the wisdom
and patriotism of Charles, submitted cheerfully to
very heavy taxes, confident in his employing them
to the best advantage, in defending the independence of the country. The assembly of estates pa-
tiently acquiesced in the imposition of the same
taxes, which the nation had paid for the ransom of
King John; and also in a tax of hearth-money, in
effect nearly the same with the *fouage*, which,
when imposed in Gascony, cost the Black Prince
so much of his popularity;—so different is the
good-will of the people in the payment of taxes,
which they conceive necessary for their defence,
compared to that with which they regard imposi-
tions which are bestowed upon objects, either altogether idle and unnecessary, or directed to unpopular and unnational purposes.

A marauding party, far less numerous than that
under the Duke of Lancaster, was commanded b

Sir Robert Knolles, that distinguished officer, who, from a mean origin, had raised himself to great distinction by his interest among the Free Companies. He was now commissioned with an army of thirty thousand men to lay waste the kingdom of France on behalf of Edward III.—a wasteful mode of warfare, inconsistent with the idea held out of permanent conquest.

Knolles took his departure from Calais at the head of his troops in the end of July, and moved forward by Terouenne and Artois, making easy marches, halting regularly every night, and burning and ravaging the country. He appears to have retained some old remnants of the adventurer, as he used occasionally to accept of sums of money, in consideration of which he spared particular districts, and forebore those violences in which he was accustomed to indulge. This was a course of conduct so misrepresented to Edward III. that in the end it had like to have cost Sir Robert dear. In the mean time, this predatory general's march was directed upon the city of Paris; not that he had any hope to gain possession of it, but merely from a desire to spread confusion and terror in the neighbourhood, and perhaps to provoke a part of the inhabitants to come out and take the chance of battle. He approached the city so near, that the fires which he raised in the neighbouring villages were plainly seen from the walls of Paris; and a knight of the English army had an opportunity, and, as it proved, a fatal one, of accomplishing one of those

A.D. 1370.

vows of chivalry which were fashionable at the period; of which the more desperate and extraordinary always added the more to the renown of those by whom they were achieved. This adventurer had, it seems, made a vow that he would strike his spear upon the gate of Paris. For this purpose, he rushed forth from the ranks, and, followed by his squire, whom he soon outstript, rode up to the gate, where he found the barriers open. There were several French knights standing by the barrier, who marvelled what this single man was about to attempt; but when they saw him satisfied with striking his lance upon the gate, and reining round his courser to return, they laughed, and said, " Go thy way for a brave knight, that hast well accomplished thy vow!" The citizens of Paris and the suburbs had not the same sympathy with the adventurous knight as was entertained by those who were his brothers in chivalry. He learned the difference of these feelings upon his return; for a butcher, who had seen him pass through the suburb, waylaid him on his return, and, coming behind him with a cleaver, struck him from his horse. The squire, alarmed for his master's fate on seeing his horse return without a rider, advanced into the suburb far enough to behold the knight prostrate on the ground, and four or five strong mechanics beating upon him at once, like smiths upon a stithy. He fled, therefore, to carry to Knolles's camp the account of the knight's misadventure.

Sir Robert Knolles encamped that night within

sight of Paris; and we shall presently give an account of the termination of his adventurous expedition, which was concluded by an engagement betwixt him and the celebrated Bertrand du Guesclin.

In the mean time, the events of the war became more and more unfavourable to England. An astrologer of that time might have said, that as a star auspicious to England had set in the horizon, so another had arisen friendly to France, and in the highest degree hostile to her enemy. Some thing of the kind actually happened in the terrestrial world; for in this year the gallant Black Prince was lost to his trade of arms, and the formidable Bertrand du Guesclin resumed that command in the service of Charles, which occasioned his being surnamed the Restorer of the French Monarchy.

CHAPTER XXIII.

Revolt of Limoges to the French—the Black Prince besieges and re captures it—Death of the Black Prince—Bertrand du Guesclin made Constable of France—the Constable defeats the English at Pont Vulant—Marriage of the Duke of Lancaster to a daughter of Don Pedro the Cruel, by which alliance Henry, the Reigning King of Castile, is rendered an enemy to England—Defeat of the English Fleet by the Spanish, off Rochelle—Rochelle delivered by the Mayor to the French—the Constable captures Poitiers—Thouars besieged, and surrenders to the French—King Charles drives the Count de Montfort from Bretagne, and declares his duchy forfeited to the French Crown—the Breton Lords rise in insurrection, and drive the French from their country—Death of the Constable du Guesclin, while besieging Chateauneuf de Randan—Charles of Navarre deprived of the Dominions he held in France—Horrible Death of Charles of Navarre—Death of Charles V., surnamed the Wise.

[1370—1377.]

You have been already informed that Edward the renowned Black Prince, had never enjoyed his usual health since the expedition into Spain. It was in vain that as difficulties multiplied around him, his high spirit struggled against the decay of strength and the increase of the debilitating disorder, which appears to have been dropsical. Yet it was not the will of fate that this celebrated champion should depart from the scene without one final ray of victory shining upon his banner. This parting favour was granted in a case in which his haughty spirit was deeply interested.

Among other advantages gained by the French in consequence of the general discontent of the Gascons against the English, the revolt of the strong city of Limoges was one of the most distinguished. This city had yielded itself up by the instigation of its bishop, whose recommendation induced the inhabitants to revolt, and admit a French garrison; the surrender was made to the Duke of Anjou, and Bertrand du Guesclin remained in the province of the Limousin, to protect this important acquisition by his presence.

The Prince of Wales, on the other hand, was dreadfully offended, not only with the bishop, who had formerly been his personal friend, but with the citizens of Limoges, who had so lightly changed their party. He could not now mount a horse; but, hastily assembling an army of about twelve hundred lances, and two thousand archers, he caused them to move forward upon Limoges, he himself being borne in an open litter at the head of his troops. The garrison treated with scorn his summons to surrender, for they confided in the strength of their fortifications, which had indeed been constructed by the Prince himself. Immediately upon receiving a scornful refusal to give up the place, the Prince of Wales laid close siege to the town, which he pressed on by means of mines driven under the walls, for which service he was provided with the best artisans of the period. Bertrand du Guesclin kept the field in the mean time with two hundred spears, with which he made incursions on the territory, which was yet English, and endeavoured by various means to divert the attention of the Prince of Wales from the siege of Limoges. It was not, however, in the power of Du Guesclin to baffle the last and almost dying efforts of this celebrated hero, who remained totally regardless of the diversions with which Du Guesclin endeavoured to amuse him. The Prince pressed on the siege with unabated vigour, attending entirely to the conduct of the mines, until the engineers informed him that they were prepared to throw down a part of the wall sufficient to admit his entering in battalion. Accordingly, the use of gunpowder in such mines being as yet unknown, the miners had orders to set fire to the props by which they supported the wall during the time they had carried on their operations. Of course, a portion of the wall, about thirty feet in extent, fell into the ditch and filled it up, while the English division appointed for the storm rushed over the ruins. The gates, at the same time, were secured by another part of the English army. All escape was impossible; and the unfortunate inhabitants had it only in their power to prostrate themselves in the streets, and implore with piteous cries the compassion of the Prince, who was determined to grant none. The slaughter was indiscriminate, and while the Prince himself was borne into the town upon his litter, the guards who attended him slew men, women, and children, with their pole-axes and swords. Four thousand persons were put to the sword, without distinguishing the unarmed from the armed, men from women, or children from adults. The sight of four gallant Frenchmen defending themselves with much bravery first awakened Edward's sympathy. Each was matched with a noble and almost royal antagonist; for the four men-at-arms were engaged hand to hand with the Duke of Lancaster and Earl of Cambridge, brothers to the Prince of Wales, with the Earl of Pembroke, his brother-in-law, and with another distinguished English warrior. The Black Prince stopped his litter to behold this sharp conflict, calculated to awaken his sense of generosity, which remained lively, though his humanity was extinguished. While the Prince's litter stood still, that he might behold the pleasing spectacle of a desperate combat, the French knights took the opportunity to surrender and yield up their swords to him. They were dismissed with praises, and the heart of the conqueror was somewhat appeased towards the vanquished by the chivalry which these combatants had displayed. But the victor's anger revived when the Bishop of Limoges, first author of the revolt of the city, was brought before him. In the first heat of his wrath, he commanded him to be beheaded; and it was with difficulty that he was finally induced to spare his life.

The recapture of Limoges was the last military feat of this renowned warrior; and we regret to trace in it so much of the cruelty of the period, and so little of its generosity. We have only farther to mention, that in the beginning of the next year, the Black Prince had the great misfortune of losing his eldest son; and, his own illness increasing, he determined to try what his native air might avail for his recovery. He left his brother, the Duke of Lancaster, as his representative in the principality of Aquitaine; and retired forever from the country where he himself had gained so much glory, and upon which he had inflicted such extensive calamities. This great prince died at Westminster, on the 8th day of June, 1376; and his father, exhausted by age, and various causes of mortification which overclouded his last years, did not long survive him. Edward III. died on the 21st of June, 1377, in the sixty-fifth year of his age. In resuming our story, we shall have to mention circumstances which happened before the date of his death.

While fate was thus removing the two greatest enemies of France, the King of that country was exerting himself, by the best means, the promotion, namely, of merit and worth, to provide for the protection of his realm. An office, always most important, but at this time particularly so, had become vacant in 1370; this was the situation of Constable of France, the highest military dignity in that kingdom, of the most important consequence, from the power which it conferred, and especially when the King, as might be said of Charles V. was not warlike in his person, or in the habit of heading his armies. The vacancy was occasioned by the resignation of a good knight, named Moreau de Fionnes, who had become, by age and infirmities, incapable of discharging the duties of the office, which he therefore resigned into the King's hands. It had been the custom to bestow this high office on persons of the most eminent rank; but, by the universal suffrages of his kingdom, Charles now resolved to confer it less with reference to the station than the merits of the person he deemed worthy of it. On this footing, all eyes were turned to Bertrand du Guesclin, as the most valiant knight, the most expert leader, the most fortunate and successful warrior, who fought under the banners of France. Nay, since the Black Prince was unable to bear armour, he was universally considered as the best general living.

Du Guesclin, summoned to the King's presence, rode from the district of the Limousin to Paris accordingly; but when he heard that the King, with full assent of all his nobles and peers, had pitched upon him to be Constable of France, he modestly stated his incapacity for such an important office, and the difficulty which he, a poor knight, must expect in making himself obeyed by the great and powerful princes of France. The King's resolution was taken upon too good grounds to be evaded by this modest plea; he insisted upon the charge being accepted by the warrior who had shown himself most capable of bearing it. Du Guesclin then asked to limit his acceptance with a condition, that in case complaints should be brought against him, the King should deign to refuse credence to any which the informer was not ready to vouch in presence of the accused; a reasonable request, which was readily granted.

But although a distinguished warrior was thus invested with full military command in France, there were still circumstances affecting in a great degree the welfare of the kingdom, the consideration and decision of which the King reserved for himself. Greatly as that wise prince esteemed Du Guesclin, he saw danger in the Constable's suffering his high ideas of chivalry to lead him into the error of precipitating a general engagement, by which France had so often suffered, and which was at all times too deep a stake to be hastily adventured. He therefore resolved, while he resigned to the Constable the unlimited direction of the French armies, that he would suffer him at no time to possess a force so strong as might encourage him to venture a battle on a large scale, trusting that when he fought upon a small one, his knowledge of war could not be excelled, if, indeed, it could be equalled, by that of any of the English leaders. This restriction the King reserved within his own breast. To have expressed it, might have implied distrust of his general, and still more of his soldiers. He therefore readily acceded to the new constable's proposal to ride after Sir Robert Knolles; yet it is said, he furnished him with no more men than should enable him to watch the enemy, but not to bring him to action. But the faithful Du Guesclin augmented his forces, by treasure of his own, and for that purpose sold a number of rich jewels and other articles of value.

The time, indeed, was very favourable for an attack upon the army of Knolles. This commander, as you have been already informed, had marched to the gates of Paris, without being able to strike a considerable blow, so that many of the men of rank who served with him, were disposed to be discontented with their commander's authority. It had been his purpose to lead his army into the duchy of Bretagne, as the safest place for winter quarters, considering that there would be then a necessity for dividing it into separate bodies, when an active enemy like Du Guesclin might, in the opinion of the experienced general, attack them with advantage. Lord Grandison, Lord Fitzwalter, and other English nobles, refused to retire into Bretagne, in obedience to Sir Robert Knolles. He was of too mean rank, they said, to command noblemen like themselves; they therefore drew off their forces from his army, which was thus much weakened, and quartered themselves in the marches of Anjou and Touraine, not even holding such communication as martial discipline required, but straggling separate, each leader according to his own pleasure.

While disunion was thus gaining ground among the English, and want of discipline arising in proportion, Bertrand du Guesclin obtained news of all their proceedings from a traitorous knight, called Sir John Menstreworth, who privately corresponded with the French, and found an opportunity of discovering to them a very important secret. The new Constable, with his forces, had already advanced on an enterprise against Sir Robert Knolles, then in quarters in Bretagne. The artful Knolles was rejoiced to hear of his approach, resolving within himself that he would assemble secretly and suddenly the troops who had lately left his standard, and thus collect a body of forces with which he had no doubt he would be able to overpower Du Guesclin, and his party. Lord Grandison, Lord Fitzwalter, and the other discontented nobles, received therefore private instructions to repair to the camp of Sir Robert Knolles, for the accomplishment of this purpose; and as the orders intimated the approach of battle, none of them hesitated to obey the summons. On the other side, Sir Robert called to his assistance Sir Hugh Calverley, and other captains of the Companions. All this plan, and these summonses, were known to the treacherous Sir John Menstreworth, and by him communicated to the Constable of France, who resolved, by his active movements, to prevent the plan of the English general, and strike a blow at the forces out of which Knolles proposed to form his army, while they were yet separated from the main body. For this purpose, aware of the march of Grandison, Fitzwalter, and their party, the Constable contrived to meet them at a place called Pont Volant, half way before they could join with Knolles, and attacking them with a force nearly double theirs, soon reduced them to extremity. The English, however, alighting from horseback, defended themselves for some time manfully on foot, with swords, spears, and battle-axes. They could not, however, long endure so unequal a combat; and as their pages, who held their horses, fled with them so soon as the day was lost, the principal part of the nobles engaged remained on the spot, either slain or prisoners. This blow, which gave the greatest spirit to the French, seemed proportionally discouraging to the English; and, as it happened so recently after Du Guesclin had become constable, it gained him honour in the eyes of the King, and of the nation, as affording an earnest of his important services. The immediate consequence of the defeat of the English at Pont Volant was, that Sir Robert Knolles, already prejudiced in King Edward's opinion for having taken rewards for sparing the country of France, fell into such suspicion, that he hesitated for some time to trust himself within the bounds of Britain. But the treason of Sir John Menstreworth becoming public, the explanations of the veteran Knolles were favourably received; and as the real traitor fell into the hands of the British, and was executed for his perfidy, Knolles became entirely restored to King Edward's favour.

The Constable of France did not long slumber after his success at Pont Volant, but, taking the field again at Candlemas, seized many fortresses, and with prevailing, though by no means uniform, good fortune, carried on the war in Guienne and the neighbouring counties.

The Duke of Lancaster now supported at Bourdeaux a princely state, not inferior to that of the Black Prince himself, whom he resembled in courage and pride, though he was unequal to him in good fortune, or rather in that military science, by which good fortune is in a great measure secured or improved. An alliance of his also, though the Duke was naturally led into it by what seemed the voice of prudence, and was certainly that of ambition, contributed to force him into the false line of policy adopted by the Black Prince himself. Don Pedro the Cruel, who died by the hand of his brother King Henry, before the Castle of Montiel, as we have already stated, left behind him two daughters, the eldest of whom was undoubtedly heiress to his kingdom of Castile. These orphan princesses were now residing in Gascony, pledges for a sum of money which had been borrowed by their father. John of Gaunt was now in the flower of his age, a widower, by the death of his wife the late Lady Blanche; and, flattered by the splendid title of King of Castile, to which he aspired, he gave his hand to the eldest of these unfortunate princesses, while the second was wedded at the same time to his brother the Duke of Cambridge. By this unhappy step, the Duke of Lancaster added to the difficulties arising from the French war, so many and so numerous in themselves, the gloomy prospect of a quarrel with Henry, the King of

Castile, who became in consequence a very violent and dangerous enemy to England, which was not long in experiencing the effects of his enmity.

In 1371, the Duke of Lancaster, having returned to England with his royal bride, the Earl of Pembroke was appointed to sail as commander-in-chief of the English forces to the principality of Aquitaine. He had a fleet of forty ships, having on board a considerable body of troops, with supplies of money and ammunition essentially requisite to the support of the sinking cause of England in the south of France. Thus provided, he sailed for Rochelle; but as he approached that place, he was encountered by a powerful fleet belonging to Henry of Transtamar, the actual King of Castile, who was called upon imperiously to espouse the cause of the French; the Duke of Lancaster having, in right of his wife the princess Constance, laid claim to his kingdom. The two navies of England and Spain encountered fiercely with each other, and the combat endured until the evening of the second day, when the Spaniards obtained a complete victory. It is said this superiority was owing not only to the size of the Spanish vessels, which were larger than those of the English, but to the use of cannon on the part of the former—a weapon for the first time made use of in naval war. The greatest part of the English fleet was burnt, taken, or sunk; and the Earl of Pembroke, often already mentioned, son-in-law to Edward III., remained, with many other knights of quality, prisoners of war to the

A.D. 1372. June 23.

Spaniards. Such were the first evil fruits flowing from the marriage of John of Gaunt with the daughter of Don Pedro the Cruel. The failure of this attempt to send supplies to Guienne, left that province, with all parts of the principality of Aquitaine, wellnigh at the absolute mercy of the Constable du Guesclin, who, alternately by address and by arms, took and garrisoned many places of strength, some with very little resistance, others with none at all.

The case of Rochelle may be mentioned as an instance how much the feelings of the Gascon people were now turned against their late masters the English. Shortly after the naval battle which we have already mentioned, and which was fought off this harbour, the mayor of Rochelle, one John Chaudron, moved, no doubt, by the issue of the battle and defeat of the English, contrived a mode of surrendering that important seaport to the King of France. The English, however, had still a garrison in the castle, of which Philip Mansel, an uneducated man of no peculiar sagacity, was the temporary governor. The mayor, having secured a party of burgesses in his plot, undertook to circumvent the thick-headed commander of the citadel. He invited Mansel to a civic feast, where he exhibited a letter under the broad seal of England (one of an old date), shrewdly suspecting that the governor could not read a word of it. "You perceive from this letter," said the mayor, boldly exhibiting it to the ignorant governor, "that the King has commanded the garrison of the castle, and that of the city, to be alternately reviewed by the commanders of each; wherefore I will make my musters to-morrow, if it pleases you to review them; and you, if it please you, shall bring your force out of the castle, that I may inspect them in my turn in the manner here appointed."

The incautious Mansel, affecting to believe and understand words which had no existence in the letter, was induced to bring his men out of the castle towards the field where the rendezvous was to be held. The mayor, seeing the stratagem so far successful, interposed a strong body of armed citizens between the garrison and the castle gate, and compelled them to lay down their arms. It was probably by the patriotism of this mayor of Rochelle, that the city, thus won from the English by the courage or ingenuity of the citizens, was not surrendered to the French Crown absolutely, but only under stipulation that the citizens of Rochelle should have leave to demolish the castle, and be secured against the erection of another; also, that they should never be separated or alienated from the kingdom of France; and thirdly, that they should be allowed to coin money upon the same conditions on which the privilege was enjoyed by the city of Paris.

The strong town of Poitiers also augmented the triumphs of the gallant Constable. A skirmish shortly after took place of little importance in itself, but of considerable weight from its consequences. The Lord de Greilly, renowned in our former history by the name of the Captal de Buche, and often mentioned on account of his gallantry, was made prisoner, and, as a captive of great consequence, was speedily despatched to Paris. His worth and character in war were not better known than the constant fidelity with which he had served the cause of the English. The King of France, therefore, followed the policy which the Prince of Wales was thought to have adopted respecting Bertrand du Guesclin, when the latter was made prisoner at the battle of Navarette, that is, he would not fix any ransom upon the unfortunate warrior, who died in the course of five years an unredeemed captive. Authors have said that the Captal, as a firm adherent of Edward and of the Black Prince, lost his health and spirits upon their decease, and pined to death of melancholy in his confinement.

In the mean time, the last post possessed by the English in Gascony was the town of Thouars, then a place of considerable strength. The Constable speedily formed the siege of the place, and pressed it on with such vigour, that the English lords who were enclosed in it, consisting of the noblest and best of those partisans whom the numerous skirmishes and sieges had left, were contented to come to a species of terms not unusual at that time. They engaged to surrender against next Michaelmas, provided the King of England, or one of his sons, should not before that time bring them succour in person.

Edward, to whom this agreement was communicated, expressed himself highly incensed, that a prince so unwarlike as Charles of France, who was seldom seen with armour on his back, or a lance in his hand, should give him so much more trouble than all his martial predecessors, and once more swore to take the field in person, with the purpose, not only of relieving Thouars, but of invading and finally conquering France. The King put to sea accordingly, with a considerable army, his destination being the seaport of Rochelle; but the winds and waves were obstinately adverse to the course he proposed; and, after a desperate struggle, King Edward, to whom fortune had been so long favourable by land and sea, saw himself absolutely obliged to return to England, without relieving the fortress.

Thouars was therefore left to its fate. The barons of Guienne, who remained faithful to England, offered indeed, at the very last, to advance with twelve hundred spears to the relief of this important place, provided the besieged would accept of their assistance. But the knights enclosed within the town had plighted their faith to surrender to the Constable, unless Edward, or one of his sons, came in person to their relief. Thouars, therefore, was given up to the French, on the terms of the treaty.

The cause of England in France being at this low ebb, the King of France thought he might very safely take the opportunity to avenge himself upon the Count de Montfort, Duke of Bretagne, whose father had been one of the principal instigators of the former war between England and

France. John de Montfort was, indeed, already wellnigh forced from his dominions by two of his own feudatories, the Constable du Guesclin, and Oliver de Clisson; and Charles now resolved, in contravention of the neutrality secured to him by a special article of the treaty of Bretigny, no longer to suffer one who had been so hostile to him to reign over Bretagne, and accordingly drove him out of his duchy, and obliged him to take refuge in England. Edward, however, on the arrival of his ally and relative in this expatriated condition, was not wanting in such exertions as might have a chance of repairing his sinking fortunes.

He raised an army of fifty thousand men, which, under the command of the Duke of Lancaster, landed at Calais, in the summer of 1372, with the purpose, on the Duke's part, of emulating his father's deeds, restoring the English affairs, and replacing the Duke of Bretagne in his government. But, as was the fate of all Edward III.'s latter expeditions, no result followed worthy of such great preparations.

The Duke of Lancaster sallied from Calais, at the head of his army. He had with him the Earls of Warwick, Stafford, Suffolk, and Lord Edward Spencer. They marched with precaution, being closely watched by three armies of the French, one commanded by the Duke of Burgundy, one by the Duke of Bourbon, a third, consisting chiefly of cavalry, headed by the indefatigable Du Guesclin, which followed in the rear of the English, cutting off all who strayed from their standard; and, thus enclosed and observed, the English could make little spoil upon the country, without exposing themselves to instant retaliation.

Their generals, too, differed in opinion. John de Montfort pressed the Duke of Lancaster to lead his troops into Bretagne, insisting that the reconquest of his duchy was the chief object of the war. The Duke of Lancaster, on the other hand, was determined to march to Bourdeaux, to restore the English power in Gascony. He accordingly precipitated his course to Bourdeaux, and at length reached that city, but not without losing four-fifths of his army in his hurried and disastrous march. Nor were the Duke of Bretagne and the Duke of Lancaster ever afterwards on the same footing of good understanding which previously subsisted between them.

King Charles, perceiving the dissension between the Duke of Bretagne and his powerful ally, thought the time was favourable to his great object of uniting to the crown the duchy of Bretagne, whose sea-coasts, and the friendship of its sovereigns, had so often afforded facility to invasions from England. He accordingly proposed the forfeiture of this powerful vassal to the Estates of France, and obtained their sentence to that effect. But the Breton Lords, although unfriendly to the Duke's English alliance, were attached to their independence, and to the De Montfort family. Instead of confirming them in their love for France, by uniting them with the kingdom, Charles provoked their resentment by this attempt at confiscation.

The nobles of Bretagne returned to the allegiance of their Duke, and readily assembling in arms, drove the French out of the bounds of the duchy, and invited home John de Montfort from his exile in England. The issue of these events belongs to the next reign. A truce had concluded the bloodshed of this war for a period of one year. King Charles himself was taken ill, with little hope of recovery.

An incident occurred which tended to sadden, in no small degree, the thoughts of his dying bed. This was the death of the valiant Du Guesclin, who had held, by the King's personal choice, with so much advantage to the country, and glory to himself, the staff of Constable of France. He had been employed in the war in Bretagne, and still more recently in that of Guienne; and had in both conducted himself with the same gallantry and success which he had all along exhibited. The last act of his life was laying siege to the Chateau neuf de Randun. He had summoned the fortress, in terms which were boldly but respectfully answered by the commandant. On his refusal to surrender, Du Guesclin pitched his tent before the place, and pressed it by a close siege. It is said, with little probability, that the melancholy inspired by the obstinacy of the resistance, first brought on disease in this great captain. Bertrand du Guesclin must, however, have been too well acquainted with the chances of war, to feel, as a great misfortune, the prolonged opposition of a petty fortress. He fell ill, however, from whatever cause, and became speedily conscious that he was upon his deathbed. Willing to expend his last spark of life in the service of the country to which it had been dedicated, Du Guesclin sent the commandant of Chateau neuf de Randon, a positive summons to surrender the place instantly, if he desired to profit by his intercession with the King of France in his favour. The commandant, moved by the resolute and severe tone in which this message was delivered, declared that he would deliver the keys of his fortress to the Constable of France, but to no leader of inferior degree. He was conducted, therefore, to the tent of Du Guesclin; but he was no longer alive; and the commandant was compelled to lay the emblems of submission at the feet of a lifeless corpse.

Thus died, in the very act of reconquering the dismembered provinces of his country, a champion than whom the rolls of history contain few braver or more successful. Du Guesclin was not exempt from the evil qualities of his time, for his valour was occasionally sullied by cruelty; but his rise from ordinary rank to greatness was the achievement of his own high talents, and, employed as they were in the service of his country, those talents could not be too much admired or praised. It was not his least merit that all the liberal donations of land and treasure conferred on him by the king were uniformly applied by him to the public service; so that Charles, though conscious what he owed to this great and successful general, could hardly devise the means of affording him a recompense for his services. To fill up the vacancy occasioned by his death, King Charles recommended to his council that Oliver de Clisson, Du Guesclin's friend and companion in arms, a Breton, too, like him, should be appointed to succeed him. Mean time, though now affected by disease, certainly incurable, whatever was its origin, Charles V. still studied the great purpose of his ambition, which was the re-union of France into one kingdom.

This desirable object had met with a great obstacle in the King of Navarre, Charles the Bad. This prince had claims, as he pretended, upon the crown of France itself; and, besides, he was entitled to various possessions in several parts of that kingdom, but especially in Normandy. To dispossess him of these was the object of King Charles's dying policy; he revived therefore against the King of Navarre an accusation of high treason, as having administered poison to the royal person of his liege lord. This, as a high feudal delinquency, necessarily inferring the forfeiture of the fief, had been reserved as a charge against Navarre, when the time of making such an accusation with effect should at length arrive. The noxious draught was said to have been so potent, that the King lost his hair and his nails, and retained to the end of his life the marks of having taken poison. Yet though various other points of discussion had arisen between the princes, and more than one truce had been entered into, the affair was never judicially brought forward, until the expulsion of the English from so many places of importance in France had rendered any rebellion of Charles of Navarre of less consequence. The wicked prince was deprived, by a sentence of the Estates, of such dominions as he still held in France. His condemnation in this celebrated process renders it unnecessary to mention him hereafter; we shall therefore anticipate the course of events, to narrate, in this place, the horrible death by which he closed an existence, which had been but a tissue of crimes.

Continuing his course of vicious habits as a man, and political intrigues as a prince, till he was fully sixty years old, the difficulties which Charles the Bad had incurred in the wars between Spain, England, and France, obliged him to demand a heavy capitation tax from his subjects of Navarre. He proposed that the wealthy inhabitants should pay ten francs, inferior persons five, and the rest of his subjects one franc each. The deputies representing the different bodies and towns of the kingdom of Navarre assured him, that as they were not yet acquitted of a tax formerly laid upon them, they were not able to endure this new imposition, and therefore conjured him to have mercy on his subjects. By way of answer to these remonstrances, Charles caused the deputies to be enclosed in a strong-walled garden, where he had conferred with them. They were there strictly confined, and sparingly supplied with meat and drink, while Charles caused the heads of three of their number to be struck off, in order to intimidate the others. How this tragedy would otherwise have ended, is uncertain; for Heaven, in its own time, and by extraordinary means, put an end to this wicked prince's tyranny.

The King of Navarre's habits of profligacy had so far reduced his constitution, that he was ordered by the physicians to swathe himself in a vestment steeped in spirits of wine. By the same advice, his bed was warmed with a pan of hot coals; and he had used these means of recovering natural heat repeatedly without accident. But while he was agitating these cruel resolutions against the deputies of his subjects, and using this course of bringing himself to warmth, "by the pleasure of God," says Froissart, "or of the devil, the fire caught to his sheets, and from that to his person, swathed as it was in matter highly inflammable." Before he could be rescued, he was burnt to the bowels, yet survived fifteen days, in indescribable agonies. Such was the horrible end of the wicked King of Navarre.

We return to the purposes of King Charles of France upon his deathbed. While he meditated and endeavoured to execute the changes already noticed, his own life was drawing to a close. He died a victim, it is said, though not very probably, to the poison so long before administered by the King of Navarre; and his death was felt by the country with deeper regret than that of a sovereign is often regarded. Calm, sedate, temperate in his passions, viewing clearly, weighing deliberately, and wisely selecting the objects of his policy, Charles never rashly changed.

Sept. 1380

and rarely ultimately abandoned them. Though born in warlike times, he was himself no warrior; a most fortunate circumstance, since he was never liable to be driven forward by the vehement desire of personal distinction, or the sense of personal shame, which hurried his predecessors, Philip of Valois and John, into the fatal fields of Cressy and Poitiers.

CHAPTER XXIV

Accession of Charles VI., when only six years of age—Regency of the Duke of Anjou, who seizes the Treasures of Charles V., which he afterwards employs in advancing his own claim to the Crown of Sicily and Naples—An English army, under the Duke of Buckingham, sent to the assistance of the Duke of Bretagne, who promises to support them, but makes a Peace with France, and compels his English Allies to evacuate Bretagne—Disorders in Flanders—Insurrection of the Ghentois, under Artavelde—The French espouse the part of the Earl of Flanders, and the English that of the Insurgents—Defeat of the Insurgents at Rosebecque—Marriage of Charles VI.—Expedition of the Bishop of Norwich—the Bishop worsted, and compelled to retreat to Calais—Expedition of the Duke of Anjou to establish his claims to the Throne of Naples—his Failure, and Death—Adventures of two Captains of Free Companions, Geoffrey Tête-noir and Amerigot Marcel—Unsuccessful Attempt of the Duke of Lancaster to conquer Castile, the Crown of which he claimed in right of his Wife, the Daughter of Don Pedro the Cruel—Wreck of a French Fleet assembled in the Harbour of Sluys for the Invasion of England—Arrest of Oliver de Clisson, Constable of France, by the Duke of Bretagne—his Imprisonment, and Ransom.

[1380—1387.]

UNFORTUNATELY for the kingdom of France, the successor of Charles the Wise, who was also named Charles, being the sixth king so called, was at this time only twelve years old; and there was a necessity for appointing a regent. The Duke of Anjou, the eldest brother of the deceased monarch, had been one of the most active leaders during his life, and was supposed to be possessed of considerable talent; he was a mortal enemy to the English, and a principal actor during the late reign in making war upon them in the south of France. He was accused by them also of treachery and bad faith; and his character in general did not stand very high for truth and sincerity.

This prince obtained, however, the regency by appointment of the Estates, but the education and personal care of the King was committed to the Duke of Burgundy, the King's uncle by the father's side, and the Duke of Bourbon, who bore him the same relation by the mother's, who were named his immediate personal guardians. The Duke of Berri, another of his uncles, was subsequently admitted to a share in the Government.

Unhappily for France, the regent Duke of Anjou had a private interest of his own entirely different from that of the kingdom at large. The last Queen of Sicily and Naples was the celebrated Joan, who possessed these fair provinces in her own right. She was a profligate and infamous woman, who, besides leading a vicious course of life, had rid herself of her husband, Andrew, by assassination. It is said, that one day this unfortunate prince found her weaving a cord made of silk and gold, so remarkable in appearance, that he was induced to ask what purpose she designed to apply it to. Joan truly answered, " it was designed to hang her husband with;" and shortly after caused this cruel assassination to be performed by the very cord in question. At the period of her death, this unhappy queen, by the council and advice of the Pope, bequeathed her crown and dominions to the Duke of Anjou, who, with the flattering prospect before him, of a kingdom which was to be his own, was little disposed to pay proper attention to the interests of that of which he was only regent for his nephew. One of his first resolutions (and certainly one which could not be vindicated on any principle of morality), was to seize upon the treasure of the late King Charles, his brother, who, by his policy and economy, had amassed large sums of gold and silver, which he kept concealed in the castle of Melun. These sums amounted, it is said, to seventeen millions of francs. Violence, and even threats of death, were unscrupulously employed, to make the old officers of Charles communicate the knowledge of his treasure. They were at length obliged to produce it; and the Duke of Anjou took possession of this mass of wealth.

The first effort of the new governors, divided as they were by the jarring claims of the princes of the blood, was exerted to procure a settlement amongst them; and for some time at least, their desire of a relaxation of taxes seemed to intimate a sincere wish to alleviate the heavy burdens of the people. This flattering prospect disappeared under the disunion of the princes of the blood-royal.

We have already said that the Regent Duke of Anjou seized upon the treasures of his brother Charles V., without having any colour of right to do so; he employed them, as I will hereafter show you, in an attempt on Naples and Sicily—a purpose which proved totally useless to himself, and dangerous to France, on which it entailed a long course of disasters.

There was at this time a schism in the Roman Catholic Church; that is, two Popes had been chosen, who were acknowledged in opposition to each other by different kingdoms of the Christian world, and both of whom aspired to wield the sword and the keys of Saint Peter. The one, who assumed the name of Urban, resided at Rome; the other, under the title of Pope Clement, held his seat of church government at Avignon, in the south of France. Each had his separate college of cardinals, and each affected the power and authority of the full papal sway.

The Duke of Anjou had no great difficulty in prevailing upon the anti-pope, Clement, to declare in favour of his title to the crown of Naples and Sicily, under the bequest of Queen Joan. He did so with the greater show of authority, as he alleged that the deceased Joan had put all her dominions and seigniories at the disposal of the church, and that, therefore, the Pope had the strongest reason for supporting and defending her subsequent bequest to the Duke of Anjou, which was made by his consent.

While, therefore, Anjou was pursuing his own

ends, the English might have made considerable, and perhaps successful efforts, for the recovery of their dominions in France. Of these extensive possessions, Calais, Bourdeaux, and Bayonne, places which required large garrisons, kept up at a great expense, were almost the only remains of Edward III.'s conquests which his successor retained. Cherbourg and Brest were also at this time in their hands, having been admitted into the former town by the King of Navarre, when he lost his other dominions in Normandy; and the Duke of Bretagne had given up Brest to them in like manner, when he found that the French King was likely to expel him from his duchy.

It was with great reluctance that the English Parliament consented to the continuance of the heavy taxes necessary to the defence of these possessions, and for the maintenance of a lingering warfare, which had not been of late years gilded over either by national glory or success. They did consent, however, and their doing so was absolutely necessary to maintain the war in Bretagne; for, although the Duke had returned to that country, in consequence of the invitation of his subjects, who were determined to resist their subjection to the crown of France, still it was impossible that he could be successful in maintaining the independence of Bretagne or his own, without assistance from England.

A large army was therefore sent into France by the way of Calais, under the command of the Earl of Buckingham, afterwards known as the good

Duke Humphrey of Gloucester, uncle to King
Richard II. This force did little more than waste
the neighbourhood after the fashion of the later
English invaders; and when they advanced towards
Bretagne, in which province they were destined
to serve, the death of Charles V. had inspired
their ally, John de Montfort, with the hopes of
making a separate peace with France, without embarrassing
himself with the claims of his allies of
England. The reason of this dereliction was, that
although his subjects were strongly attached to his
person, and determined against subjection to France,
they disapproved of his strict alliance with England,
and were unwilling to admit these confederates
into their strong places and castles. The
Duke was therefore induced to try whether he could
be admitted to peace with the French government
of the day by a separate treaty, now that the death
of the King, who hated him personally, had removed
every obstacle to his becoming connected with
France as a vassal. With this view, following a
policy which was that of a perfidious age, De
Montfort, on the one hand, invited the English to
lay siege to Nantes, the capital town of Bretagne,
assuring them that he would support them with a
sufficient army; while, on the other, he negotiated
for a separate peace with the authorities
who had succeeded to the government of France.
He found little difficulty in the execution of the
latter purpose; and, being received by the French
into their alliance, he dictated to his late allies the
English, as a measure of necessity, the evacuation

of the territories of Bretagne, which they had entered at his request. It is remarkable, that notwithstanding this double dealing conduct of the Duke of Bretagne, he retained so much influence with both French and English as to be able again to impose himself upon them in the character of a mediator.

Both kingdoms, indeed, were at this time in a situation alike unfavourable to any vigorous course of foreign or domestic policy, and which obliged them to submit rather to the course of events, than attempt to direct them. Charles VI. of France, and Richard II. of England, were both minors. Neither king was of distinguished capacity, though both of good dispositions. Each was held in the management of uncles or near relations, who quarrelled among themselves, pursued their own interests with little regard to those of their sovereign, and entirely neglected the duties which they had solemnly bound themselves to discharge.

The condition of the two kingdoms was similar in other respects, as well as that of the sovereigns. The people of both countries, exhausted with taxation, and with all the evils of a burdensome war, had shown themselves mutinous and insubordinate; and the great insurrection of Wat Tyler and the commons of England rivalled in its horrors the Jacquerie of France, and the still-continued mutinies of Paris. In a word, the state of the two kingdoms resembled that which is told of the hound and the deer, who exhausted themselves in a long course, until the stag became unable to make a last effort at escape, while the dog was equally incapable of a final attempt to secure his prey.[1]

Abroad, both kingdoms were embarrassed with restless neighbours;—France, for example, by the Flemings, whose numerous and constant intestine divisions formed a temptation to the French and English to take a part in their dissensions.

Before giving an account, therefore, of the intestine discords of the princes of the blood at court, the rash expedition of the Duke of Anjou to Naples, and other matters concerning France alone, we will say something of the disorders of Flanders, in which France and England were as usual interested.

You may remember the fate of Jacob van Artavelde, the brewer, at one time the uncontrolled demagogue among the citizens of the great towns in Flanders, and at length slain in a tumult by the inhabitants of Ghent. This person had a son named Philip, who, undeterred by his father's fate, and possessing his father's popular talents, contrived to raise himself to as much authority among his fellow-citizens as ever was possessed by his father, though the ally of Edward III. This was no sudden achievement. Philip van Artavelde, appalled perhaps by his father's fate, remained during early life estranged from all the objects of popular ambition, and living much as a private citizen. But a series of events was on the eve of taking place, which tended in their consequences to call him into public view and action.

["Hercules killed Hart o' Greece,
And Hart o' Greece killed Hercules."]

INSURRECTION OF GHENT.

The people of Bruges, with the consent of the Earl of Flanders, had meditated certain improvements on the channel of the river Lys. This gave great umbrage to the citizens of Ghent, lest the course of the river should be interrupted; and a faction was formed in that city, distinguished by wearing white hats, at the head of which was placed John Lyon, a burgess, who had once been in great estimation with the Earl of Flanders, but now adopted the popular side, and became that Prince's bitter enemy.

The wearers of the white hats rose in mutiny, defeated and killed the provost of Ghent, who attempted to subdue them in the name of the Earl, and made sallies from the town, burning the Earl's castle of Andreghen. Several places in Flanders made common cause with Ghent; while the Earl threatened the city with severe punishment for the loss and insults to which he had been subjected: and with that purpose he besieged, or rather blockaded the town, with little effect. The great population of the Ghentese enabled them to keep the field, notwithstanding the displeasure of the Earl; and although many citizens disapproved internally of the violence of the white hats, no burgher dared publicly dissent from their proceedings. The insurgents obtained several advantages over the Earl, and even compelled him to raise the siege of the place. Still it was apparent to wise men, that the white hats were falling in reputation; and their leader John Lyon having died under suspicion of poison, it was thought impossible to find any man of sufficient courage or influence to supply his place; and thus a severe attack from the opposite party was likely to overthrow the insurgent faction. At this crisis Philip van Artavelde emerged from obscurity, and rose to the head and management of the insurgents of Ghent, securing his authority by many acts of arbitrary power. Artavelde was specially encouraged to the part he acted by the instigation of a subtle citizen called Peter Dubois, who, before promising him his interest in the city, thus questioned him whether he possessed the qualities necessary for a demagogue. "Can ye bear yourself high," said he, "and be cruel among the commons, and especially in such things as we shall have to do? A man is nothing worth, unless he be feared and dreaded, and at the same time renowned for cruelty. Thus must the Flemings be governed; and you must have no more regard for the life of man, or pity for their sufferings, than for the life of the brutes which we kill for food." Philip Artavelde assented to this lesson; and by the recommendation of Dubois, and the recollection of his father's original popularity, he was chosen governor of Ghent, and leader of the insurgents in Flanders.

Thus were the Earl of Flanders, and the citizens of his towns, once more in open arms against each other. The French, espousing, as formerly, the cause of the Earl of Flanders, sent forces to his assistance; and the English government, though distracted by domestic confusion, failed not, as usual, to send to Calais an army to assist Artavelde and the insurgent citizens.

BATTLE OF ROSEBECQUE.

The French prince who had the greatest personal interest in this revolt of Flanders, was Philip, Duke of Burgundy, son-in-law and heir to the Earl of that country. To him, therefore, the Earl of Flanders naturally carried his complaint, stating, that these traitors, the insurgents of Ghent, his own native liegemen, had destroyed the house in which he was born, broken to pieces the font in which he was christened, done him every manner of despite, and were now likely to ruin his remaining heritage. In all this the Duke of Burgundy saw the necessary desolation of a heritage that would one day be his own, and therefore, having much influence in the administration of France, he resolved that the King, his nephew, and all his peers, should march into Flanders, and fight against those insurgent burgesses, who were likely to lay that fine country entirely waste, or declare it independent of its Earl and his nobility. Accordingly, the King of France, under the guidance of his uncle the Duke of Burgundy, marched into Flanders, at the head of eighty thousand men.

The war was conducted with great vigour on the part of the French. Yet Philip Artavelde, on this trying occasion, showed both dexterity and courage. From Ghent and the confederate towns he collected a numerous army. Those who fought under him were arrayed in cassocks of different colours, to mark the various towns they belonged to; they were armed chiefly with pikes, and fought entirely on foot, forming one main battalion or division. Artavelde alone kept a good horse beside him, not for the purpose of flight, but for that of following the French in the pursuit which, he doubted not, would be the consequence of the battle. The country, divided by rivers and canals, was favourable to the Flemings.

After some lesser skirmishes, the two armies encountered each other in a pitched battle near the town of Rosebecque. The Flemings, for a time, made a most desperate and gallant defence; but as they were attacked by the flower of the French chivalry, headed by the princes of the blood, and by the King in person, the insurgents were at length broken by the charge of the horses and lances. As the knights and men-at-arms gave no quarter to an enemy, whom they reckoned so inferior to themselves, twenty-five thousand men were left dead upon the field. Philip Artavelde fell, fighting bravely; and the victory was so well improved, that most of the towns which had been in insurrection submitted peaceably to their sovereign, though Ghent still held out.

A.D. 1381.
Nov. 27.

Shortly after he had been thus replaced in his dominions, Louis, Earl of Flanders, died, and the Duke of Burgundy became established as a very great prince, enjoying not only his deceased father-in-law's seigniories, which comprehended the whole country of Flanders, but his own dominions of Burgundy and Artois—forming together a strong, compact, and powerful principality, which, though now its lord was so nearly connected with the crown of France as to be its principal regent, became in after times a dreaded enemy of that power.

About this time, by the advice of the Duke of Burgundy, the King of France was wedded to a beautiful German princess, Isabella, daughter of the Duke of Bavaria. It was remarkable that the young Prince declined acceding to the match, until, contrary to the usage of princes, he was permitted to see the princess to whom he was to be betrothed. He was delighted with her external beauty, but had no means of perceiving the bad qualities of the mind which was lodged in so beautiful a form. Mean while the Duke took the opportunity of the King's German match, to make an advantageous match for his own son with the daughter and heiress of Albert, Count of Zealand, Hainault, and Holland, affording the prospect of a succession which would make a formidable addition to the dominions of Burgundy and Flanders.

From the bloody field of Rosebecque, in which the power of the insurgent Flemings had been broken, the young King of France hurried back to his own capital, which had been for a considerable time more or less in insurrection against him, as formerly against his father Charles V. The Parisians had rendered their city in some degree tenable by building walls, digging trenches, drawing barricades across the streets, and thus impeding the entrance of the military; and they themselves had assumed the title of *Maillotins*, or malleters, from the mallets with which they were generally armed. In order to overawe the young King, they displayed before him this force, amounting to thirty thousand men; but, instead of being daunted, Charles was provoked by their menacing appearance, and, despising their numbers, entered his capital as if by force of arms, and seized, without scruple, upon two or three hundred leaders of the Malletors, many of whom were put to death during several successive days, in requital of former acts of insubordination. The gates of the city were also pulled down, the citizens disarmed, and the insurrection was for the time effectually subdued.

England, weakened as she was by external losses and internal mutiny, was still too powerful not to be appealed to during these times of confusion. When the Flemings were in insurrection, the English, though they refused to give the pecuniary assistance which Artavelde required, were yet disposed to send troops to the Continent, to operate as a diversion in his favour.

With this view, two propositions were made to the British Parliament. By the one, John of Gaunt, on receiving an allowance of forty thousand pounds, or thereabouts, declared himself willing to undertake an expedition into Castile; but as the purpose of this must have been a conquest for his own benefit, without any corresponding national advantage, the Parliament declined entering upon this proposal, which was afterwards, however, unfortunately resumed.

The other proposal was made by the Bishop of Norwich, for the support of the Flemings. This military prelate had already distinguished himself by quelling some insurrections in his own bishopric. He now offered his services, upon certain terms of money to be paid, to raise three thousand men-at-arms and three thousand archers, whom he proposed to transport to Calais, and from thence to march in aid of the Flemings. This was also in some measure a religious undertaking; for the warlike bishop, who declared stoutly for the rights of Pope Urban in the schism of the church, made it a principal object of his expedition, to remove his competitor Clement, whom he held to be the antipope, from the city of Avignon. The nobles of England thought well of this enterprise of the bishop; but while they were yet in deliberation upon the subject, the news of the battle of Rosebecque, the death of Artavelde, and the total defeat of the Flemish insurgents, arrived. Then, indeed, the English government blamed their own indecision, and began to censure each other for not having sent timely succours to Artavelde. "Had these poor Flemings," they said, "who fought so well in their own rude manner, been joined by only two thousand English spears and six thousand archers, not a Frenchman would have escaped death or captivity. But there is a good time to come. The French King has conquered Flanders; we will conquer it again for Richard of England." This species of reasoning induced many distinguished men, as Sir Hugh Calverley and others, to join the expedition under the Bishop of Norwich, although its chance of success was greatly diminished by the defeat of Rosebecque.

The martial prelate took the sea accordingly, and
landed at Calais on the 23d day of April, 1383.
He was in great haste to march against the Earl
of Flanders; although, strictly speaking, his commission limited him to attack and destroy those
only who owned Clement as the Pope. Some
disputes there were upon this subject; but the
fiery prelate was not to be restrained by remonstrances, nor disposed to limit his commission to
the letter. He defeated an army of thirty thousand French and Flemings, in the French interest,
and made himself master of Gravelines and Dun-
kirk, Burburgh, and several other towns; and
besieged Ypres, which was valiantly defended.
The besiegers sent to the people of Ghent, who
had still, notwithstanding the defeat at Rosebecque,
remained in insurrection against the Earl of Flanders; and as they joyfully obeyed the summons,
and came in large numbers, with great hope of
success, the siege was closely pressed. The King
of France, therefore, instigated by the Duke of
Burgundy, his uncle, assembled an army of twenty
thousand men-at-arms, and more than threescore
thousand of other troops, for the purpose of relieving Ypres.

This news alarmed the bishop, whose force was
too weak to cope with such an adversary. The siege
was raised in such haste and disorder, that the
besiegers took different routes to secure themselves; one portion marching towards Burburgh,
under Sir Hugh Calverley and Sir Thomas Trivet;
and the rest of the army, under the personal com-

mand of the bishop, retreating towards Gravelines. The party under Calverley halted for some time at the town of Bergues. The French host approached them just after they had occupied the place. "It was beautiful," says Froissart, "to behold this royal armament, their banners and pennons flying, their spears and helmets glistening against the sun, their number so great that it could not be ascertained, and their spears appearing like a thick wood!" Sir Hugh Calverley was at first inclined to have fought the French at Bergues, regardless of the great disparity of numbers; but on better reflections, he retreated to the town of Burburgh, which was stronger, though unfortunately the houses were most of them thatched, and thus liable to be set on fire.

Here the party of English defended themselves valiantly for some time, until the King of France ordered a great number of fagots for filling the ditches of the place, as one determined to carry it by storm. A small piece of silver, called a blank, was paid to each peasant who should bring a fagot, and on these terms the ditches were soon filled. In this extremity, the English leaders were glad to compound for permission to evacuate the place safely, and return to Calais. Gravelines, whither the main body of the English had retired, and where the Bishop commanded in person, was surrendered in like manner, and on the same conditions as Burburgh.

This expedition of the Bishop of Norwich gave little satisfaction to the English; and though it

certainly was not more useless than most of those
which had lately been undertaken in France, the
Bishop underwent both censure and fine for its bad
success. John of Gaunt, the Duke of Lancaster,
was rather pleased than otherwise with the unfortunate issue of the Bishop of Norwich's attempt:
yet he might have learned, from the fate of the
Duke of Anjou, whose situation in the court of
France nearly resembled his own in that of England, that he might be a loser, rather than a gainer,
by the enterprise which he himself meditated, even
if he had succeeded in the commencement. The
following is a brief account of the Neapolitan expedition, which we have postponed till now, though
it began in the middle of the year 1382:—The Duke
of Anjou, I have told you, had appropriated to
himself the treasures of his brother Charles V., in
order to support the legacy which Queen Joan had
bequeathed him of the throne of Naples, and Pope
Clement had sanctioned. Dazzled with the prospect of a kingdom, he unwarily sacrificed the real
power which he possessed as Regent of France,
for the shadowless project of making himself a king
in Italy. His brother, the Duke of Burgundy,
who expected to succeed him as regent, encouraged
him in his desperate enterprise.

The Duke of Anjou employed the wealth which
he had acquired in levying an army, which, in the
days when the Free Companies were everywhere
to be found, was, so long as there were funds to
pay them, a matter of much ease. He acquired the
aid of the Earl of Savoy, who joined him with a

considerable body of followers. In his progress through Sicily, the French prince coined money, and assumed the titles of King of Naples, of Sicily, and Jerusalem, Duke of Apulia and Calabria. On the other hand, his competitor, Charles du Durazzo, as nearest heir of Queen Joanna, claimed her kingdom as his inheritance, and his title was affirmed by Pope Urban on similar grounds to those which moved his rival Clement to prefer that of the Duke of Anjou.

This prince had no means of withstanding such an army as that led by the Duke of Anjou. Upon the Duke's first arrival, therefore, in full strength, he resolved to avoid fighting, and watch the course of events. He saw with considerable equanimity his country laid waste, and the city of Naples taken possession of by his rival. Being satisfied in his own mind, however, that the wealth of the Duke of Anjou must, in a short time, be exhausted, and his army disbanded for want of supplies, he continued to protract the struggle.

Accordingly, the sums required for paying and supporting an army, which consisted of fifty thousand men at least, soon exhausted all the treasures which the Duke of Anjou had been able to collect. His rival exercised effectually the arts of Italian policy, and, by protracted hostilities, provoked the French prince to send him repeated personal challenges, to which Charles paid no attention; so that at length, his army being almost totally dissolved, and his treasures entirely exhausted, Louis of Anjou died of depressed spirits and disappointed hopes, at the village of Bari, on the 10th of October, 1384. Charles of Durazzo, as if to carry on his dissimulation to the last, wore mourning for thirty days for the death of his competitor and mortal enemy—after which he resumed possession of the kingdom, and reigned as Charles III.

It is said, that one of the main causes of Anjou's failure was the treachery and faithlessness of one of his followers, Peter de Craon, a powerful Breton, and relation of the Duke of Bretagne. He was a man of talent and social habits, for which he was highly valued at the profligate court of France. The Duke of Anjou, in his necessities, had sent him from Italy to bring some supplies of money, which he had left in France under the charge of his princess. The money was delivered to Craon, but, instead of conveying it safely to his master, he had either spent or appropriated it to his own use. Having, notwithstanding, ventured back to Paris after the Duke of Anjou's decease, Craon fell at first under the displeasure of the King, for his breach of trust; but afterwards contrived to obtain his pardon from the King, and to insinuate himself into the favour of the Duke of Orleans, the King's brother.

About this time, the Duke of Bretagne, who had borne arms in the camp of the King of France during the expedition of the Bishop of Norwich, ventured to make his appearance in the character of mediator of a peace between France and England—a character somewhat singularly assumed by one who, like John de Montfort, had been unfaithful to both kingdoms. Neither, however, were prepared, by the course of events, to agree to moderate terms; and while the English refused to hold in vassalage of France the few places which they still retained in that kingdom, the French were equally unwilling that a foreign nation should enjoy even the slightest independent possession on their soil. No solid terms of peace, therefore, could be adjusted between the contending powers.

In the mean time, France, more especially its south-western provinces, continued to suffer from the Free Companies, or bands of armed men, of whom I have often told you before; they owned no king or country, but assembled in towns and castles, where they made their living by force, and at the expense of the neighbourhood. Many of them, we have seen, rose from being captains of such robbers—for such was their true description—into knights and generals of great consequence. I think, however, you will better understand the character of this sort of persons, and conceive the scourge they must have been to a peaceful country, by a short account of the history and death of two of their number.

The province of Auvergne was particularly haunted by these banditti, because it abounds with passes, rocks, hills, and strongholds, of which the Free Companions knew admirably how to take advantage in war. Several of the most renowned leaders had settled themselves there, for the same reason that a mountainous region is peopled by eagles, hawks, and other birds of prey, to whom it affords opportunities of rapine, and means of concealment. Two of these freebooters were distinguished above the others by their courage, intelligence, and activity; their names (at least the epithets by which they were distinguished in the wars) were Amerigot Marcel, and Geoffrey Tête-noir, that is, Black-head. They both professed to espouse the English cause; but it may be supposed that they only chose it because it afforded the most unlimited privilege of plunder. Froissart's account of the death of these two celebrated Companions is one of the most picturesque passages of his lively work, and will make you better acquainted with the lawless men who existed in that distracted time, than a long dissertation of mine.

Geoffrey Tête-noir obtained, by bribing a domestic, the means of obtaining possession, for himself and company, of the strong castle of Ventadour, belonging to an aged earl of that name, a quiet, peaceful man, whom the robbers dismissed without injury: such, indeed, had been the bargain of his treacherous squire, who surrendered the place. Geoffrey Tête-noir here prosecuted his profession with great success. "He was a hardy man," says the historian, "who knew neither fear nor pity, and would put to death a knight or squire as soon as a peasant, for he cared for no one; and he was so much dreaded by his men, that none dared displease him." This chieftain assembled a band of four hundred men, to whom he paid high wages monthly with the utmost regularity. He protected the country around Ventadour, so that no one dared make incursions upon the territory. In his castle he held a kind of open market, where goods and furniture, cloth of Brussels, peltry and mercery, with iron and steel ware, leather, and other commodities, were to be found as plentiful as in the city of Paris. The castle was fully victualled for a siege, had it been to last seven years. Nay, occasionally, to show his independence, Tête-noir chose to make war on the English as well as the French; and this jovial course of life he led for many years, more dreaded than any lawful authority in the country where he lived.

But when the French interest began to recover itself in these districts, the nobles and knights united themselves together for the purpose of besieging the forts and castles of which these robbers had possession, and delivering the country, by fair means or by force, from these lawless companions.

Accordingly, Sir William Lignac, Sir John Bon-lance, and many others, knights of Auvergne and of the district of the Limousin, formed the siege of Ventadour, for the safety of which Tête-noir was no way distressed, having plenty of ammunition and provisions. But one day, as he was heading his men in a sally, he received a crossbow shot in the face. The medical persons thought that the wound was unattended with danger, had the patient observed the regimen prescribed; but he was a free-living person, unaccustomed to self-denial of any kind. The consequence of his careless course was, that the wound proved mortal. When Geoffrey Tête-noir found his end approach-

ing, he summoned the principal officers of his Free
Company to his dying bed. He reminded them that
he had long been their true captain, and, being now
about to die, was desirous to see them unite to
choose a chieftain in his stead, who might be able
to defend this strong and well-furnished castle, until the French should raise the siege. " I have
served," he added, " chiefly under the shadow of
the King of England, holding the service to be one
in which there is much to be got, and you will do
well to choose one who shall follow the same
policy." The Companions heard their commander's words in silence, and when they answered, it
was to offer to Tête-noir the choice of his successor. Having named a kinsman of his own to this
office, the patient proceeded to make his will; and
it was one which, while it shows the wealth acquired by such people, is a curious evidence of
their superstition, and their wild and irregular
ideas of property, even when it was their own.
" In yonder chest," said the dying brigand, " are
thirty thousand marks. I will give them according to my conscience. First, to the chapel of Saint
George, in this castle, fifteen hundred marks, to be
spent in repairing the same; next, to my mistress,
who has truly and faithfully attended me, two
thousand five hundred francs; to Allan Roux,
whom I have named your captain, four thousand
francs; five hundred to the varlets of my chamber;
fifteen hundred to the officers of my household;
the rest I give and bequeath thus:—Ye be about
thirty Companions, all of one band; ye ought to

be brethren, without debate, anger, or strife among you. Having paid these legacies, I will that you divide the residue of the money, which you shall find in yonder chest, truly and equally among you thirty. But if you be not content with my bequest, and the devil do set debate amongst you, there stands a stout axe, break up the coffer, scramble for the money, and get it who can!" The residuary legatees replied, that as they had always regarded their captain, while living, with love and reverence, they would follow his behests when dead.

They continued to respect Geoffrey's testament after his death. But his successor, Allan Roux, being surprised in a piece of intended treachery, was put to the sword, and the castle of Ventadour taken.

The history of Amerigot Marcel, whom we have mentioned as a brother in the trade of war, and an occasional partner of Tête-noir, gives us a similar picture of their life. This worthy had, in like manner, acquired the strong castle of Aloys, in Auvergne; from it he made many successful inroads upon the country, which produced him a revenue of twenty thousand florins. But about the time of Tête-noir's death, the Earl of Armagnac, and several French lords, were commissioned to get these robbers out of the country by bribery, if that should be necessary, since force was a doubtful and dangerous remedy. Marcel was, after a time, persuaded that he had better accept the offer made him, renounce his unlawful and violent proceedings, and, by means of the treasure he had acquired, live in future a peaceful life. In these sentiments, he delivered up to the Earl of Armagnac the castle of Aloys, situated in the very heart of Auvergne.

But after he had resigned this stronghold, he began to repent of having done so, and of having adopted reformed courses. He felt that there was a diminution of the respect and awe which he formerly inspired whenever his name was pronounced. The brigand is said to have lamented his change of condition to the old companions of his rapine; and his recollections, as delivered by the historian, give a lively picture of his successful robberies.

"To pillage and rob," he said, "all things considered, was a good life;" and so he repented him of his good resolutions, and thus addressed his old companions:—" Sirs, there is no sport or glory in this world among men of war, but to use such life as we have done in time past. What a joy was it to us when we rode forth at adventure, and sometimes found by the way a rich prior or merchant, or a route of mules of Montpelier, of Narbonne, of Toulouse, or of Carcassonne, laden with Brussels cloth, or with furs coming from the fairs, or of spicery ware from Bruges, from Damascus, from Alexandria! Whatever we met, all was ours, or else ransomed at our pleasure. Then, for our living, the peasants of Limousin daily brought to our castle, wheat-flour, ready-baked bread, forage for our horses, good wines, beeves and fat sheep, pullets and wild fowl. We were furnished as though we had been kings; when we rode forth, the whole country trembled for fear; all was ours, going and coming. How we took Carlusbe, and James the Bourge of Compiegne; and how I and Perrot of Bernoys took Chalucet! How did we scale with little aid the strong castle of Marquel, and how I received in ransom thereof five thousand francs, told down on a fair table, and showed my gentleness by forgiving another thousand, out of respect to the Dauphin's children! By my faith, this was a fair and a good life! and I repute myself sore deceived when I rendered up the fortress of Aloys; since, well victualled as it was, I could have kept it against all the world."

Marcel's regret for the license of his early life naturally led to his return to his old profession. It would be useless to trace his further exploits, though they are singular enough. His mode of life was rendered more difficult by the close alliance of the French knights, which, as we have already noticed, had for its object the suppression of the Companies. Nor did the English afford him any effectual support, there being a truce between the kingdoms at the time. At length he intrusted himself to the confidence of one of his kinsmen called Turnemine, who delivered him up to the French. When he was brought to Paris, Marcel offered threescore thousand francs for his ransom. The cold reply was, that the King was rich enough. The brigand was dragged on a cart to the Halles, and, being first exposed on the pillory, was afterwards hanged and quartered, his quarters being placed over the gates of the city. These two leaders of banditti, their sentiments, and their fate, may serve to give you some idea of the life they led, and the manner in which France was finally relieved of them.

To return to our history. The Duke of Lancaster, having at length, by his extensive influence, obtained the means of prosecuting the great but ill-placed object of his ambition, had sailed with twenty thousand English troops, to make good his claim to the kingdom of Castile, lately possessed by his father-in-law, Pedro the Cruel. It is unnecessary to say more of his adventures in Spain and Portugal, than that his troops maintained the English character for bravery; and acquired, as has been their usual fate, little or no advantage to their country from their brilliant exploits. The unhealthy climate, and intemperate use of the wines and fruits of the country, spread contagious diseases among them. But when we remember that port wine is now a general, and supposed a healthy beverage, for Englishmen of the higher and middling ranks, we cannot suppress a smile when we read Froissart's assurances, that the hot and fiery wines of Oporto were fatally noxious to the English of his day, who were accustomed only to drink the light and generous wines of Gascony, or the mild ale of their own country.

It occurred to the French King and his counsellors, that when the realm of England might be supposed exhausted by the insurrections of the peasants, and the two expeditions under the Bishop of Norwich and John of Gaunt, the proper season had arrived for transferring the war into the territory of England. On this, as on later occasions, the preparations for invasion were made to a cumbrous, rather than useful extent, and with great and unnecessary splendour. Upwards of seven hundred ships were prepared to transport the large army which was collected for this enterprise; the frame of a wooden town was put on board, which was designed to be taken to pieces, and carried from place to place for the King's lodging, should he attend the expedition. The severe equinoctial storms of 1386 destroyed this great fleet of transports, which had rendezvoused in the harbour of Sluys The King showed his favour to his uncle, the Duke of Burgundy, by bestowing upon him the harbour of Sluys itself, and the various wrecks with which the tempest had filled it, including the fragments of the great wooden town already mentioned.

About the same period, the affairs of Bretagne began again to assume peculiar interest. John de Montfort, Duke of Bretagne, whom we have so often mentioned as a man of bravery and talent, had a difficult part to play between France and England, and might, therefore, have been taught prudence by his situation. Yet, on the present occasion, he ventured upon a line of conduct which would have been destructive to him, had circumstances permitted the French King to have driven the matter to extremity.

You cannot have forgotten the long wars betwix' John de Montfort and his parents on the one side, and Charles de Blois, on the other. Among the greatest partisans of the latter family was Oliver de Clisson, a Breton lord, now Constable of France. The Constable's father had, as has been mentioned, lost his life for his attachment to the house of De Montfort: but he himself had long since changed sides, had become the most bitter enemy of the English, and fought for Charles de Blois, at the battle of Aurai, in which Charles was slain.

A.D. 1387. Oliver de Clisson had recently and secretly agreed to ransom, at his own cost, the only surviving son of Charles de Blois, the Duke of Penthievre (who had been for 23 years a prisoner in England), on condition of his marrying Clisson's daughter. The Duke of Bretagne had been duly informed of the progress of this negotiation, and looking upon it, probably not unjustly, as a scheme of the Constable to aggrandize his own family at his expense, by reviving the claim of his intended son-in-law upon the duchy, he determined to be beforehand with him, and to put it out of his power to do him any mischief for the future. For this purpose, he took the opportunity of the Assembly of the States at Vannes, in June 1387, and after the affairs of the province had been discussed, he invited all those who had been present, including the Constable de Clisson, to a grand entertainment, before their departure. Clisson gave a similar entertainment to the same parties on the following day, and was to set out immediately afterwards for Treguier, to superintend the armament then preparing for the invasion of England. The Duke on that occasion invited Clisson and the others to go and see a castle which he was then building by the sea-shore, and to which he gave the name of l'Hermine (Ermin). They were shown all over the building, and when they came to the principal tower, the Constable was requested to enter it and give his opinion, as a competent judge of the masonry. No sooner had he reached the first story, than he was laid hold of by the persons who had been lying in wait, and loaded with irons. His brother-in-law, the Lord De Laval, who saw the gate of the tower shut suddenly, and observed by the Duke's change of countenance that something remarkable had happened, threw himself upon his knees, and demanded mercy for the Constable. "Are you willing to share his fate?" answered the Duke, obviously in a high passion. "I am," answered Lord De Laval, in more anxiety for his friend, than apprehension for himself. "Then," said the Duke, drawing his dagger, "you must be content to lose one of your eyes, for Clisson has but one." (He had lost the other, it must be observed, at the battle of Aurai). After a moment, however, the Duke abstained from the violence which he meditated, and caused De Laval to be apprehended, saying, that he should have neither worse nor better treatment than his friend. He was led, accordingly, into a prison-chamber, and loaded, as was the Constable himself, with three pair of irons. The Lord De Laval continued to make intercession for the Constable; and though the Duke repeatedly threatened to put both his prisoners to death, he succeeded in diverting him from his purpose. Finally, the Duke consented to accept a ransom for his liberation, amounting to the large sum of one hundred thousand francs, besides three castles, and the town of Guyon.

The consequence of this successful plot against the Constable was fatal to the success of the projected invasion of England, as immediately on the news of his captivity, the preparations both at Harfleur and Treguier were suspended, and the leaders returned to Paris to learn the King's pleasure as to their farther destination. The Duke of Bretagne, however, not long afterwards, contrived to reconcile himself with the King of France, at the expense of returning the sum he had extorted as the ransom for Clisson, and giving up the castles which he had received from him. The Duke of Penthièvre returned from England about the same time, and married the Constable's daughter, as had been agreed upon.

CHAPTER XXV.

Charles VI. takes the Government into his own hands—his choice of Counsellors—Attempt of Peter de Craon to assassinate Oliver de Clisson, Constable of France—the Assassin takes refuge in Bretagne, whose Duke, John de Montfort, had been privy to his design—King Charles, in marching towards Bretagne, to avenge himself upon the intended Murderer, is struck with Insanity, whereupon the Expedition is abandoned—Accident at a Masque, in which the King, during one of his lucid Intervals, performed a part—The Duke of Burgundy appointed Regent, in opposition to the claims of the Duke of Orleans—Burgundy drives Oliver de Clisson from Court, who retires to Bretagne, and engages in a war with De Montfort—Peace concluded between them—Death of John de Montfort, Duke of Bretagne—Death of Oliver de Clisson—Administration of the Duke of Burgundy—Assistance afforded by France to the Scots Expedition to protect Hungary from the Turks—the French and Hungarians defeated by the Sultan Bajazet near Nicopolis—Massacre of the Prisoners—State of France at the Close of the Fourteenth Century.

[1388–1399.]

THE next year was far advanced, when King Charles VI., having completed his twentieth year, assembled a council of state at Rheims, to which he had summoned his uncles, the Dukes of Berri and Burgundy, and by the advice of his council, after expressing his grateful thanks

A.D. 1388.

to them for the services they had rendered him, declared his determination to take the reins of government into his own hands. This important step, it should be mentioned, had been taken at the special instigation of several of the ministers of Charles V., who were subsequently members of the council appointed to aid the King with their advice.

The nation were not sorry to see that the Duke of Bourbon, who had made himself generally popular, was the only one of the King's uncles included in the list of counsellors. The Dukes of Berri and Burgundy, however, both of whom were ambitious men, though Burgundy alone was an able one, were highly offended at their sudden dismissal and subsequent exclusion from power. The King himself, as far as the character of so young a man could be guessed at, possessed the most promising dispositions. His education, however, had been neglected; and, as was probably the policy of his uncles, who wished to keep him detached from business, he had contracted an extravagant passion for hunting, and other youthful exercises, together with a love of public show and festivities, inconsistent with the economy which the state of the nation highly demanded. These failings, added to untoward circumstances, and to a melancholy alteration in the state of his health, rendered Charles VI. one of the most unfortunate princes that ever sat upon the throne of France, even though he had been preceded by the vanquished Philip and the captive John. In the commencement of his reign, however, these defects were far from being visible. He was attentive to business, careful to render justice to those who presented petitions to him, liberal in the remission of taxes, active in his administration, and so amiable in his general deportment, as to acquire the epithet of Charles the Well-beloved.

In this, the happiest period of his reign, the death of the Duchess of Orleans enabled him to bestow that title, and its appanage, upon his only brother, the Duke of Touraine.

One of the principal members of the new administration which had superseded the King's uncles, and who enjoyed a high place in the public estimation, for his civil as well as his warlike qualities, was the Constable de Clisson, already so often mentioned. To this nobleman, the King's uncles, Berri and Burgundy, regarding him as the person by whose influence they had been principally excluded from the royal councils, conceived a deep hatred, which displayed itself on several occasions; and these princes are, therefore, supposed to have aided the Duke of Bretagne in escaping, so easily as he did, from the consequences of his treacherous attack upon the Constable's person, at the castle of l'Hermine, and to have been at the bottom of a foul attempt to assassinate him, which took place a few years afterwards. A.D. 1392.

The agent in this vile deed was the same Peter de Craon, of whom we have spoken as the unworthy confidant of Louis of Anjou. Craon, who was a bold and intriguing person, had acquired so great an influence over the Duke of Orleans, the King's

brother, as to give him opportunities of turning it
to his own purposes, which it was not in his nature
to let slip. It was said that the King and the
Duke had, on the report of Craon's making himself
busy in fetching and carrying tales betwixt the
latter and his wife, intimated to him that they had
no farther occasion for his services. Craon himself
gave out publicly that he had offended the Duke by
warning him against the wizards and sorcerers who
had got possession of his ear, and were filling him
with idle visions of future greatness. Be that as
it may, Craon retired into Bretagne, of which
duchy he was a native, and where he had property,
full of indignation against the Constable, to whom
he probably attributed his disgrace; this was at
the time that the feud between the Constable and the
Duke of Bretagne, to whom Craon was also related, was still fresh, on account of the surprise of the
Constable's person at Hermine, and the subsequent
transactions. On a visit to the Duke, these two
had been talking over their mutual grievances
against De Clisson, and the Duke expressed his
regret for having, at the time he was so completely
in his power, allowed his enemy to escape; to this
observation Craon replied, that the opportunity
which had occurred once might occur again, and
took his measures accordingly.

Though banished from Paris, Craon still retained there a handsome hotel of his own, into
which he caused to be introduced, secretly, and one
at a time, as many as forty men, the most desperate
ruffians whom he could find, and furnished them

with arms and provisions, with orders to keep themselves concealed and wait his instructions. He returned to Paris on the 2d of June, 1392, and remained shut up till the 13th, when he proposed to strike the blow which he had so long kept suspended. On the evening of that day, there was a grand entertainment at court, upon which Craon kept a close watch, in order to be apprised of the motions of his victim. The knights jousted in presence of the King and Queen; supper was served; dancing ensued; at length the company took their leave. As Constable of France, Clisson, was the last to retire. It was then past one in the morning. Attended by his retinue, consisting of eight domestics, two of them bearing torches, the Constable, on horseback, was pursuing his way homewards through what was then called the street of Saint Catherine, when at the corner of the street of Saint Paul he was met by Craon at the head of his band of assassins, all of them fully armed and on horseback. They struck the torches immediately, according to orders, from the hands of the bearers. The Constable, conceiving this to be a frolic of the Duke of Orleans, from whom he had just parted, exclaimed, "Ah! sir, this is a bad jest; but I pardon your youth and love of frolic." On this, Peter de Craon drew his sword, and cried, "Death to Clisson—Clisson, you must die!"—"Who art thou," said Clisson, "that utterest these words?"—"I am Peter of Craon, your mortal enemy, whom you have so often provoked; I must now have amends." And turning to his men, "Advance!" said he, I have

what I asked for, and what I am determined to
have." Urged by their master's cries, Peter de
Craon's men struck at the Constable, yet it was but
faintly, " for," says the chronicler, " what is done by
treason is seldom done hardily," and scarcely any of
them knew beforehand their intended victim. Clisson defended himself manfully with a sword scarcely
two feet in length, the only weapon which he had,
and warded off many blows. At length, having
received some severe wounds in the scuffle, he fell
from his horse, and his head struck against a baker's
door, which was forced open by his weight, and the
baker, who was up early to attend to his oven, drew
the wounded man within his house. The ruffians,
having no idea beforehand who was to be their
victim, no sooner heard who it was than they became alarmed at the consequences. Supposing,
from his fall, that the Constable was dead, they
urged Craon to make his escape, and immediately
dispersed themselves. Putting his horse to his
speed, Craon reached Chartres at eight in the
morning, changed horses, and never halted till he
reached his chateau at Sablé in Maine. Intelligence of the crime was conveyed to the King before he had retired to rest. Without dressing
himself, and merely throwing a cloak over his
shoulders, he hastened to the baker's shop, where
Clisson was still laying, somewhat recovered from
his stupor, and able to indicate the assassin, on
whom Charles vowed to take signal vengeance.
He instantly ordered the Provost of Paris to make
a hot pursuit after the assassins, a few of whom

were taken and beheaded. The trial of Craon himself, *par contumace*, was immediately proceeded with. He was condemned to death, his property confiscated, his houses rased to the ground, his most valuable effects taken possession of by the treasury, and his estates bestowed on the Duke of Orleans and some of the courtiers; and last of all, his wife and daughter were driven out, *en chemise*, from the chateau where they were residing at Ferté Bernard.

Clisson, though much hurt, recovered from his wounds, although he thought his end so near, as to make his testament. This turned out an extremely impolitic step, as its contents confirmed reports which were current respecting the immense wealth which he had amassed, and greatly increased the animosity entertained against him by the King's uncles on that account. His property was said to amount to seventeen millions of francs, exclusive of his lands and lordships, forming a strong contrast to the honest poverty of Bertrand du Guesclin, his predecessor in office.

In the mean time, the intended murderer, learning that the Constable was not only not dead, but in a fair way of recovery, and the proceedings against himself, immediately made his retreat into Bretagne, where he met with but a sorry reception from the Duke; not because he had attempted the deed, but because it was not fully executed. "Ah! Sir Peter of Craon," said the Duke, "you are very unlucky, that you could not slay your enemy when he lay under your sword!"—"Sir," answered Craon, "I think all the devils had con-

jured him out of my hands! I am sure more than
sixty blows were dealt at him with swords and
javelins; he was felled from his horse; and had
he not tumbled in at a half-open door, he had been
but a dead man." The Duke of Bretagne answered, " that as it was so, he would conceal Sir
Peter of Craon, since so far he had promised to aid
him."

It was soon ascertained at court where De Craon
had taken refuge, and the King immediately wrote
to the Duke of Bretagne to require him to be delivered up; the Duke evaded compliance, by pre-
tending ignorance of Craon's place of retreat. This
conduct incensed the King still more, and he swore
he would never rest till he had punished both the
assassin and his abettors. The offenders, however,
had friends about the King's family and person;
the Dukes of Berri and Burgundy, enemies to
Clisson, would have had the matter considered as a
mere brawl between two Breton lords, with which
the King of France might dispense with inter-
meddling. The King, notwithstanding this opposition, persisted in his determination, and ordered
his army to be assembled, with the intention of putting himself at its head, and marching into Bretagne. He quitted Paris at the beginning of
July, but did not reach Mans till the beginning of
August.

His uncles of Berri and Burgundy remonstrated
with him on the determination he had taken without their advice, but the King was furious, and
would listen to no argument, and gave orders for

the army to march on the following day, August 5. For some days previous to this, the King had betrayed evident symptoms of mental derangement—the apparent effects of a slow fever, from which he had newly recovered, and the vexation he had suffered from the attempt upon Clisson—probably increased by the extreme heat of the weather. The day on which the army commenced its march was the hottest that had been felt for several years. Charles himself rode like a man-at-arms of the day, fully sheathed in mail, except his head, and having two pages bearing before him his helmet and his lance. The armour, being covered with black velvet, chafed and heated him excessively. His brother, his uncles, and one or two principal persons of the army, attended immediately on his person. In passing through a forest on the line of march, he himself being in a moody fit, a tall figure dressed in rags, and hideous in appearance, rushed out of a thicket, and, seizing the King's bridle, exclaimed, in a singular tone of voice, "King, go no farther. Thou art betrayed!" Who this man was, or what was the purpose of his wild warning, it is difficult to conjecture. The King's servants, who paid no attention to his words, suffered him to escape into the thicket, after having dealt several blows at him, and he was nowhere afterwards to be found. The King himself seemed struck at his words, but said nothing. In the mean time, the army emerged from the forest, and entered a broad, sandy plain, where the sun, at the height of noon, was still more oppressive than before. Here the

pages with the spear and helmet rode close behind
the King, and his uncles, the Dukes of Berri and
Burgundy, with other high nobles, kept at a little
distance, to be free of the columns of dust which
arose from the tramp of so many horses. In these
circumstances, the page who bore the spear having
from drowsiness, or through carelessness, allowed
the lance to drop upon the casque of him who bore
the King's helmet, that slight accident was sufficient to produce the catastrophe which followed.
All at once, the King drew his sword, and, rushing
like a madman on the page who had caused the
noise, struck him a mortal blow, killed three or four
others, and continued hewing at all around him
with so little distinction, that it became obvious he
was wholly deranged. There was no other remedy
but to seize upon him by main force, disarm and
bind him, and in this unhappy condition to convey
him back to Mans, where he arrived, exhausted
with his frantic fit, speechless, motionless, and almost lifeless. He recovered, indeed, after some
weeks' illness; but both mind and body had received
such a shock, as was never afterwards repaired.

This was a melancholy conclusion of the expedition to Bretagne, all thoughts of prosecuting
which were immediately abandoned. There was
the less hesitation about this, that the King's uncles
had always disapproved the expedition; added to
which, Burgundy mortally hated Clisson, regarding him as the person by whose advice he himself,
and his brother the Duke of Berri, had been excluded from power, ever since Charles personally

assumed the management of public affairs. The same Duke of Burgundy, at a period somewhat later, accused the King's sister-in-law, the Duchess of Orleans, of having, by means of spells, brought on the King's malady. The Duchess was an Italian, daughter of Galeazzo, Duke of Milan, beautiful, accomplished, and possessed of high talent; and it would have been indeed ungrateful in her to have sought to do any injury to the King who had always shown her a particular degree of regard, spoke to her with tenderness by the name of my "fair sister," and always knew her, even during his fits of insanity, though he could distinguish no one else. Neither did the Duke of Orleans succeed to any considerable increase of power by the King's malady, at least in the first instance, so that there was no motive to induce him to be guilty of practising upon the King's life in any way.

At first it seemed as if the King was not unlikely to recover permanently from his malady, when his fits of insanity were again brought on, after a temporary convalescence, by an accident as extraordinary as that by which his disease had originally been manifested. Six months had elapsed, and Charles was so far recovered as to take an interest in the festivities of his court, though not in the affairs of state. There was one A.D. 1393. night exhibited at court a masque of particular splendour, in which the King himself acted a part. Six personages of the highest rank, of whom the King was one, appeared, for the amusement of the party, disguised in the character of Silvans or Satyrs. Their dress consisted of canvass coats, pitched over, to which wool or flax was attached in loose flakes, to represent the character which they had assumed. They were linked together with chains, and formed a pageant which excited general curiosity. The Duke of Orleans used the privilege of his rank, to approach the masquers with a torch, in order to discover who they were. Unhappily, their dress being highly inflammable, the whole group was on fire in an instant. Linked together, in the manner described, there was little chance of escape; yet the general cry of the perishing group was to save the King, even while they themselves were in the agonies of a death so painful. The Duchess of Berri, who was speaking with the King at the moment the accident took place, had the presence of mind and resolution to wrap the unhappy monarch in her mantle, and save him from a death, which, in his condition, however painful and horrible, might have been a merciful dispensation. Another of the unhappy masquers plunged himself into a cistern of water which chanced to be near. The remaining four were so dreadfully burnt, that they all died in great agony.

The natural consequence of so dreadful an accident was to produce a return of the King's malady in its fullest extent; and, as he never afterwards recovered the perfect use of his reason, he must be considered henceforward as an incurable lunatic, whose insanity was only checkered with occasional intervals of reason during the thirty years he still continued to reign.

It became absolutely necessary, therefore, to provide a regent to carry on the business of the state; and great disputes arose in the royal family which of them should be appointed, but the choice lay between the Duke of Orleans and the Duke of Burgundy. The first, as the King's brother and heir, might be considered to have the superior claim. the King, during his rare intervals of reason, gave his opinion to this effect: nor was this Prince unfitted for the situation by personal qualifications. He was a handsome man, and possessed all those exterior accomplishments which gain the admiration of the inferior orders. But as a set off, the Duke was a licentious voluptuary, preferring pleasure to principle, and not extremely select in choosing the road by which he sought the former. He was also only twenty years old at the time when the King's incapacity was first admitted, and was not, therefore, considered sufficiently ripe in years to take upon him the high responsibility of the regency.

The Duke of Berri was the oldest of the King's uncles, but he was a man of weak parts, extremely avaricious, and also unpopular from his mal-administration, upon a former occasion, of the province of Languedoc. Accustomed likewise to defer on most occasions to the superior talents, and influence of his younger brother, his weight was thrown into the scale in Burgundy's favour.

The Duke of Burgundy was, therefore, raised to the regency, and his Duchess appointed to have the care of the King's person, and to attend upon

the Queen, who was then pregnant. At this
period commenced that desperate struggle between
the rival houses of Orleans and Burgundy, which
so long distracted the kingdom of France with
civil violence, and deluged it with oceans of blood.

No sooner had Burgundy assumed the reins of
government, than he took the first opportunity to
visit upon the Constable, Oliver de Clisson, the
resentment which he had long nourished against
him. When the latter appeared in his presence to
require payment of the expenses of the meditated
expedition to Bretagne, the Duke took the opportunity to insult him, upbraiding him with having
too long, and too busily, interfered with the affairs
of the kingdom, he taunted him with having
amassed so much wealth, and concluded by bidding
him begone, as he valued the sight of his remaining eye. Clisson, apprehending worse treatment
from so brutal a reception, retired from the city of
Paris, and took refuge upon his own territories in
Bretagne.

Immediately afterwards, the Duke of Burgundy
caused Clisson to be summoned before the Parliament of Paris, to answer the charge of extortion
in his office of Constable. As the Constable did not
appear before an assembly in which his enemies
were predominant, he was, in all form, banished
from the realm of France, condemned to pay a fine
of one hundred thousand marks of silver, and deprived of his office of Constable for ever. In the
following year, Burgundy conferred the office upon

Philip of Artois, Count d'Eu, who had recently married his daughter.

Clisson's old enemy, the Duke of Bretagne, was not disposed to let him remain quiet in his dominions, and with the countenance of the Duke of Burgundy, had the advantage of turning the tables upon his adversary, as an enemy of the King of France, whose authority Clisson had so recently directed against himself. Clisson, however, was not deserted by his friends, and received aid and support also from the Duke of Orleans.

For nearly three years, with some short intervals, a cruel war was carried on between Clisson and the Duke, principally in Lower Bretagne, distinguished as usual by skirmishes, mutual taking of castles, and butchering of prisoners, as both parties allowed no quarter to each other. The Duke of Bretagne, notwithstanding his being sovereign of the country, found the majority of his vassals disposed to remain neuter in the contest; the parties, therefore, were more upon an equality than might have been expected; in fine, the Duke finding age creeping upon him, and his health decaying, was fain to make peace with him as an equal, and upon terms which Clisson considered advantageous. An act of generous confidence on the part of Clisson closed the feud, and serves to show us, that however regardless of equity and good faith the nobles of that day were, when they interfered with the gratification of their revenge, they yet were fully sensible of the obligation arising from noble actions and frank reliance. The Duke of Bretagne having desired an interview with Clisson, and the latter, remembering the treacherous arrest at Château l'Hermine, having required a hostage for his personal security, the Duke sent him one of his sons without hesitation, thereby showing the strongest confidence in Clisson's honour. Not to be outdone in generosity, Clisson immediately proceeded to the Duke's residence, accompanied by the youthful hostage, and restored him to his father. John de Montfort showed himself highly sensible of this mark of confidence; and the more so, as he might be conscious it was undeserved. A long and amicable conference then took place between these two illustrious persons, to which no third person was admitted, the result of which was seen a few days afterwards in a treaty, by which all differences between them were terminated,—to be revived, however, by their families in the next generation.

I may also mention in this place the fate of Peter de Craon, the deviser and perpetrator of so many crimes. He was included in the reconciliation between the Duke of Bretagne and De Clisson, and absolved from the consequences of his attempt upon the Constable. Immediately afterwards, judgment was pronounced against him in the civil suit brought for the recovery of the money of the Duke of Anjou, which he had embezzled, and he was shut up in prison. From the effect of this also he contrived to get free. During the treaty of marriage betwixt France and England, Richard II. solicited and obtained his pardon and

A.D. 1396.

liberation. A singular monument long after existed at Paris, in the shape of a stone cross, with his arms carved upon it, which this man caused to be erected near the place of execution, where criminals on their way thither were detained and made their confession to the friars, to whom Craon left a perpetual legacy for the purpose. Such was the shape in which his repentance for the misdeeds of his past life exhibited itself.

John IV., Duke of Bretagne, died in 1399, leaving his eldest son, still a minor, in tranquil possession of his inheritance. By this son the ancient feud between the families was revived, for in 1407, when the aged Clisson was quitting this world, the young Duke was preparing to besiege him in his castle.

During his lucid intervals, King Charles was entertained with hunting-matches and other pastimes, in order to divert his thoughts from more serious subjects; and it is said that playing-cards were invented for his amusement. But, while in his fits of lunacy, the expenses of the unhappy monarch's establishment were reduced to the least possible compass which decency would admit, and often restricted within it. These instances of economy, and others, doubtless of a more praiseworthy character, enabled the Duke of Burgundy to pacify the complaints of the common people, by reducing the public taxes; nor was he altogether negligent of the affairs of the kingdom. He was regularly guided by the advice of parliament, who were convened every year; and, using the counsel of his brother, the Duke of Berri, as a species of colleague, the laws which they promulgated, with the consent of that body, were in many instances of a praiseworthy character.

During the Duke of Burgundy's administration, also, of which much that is evil may be said, the public peace was not disturbed by the destructive war with England, by which France had been so long ravaged. This was, indeed, owing rather to the weakness of England, than to the prudence of the French regent. The reign of Richard II. of England had been marked by public discord, popular tumult, and almost every event which can render a country incapable of foreign war; and during this general confusion, the quarrel with France, if not made up, was lulled to sleep from time to time by continued truces, until the year 1396, when Richard, then a widower, sent an embassy to demand in marriage the princess Isabel, eldest daughter of the reigning monarch Charles, then a child of only six or seven years old. The French administration agreed to the match; but though the princess went to reside in England the marriage was broken off by Richard's dethronement and death three years after. The most important consequence of the treaty of marriage, otherwise so ill assorted, was the accommodation of all disputes between France and England, and amongst other articles, the restoration of Brest to the Duke of Dretagne, and of Cherbourg to the King of Navarre. Of the connexions of France with other foreign powers at this time, it will be necessary here to say something.

EXPEDITION TO SCOTLAND.

The unfortunate fate of the Duke of Anjou's expedition against Sicily and Naples has been already sufficiently dwelt upon; but the intercourse of the French with the Scottish nation is also worthy of some notice. We have already observed that love to the French, hatred to the English, and the distribution of considerable sums of money, had induced a nation, generally reckoned both poor and warlike, to attempt an invasion of England, in order to create a diversion in favour of Calais, which Edward III. was then besieging. In this enterprise the Scots had the misfortune to lose a fine army, and to leave their king, David II., a prisoner in the hands of the English. In the battle of Poitiers, a body of Scottish gentry, the flower of their kingdom, commanded by the celebrated Earl Douglas, shared the disasters of that bloody day. The French had always expressed themselves grateful for the assistance which the Scots had meant to give them, sorry for the loss which their allies had sustained, and willing to return the obligation when circumstances should put it in their power.

A period occurred in 1385, when such an opportunity of assisting the Scots, and carrying war into the northern limits of England, appeared favourable. A.D. 1385. The spearmen of Scotland formed a body of infantry whose impenetrable phalanx defied even the shock of the men-at-arms. Their irregular cavalry were unequalled for the width to which they could spread devastation. But their archers, whom they drew from the Highlands, were far inferior to those of the

English; and the general poverty of the country rendered their regular cavalry comparatively few and ill appointed.

The French council conceived, that by assisting the Scots with forces of the latter description, they might place their allies upon a footing with the English. A thousand men-at-arms were sent to Scotland under the Admiral of France, John de Vienne, a warrior of approved talents. He was also furnished with a large sum of money to distribute among their Scottish friends. At first, allies who came so well provided were received with general gratulation. But the strangers speedily found that they had come to a wild and savage country, destitute of the useful arts, and dependent upon Flanders even for horse-shoes and the most ordinary harness. On the other hand, the Scots were irritated and displeased with the natural petulance of these military strangers, who interfered in their families with an alert gallantry, which the French conceived to be a mark only of breeding, and a privilege of their rank. The Frenchmen were yet more disappointed upon finding the cautious manner in which the Scots proposed to conduct the war, which, though admirably calculated to distress the English, afforded little prospect either of gain or glory to adventurers like themselves. Instead of rushing on with precipitate rashness to a general action, as the French wished and desired, the Scottish warriors, taught by experience, suffered the English army to enter their eastern frontier, and to do such damage as they could, which was very small, where flocks, herds, and cattle, forage, and all that could support an army, had been previously driven away, or destroyed. In the mean time, while the English were engaged in traversing what may be called a howling desert, the Scots, who even excelled their neighbours in the arts of devastation, poured a desultory but numerous army upon the western frontier of England, laying all waste, and doing more mischief than their own eastern provinces could have received from the southern foe, had they been plundered from sea to sea.

In this species of warfare the French men-at-arms could acquire neither fame nor profit; they lost their horses, lost their armour, and at length lost their patience, execrating the poor, rude, and pitiful country of Scotland, on account of which they had suffered so much trouble. What was worse, they found great trouble in obtaining permission to return to France. Wine they had little; their bread was of barley, or oats; their horses were dead from hunger, or foundered with poor living; and when they would have brought them to sale, to relieve their pressing occasions for money, there were no purchasers in Scotland disposed to enter upon such a bargain. The Scots also insisted on being paid a large sum, due, they said, for the expense of their allies' maintenance, and for the damages which they had in different ways done to Scotland. De Vienne himself was actually obliged to remain a hostage in Edinburgh, until the fact of the payment of the sum by the

government of France to the Scottish factors at
Bruges was fully ascertained. The allies therefore
took farewell of each other with mutual pleasure,
the Scots execrating the affected delicacy and epi-
curism, the self-importance and insolence of the
French, while the French inveighed with no less
justice against the barbarity of the Scots, and the
miserable poverty of their country.

France, however, was in this reign to send forth
an expedition still more important, and doomed to
terminate in a far more disastrous manner, than
that to Scotland. Crusades had long ceased to be
the fashionable employment of Christian monarchs;
but it was not possible that they could see with indifference the progress which the victorious Turks
were daily making, both in the Grecian empire,
and in the kingdom of Hungary. The Emperor
Sigismund was so apprehensive of the danger to
which Europe was exposed from these infidels,
whose Sultan was at that time the celebrated Bajazet, who had already for eight years besieged
Constantinople, and was now threatening the frontiers of Hungary, that he endeavoured, by the most
humble applications to the court of France, to obtain the assistance of a body of volunteers, who
would merit Paradise, by combating against the infidels; "making use," says the chronicle, "of many
words of great love, such as kings and such persons
write to each other in circumstances of necessity."
Similar letters were written by Sigismund to the
other European monarchs.

John, Count of Nevers, son of the Duke of Burgundy, was appointed to command the expedition which the French Government agreed to send to the Emperor's assistance. He was accompanied by the flower of the French chivalry, including his brother-in-law the Constable of France, several others of the blood royal, and the first nobility of the land, to the number of a thousand persons.

The army which assembled on this occasion, under the command of their princes and nobles, made such a splendid show when it reached Hungary, that Sigismund proudly exclaimed—" Why should we fear the Turks? If the heavens themselves should fall, we are numerous enough to uphold them with our lances." A.D. 1396.

The impatience of his auxiliaries to advance induced the Emperor to move forward with his allies, so that they might the sooner come to deeds of arms. They crossed the Danube, entered Bulgaria, took several of its towns and formed the siege of a town called Nicopolis, which was garrisoned by the Turks. Bajazet, in the mean time, had raised a very large army, with which he approached the camp of the besiegers, showing only a small part of his force in the centre, and concealing a very large force upon each wing. A party reconnoitring brought news to the Christian camp that the Turks were advancing, but without any exact account of their numbers or disposition. The Christians instantly took arms, but were considerably heated with the wine they had been drinking. The French claimed the honour of making the onset; and they were drawn up in front of the centre of that part of Bajazet's force which was open and uncovered.

The King of Hungary's mareschal then advised the strangers to halt, and keep their ground without advancing, until a reconnoitring party, which Sigismund had sent out, should bring more exact intelligence than they had yet received concerning the enemy's force. The Hungarian had scarcely turned his horse, ere Philip of Artois, Constable of France, out of pure spite and insolence, commanded his banner to advance, in defiance of the orders, or rather advice, received. The Lord de Coucy, a knight of great fame, considered this a presumptuous proceeding; and, looking towards the Admiral of France, John de Vienne (the same who had commanded the French auxiliaries in Scotland), demanded what was to be done. "Sir," answered the veteran, "where reason cannot be heard, pride must reign; since the Constable will needs advance, we must follow him, and support him." They rushed forward, therefore, on what appeared to be the main body of the Turkish army, which retired before them, according to the Sultan's previous orders. In the mean time, as the French advanced upon the centre, two strong wings on either flank of the Turkish army, which had been hitherto concealed, threw themselves in the rear of the men-at-arms, and cut off the French chivalry from the main body of the Imperial army. This manœuvre was executed with the characteristic rapidity which procured for Bajazet the epithet of Ilderim, or Lightning. The army of Sigismund, being fifty or sixty thousand men, might still, by a desperate charge, have rescued their allies, and perhaps gained the battle. But the Imperialists, losing courage on seeing many of the French horses running back without riders, concluded that their vanguard was defeated, and fell, from the very apprehension, into great disorder, and retired, or rather fled, in confusion. The Turks, whose armies consisted chiefly of cavalry, made great havoc in the pursuit. The King of Hungary himself, with the Grand Master of the Hospitallers, escaped with difficulty; and the slaughter and carnage, both among the Hungarians and their auxiliaries, was very great; while most of the French knights who escaped death on the field of battle, had the sad alternative of becoming captive to the infidels.

Bajazet, greatly elated by his victory, took possession of the King of Hungary's tent, and, with the usual caprice of a barbarian, evinced at first a desire to be civil to, and familiar with, such nobles as were brought prisoners to his presence. He took credit to himself naturally for the great victory he had won, and boasted, it is said, a pretended descent from Alexander of Macedon, in whose steps he affected to tread. But when the Sultan had refreshed himself, and came to view the field of battle, the loss of his best and bravest Turks was so much greater than he had conceived, that his tiger propensities began to show themselves. He caused to be pointed out to him some few of the knights who were of the highest rank, and likely to pay the best ransom. These being

set apart, with a view of preserving their lives, the
rest, stript to their shirts, were brought before him,
previous to being put to the sword.

There were present a great number of captives,
of the highest blood and character in France, and
other states of Europe; in all, more than three hundred gentlemen. The Turks stood around them with
their drawn scimitars. Bajazet appeared, and received the supplications of all, for all were at his
mercy. He looked upon his prisoners for a few
moments, as a wild-beast beholds his prey when
he has made sure of it; and then turning away,
made a sign to his soldiers, in obedience to which
the unarmed prisoners were hewn to pieces without
compunction.

The Sultan, however, was not wanting in a
species of clumsy courtesy which intermingled
strangely with his cruelty. He caused to be brought
before him the Count of Nevers, to whom, on account of his high rank, he showed some deference,
and asked him, which of three knights he would
wish to despatch to Paris with the information of his
captivity. The count fixed his choice upon one
whom Froissart calls Jacques Helley, who had
been formerly prisoner with the Saracens, and
whose knowledge of their language and manners
had been of great service to his countrymen. The
other two knights were presently put to death; and
Helley departed with instructions to return to the
court of Bajazet when he had discharged his
embassy.

The arrival of this messenger at Paris, with

tidings so dismal, threw almost the whole kingdom into mourning; and it was the general feeling that France had sustained no defeat so disastrous since the fabulous combat of Roncesvalles, in which romance stated the twelve peers of Charlemagne to have fallen. Amid the number of tears which were shed, and the grief which was displayed on every side, the Regent Duke of Burgundy was the only person who experienced some comfort in the general distress. It is said, he contrived to extort from the subjects of his duchy, for the ransom of his son, the Count of Nevers, a much larger sum than was necessary for the purpose, or than was actually paid to Bajazet.

Thus closed the fourteenth century upon the kingdom of France, neither leaving it healed of its disorders, nor in a way to be speedily cured of them; fortunate, however, in this, that the dissensions betwixt York and Lancaster, now commenced by the rebellion of Bolingbroke, were likely to occupy the attention of the English nation, and prevent the renewal of a war which had been long the scourge of both nations.

CHAPTER XXVI.

Factions of Orleans and Burgundy—Threatened Rupture with England—The Duke of Orleans appointed Regent, and again deprived of that office—Death of Philip of Burgundy—John the Fearless succeeds him, and the Dissensions with Orleans continue—Reconciliation of the two Dukes—their hatred again bursts out—Murder of Orleans—Burgundy, who instigated this crime, obtains a full pardon, but, having gone to quell an Insurrection at Liege, the Doom of Treason is pronounced against him—Burgundy advances upon Paris—The Adherents of Burgundy termed Cabochins, those of Orleans, Armagnacs—the Armagnacs obtain assistance from England—King Charles, during an Interval of his Malady, manifests the utmost indignation at this League with England, and marches in person against the Armagnacs—the French Nobles assemble in Paris, and compel the Armagnacs and Cabochins to be reconciled to each other—On an Insurrection of the Parisians, the Dauphin calls to his assistance, and re-organizes, the Orleans Party—Burgundy retires from Paris, but is recalled by the Dauphin, on some disagreement between him and his mother, Queen Isabella—On the approach of Burgundy, the Dauphin again invites the Armagnacs to join him—Charles himself, partially recovered, marches against Burgundy, and compels him to sign a Pacification—State of England—Conclusion.

[1399—1414.]

Our last chapter left France in a situation equally extraordinary and disastrous. The unfortunate monarch Charles VI. was so incurably deranged, that a light like that of a sunbeam in a tempest seemed only from time to time to gleam on his clouded intellect, and enabled him to express his approbation of the particular measures which it was the interest of those of his relatives who had for the time the nearest access to his person, to obtain for the furtherance of their own purposes. Thus, without having, properly speaking, any will or opinion of his own, the unfortunate prince, during his lucid intervals, was always ready to adopt those of the person who last spoke to him; he was sometimes brought forth to do so even in public, which, as his deficiencies were well known, could only have had the effect of degrading his government.

At other times, the person of Charles was strictly secluded. His tent and his banner were displayed in marches and sieges; but the curtains of the pavilion were never raised, nor was the person of the sad inhabitant ever visible to his soldiers.

During the first twelve years of the King's malady, the two factions of Orleans and Burgundy, although their representatives were connected in the near relation of uncle and nephew, maintained a most violent struggle for the largest share in administering the government. The Queen Isabella, wife of Charles VI., a weak and easily influenced woman, was supposed to have espoused the interest of the Orleans party, with a warmth which, as the Duke was a notorious libertine, was prejudicial to her reputation. The Duke of Orleans, therefore, and his wife Valentina, who possessed a strong personal interest with the King, were for the present leagued with Queen Isabella, for the purpose of supplanting the Duke of Burgundy in the share which he held in the administration. We shall afterwards see this intrigue assume a different form.

Each of these factions took the most violent and unscrupulous mode of doing whatever might injure their rivals in the public opinion. Both of them called in the aid of physicians, in the hope of devising some cure or alleviation of the King's malady; and as the empirics who were permitted, if not encouraged, to make new experiments upon the royal patient, usually left Charles worse than they found him, their want of success was always laid to the charge of the party which had employed them. The Duke of Orleans condemned to the flames, as a magician, a learned man, named Jean de Bar, who had been employed by the Duke of Burgundy to effect the King's cure. Burgundy, in retaliation, commanded the prosecution of two Franciscan friars, who had been brought by the Orleans faction to attend the King as physicians, and whose experiments had consisted in deep and dangerous incisions made on the head of their royal patient. The Duke of Burgundy caused them both to be hanged.

In the mean time, the external peace of the kingdom of France was threatened, while the government of the country was a prey to discordant factions. The contract of marriage between Richard II. and the young Princess of France, Isabella, though absurdly ill-suited as regarded the age of the parties, had yet the great advantage of procuring a prolonged and solid peace betwixt two nations, whose chief miseries for two centuries had been occasioned by inveterate and senseless hostilities, from which neither had gained advantage, while both had suffered immense loss in blood and treasure. But the dethronement and death of Richard II. was an unexpected stroke, which dissipated all these happy prospects; and the unfortunate Charles, who happened to be in one of his lucid intervals at the time, was so much affected by the melancholy tidings, that he relapsed into one of his most outrageous fits of insanity. A.D. 1399.

The French Princess, the intended wife of Richard so soon as she should have arrived at a proper age, was still residing at the court of England; and although her proposed husband was dethroned, and it is believed murdered, Henry IV. would fain have retained her there as a future bride for his son, afterwards Henry V. This match, which would in all probability have secured a stable peace between the countries, must have been highly to the advantage of both. But the French nation were incensed at the death of Richard, whom they looked upon as their ally; and the lords of Gascony were ill disposed to his successor, from their attachment to the deposed monarch, as the son of their great Prince Edward, and their countryman, Richard having been born at Bourdeaux. The French, aware of this feeling, were

universally disposed to go to war for the recovery
of Bourdeaux and the other English possessions
in France, in preference to a peaceful alliance with
that power under its new dynasty. But the malady of their King, and the contests between the
factions of Orleans and Burgundy, rendered the
French quite incapable of prosecuting the war, in
spite of their aversion to continuing at peace; and
thus a reinforcement from England, under command of the Earl of Worcester, easily secured
Bourdeaux to the English crown.

In the year 1402, during a casual absence of the
Duke of Burgundy from court, the opposite party had the art to extract from the
King, then in one of his twilight intervals, a commission, appointing his brother, the Duke of Orleans, his lieutenant and regent of the kingdom, at
such periods when he himself should, by the visita-
tion of God, be prevented from administering the
government. This commission was partly obtained
by the influence of the Queen, who at this time
hated the Duke, or rather the Duchess, of Burgundy; and it was received the more willingly
by the people, as, by the law of France, the Duke
of Orleans was the rightful claimant of the regency,
and his youth could not now, as formerly, be objected to.

A.D. 1402.

But the new regent used his power very unskil-
fully. In the quarrel between the two Popes,
which still subsisted, the Duke of Orleans espoused
the cause of Benedict, which was the most unpopular in France; he likewise imposed taxes both

on ecclesiastics and on the laity, which, joined to a casual scarcity of provisions, rendered his government intolerably oppressive. A crisis speedily followed, in which the Duke of Orleans was deprived of the regency by an assembly of the great men of the kingdom. Both dukes then took arms, and a civil war seemed inevitable, when, by the interference of the Dukes of Berri, Bourbon, and other princes of the blood, it was declared that, to end the family dissensions, both Orleans and Burgundy should be excluded from the government of the kingdom, which was vested in the Council of State, over which the Queen was appointed to preside. This suspended, in appearance, the quarrel between the rival princes, and, for a time, neither attempted to assume the regency in person, though both exercised an indirect influence upon the different members of the council.

Philip, Duke of Burgundy, was afterwards again raised, by his nephew the King, to a more active share in the government, when he suddenly died upon a journey, so overwhelmed with debts that his sons were obliged to sell his furniture and jewels to pay the expenses of his funeral, and his Duchess to renounce all share in his movable succession; in testimony of which, she laid in the coffin of the deceased Prince the keys of his household, and the girdle at which she wore them—a strange ceremony to take place at the funeral of a prince, possessed of such immense revenues of his own, and having also those of France under his control, and who was not suppos-

A.D. 1404.

ed to be over scrupulous in employing them to his own purposes.

John, Duke of Burgundy, who succeeded Philip (the same who, as Count of Nevers, headed the unfortunate expedition to Hungary), was called the Fearless. He inherited his father's power and extensive dominions, although he had two brothers, each of whom succeeded to considerable territories, namely, Anthony, Duke of Brabant, and Philip, who took the title of Count of Nevers, on his elder brother's succession to the dukedom of Burgundy The young Duke inherited also to the full his father's ambition, and took up the family quarrel with the house of Orleans exactly where Duke Philip had left it.

The discord between the uncle and nephew came thus to subsist in full force between the two cousins. They disturbed the whole kingdom by their intrigues; and the Duke of Burgundy had, like his father, the address to secure a very strong party in the city of Paris, to which his house and faction had represented themselves as the preservers of the privileges of the city and university, and enemies to the imposition of excessive taxes. In the dissensions which followed, the Dauphin, a young man of feeble talents, and no fixed principles, would have fled with his mother to the town of Melun, but was pursued by the Burgundian party, and brought back by force. Bloodshed seemed so near, that each prince chose his device. Orleans, to indicate his possessing the right of regency, displayed a hand grasping a club full of knots, with the motto—*I envy it*—alluding to the feeling which he attributed to the opposite house. Burgundy, on the other hand, showed a carpenter's plane, with a Flemish motto—*Ik houd*—that is, *I hold*—the means of smoothing the knotted club.

Mutual friends and relations, chiefly of the blood royal, once more interfered, and brought the two contending princes to a solemn agreement. A.D. 1407. They dismissed their troops on each side, met together at the palace of the Duke of Berri, embraced each other, and took the sacrament at the same time.

It would appear that the hatred of the two dukes became only the more bitter, as on the 23d of November, the very day after this apparent reconciliation, the Duke of Burgundy caused to be carried into effect the plan he had arranged for ridding himself of his rival.

On the evening of that day the Duke of Orleans, who was at the Queen's apartments, where he usually spent the evening, received a summons, just after supper, to wait on the King immediately. Suspecting nothing wrong, the Duke hastened to obey this command, and traversed the streets mounted on a mule, accompanied only by two gentlemen and a few valets on foot, when he suddenly fell into an ambush posted for the purpose. The leader of these ruffians was one D'Hacquetonville, personally injured, as he conceived, by the Duke of Orleans. One of them struck at the Duke with his battle-axe, and, missing his head, the blow fell on his right hand, which it struck off. " I am the

Duke of Orleans," cried the party assailed. "It is he whom we seek," answered his assassins, with wild exultation, and, striking the Prince from his saddle, they cut him limb from limb by their furious and united assault. They had taken every precaution to ensure the perpetration of the crime, and their own subsequent escape. The streets were strewed with caltrops, for laming the horses of such as should attempt a pursuit: a house was set fire to by the assassins, who cried " Fire, fire!" to distract the attention of the people, while the Duke of Orleans's retinue were crying "Murder!"

In the morning, the Duke's body was discovered, so much hacked and dismembered, that the streets were sprinkled with his blood and brains, while some of the limbs could scarcely be found by his weeping attendants. Such, indeed, was the inveteracy of the factions, that the Burgundians only said to each other, with a sneer, " See, if the knotty mace has not been well smoothed by the plane!"

The Duke of Burgundy at first affected innocence and surprise. On the proposal, however, to examine the household servants of the King and the different royal Dukes, with a view to discover the murderer, the Duke took two of his uncles aside, and confessed that he had incited the crime, on which the princes advised his immediately retiring from Paris, which he did with much precipitation. But no sooner had he reached a place of safety, than he recovered his spirits; and, finding that his party were willing to support him, without much regard to his innocence or guilt, he returned in less than two months, at the head of an army of his own subjects of Burgundy and Flanders, and entered the capital, having with him, as an apologist, or rather vindicator, a doctor in theology, named John Petit, who, in Mar. 1408. the face of the Dauphin and princes of the blood, preached a sermon, arraigning the late Duke of Orleans as a traitor, and justifying the Duke of Burgundy for the murder of his near relation, as an act of necessity for the safety and advantage of the state. The Duke of Burgundy was already secure of a judicial acquittal, for, three days before this, he had obtained from the King letters of remission for the crime, conveying as full a pardon as could be put into words. The sovereign authority, therefore, at this time, was transferred without control into his hands. One of his first acts was to remove the Admiral of France from his office, the penalty, no doubt, of his having offered with two hundred knights to pursue the murderer of Orleans, when he fled from the capital.

A few months afterwards, his triumphant career received a temporary check by the intelligence that the people of Liege were in arms against his brother-in-law, their bishop, on account of his oppressive conduct; for no sooner had Burgundy left Paris with his forces, to quell this insurrection, and prevent its spreading into Flanders, than the Queen, the Dauphin, and the other princes of the blood returned to the capital, assembled a council, and deliberated on the measures to be taken against the formidable Burgundy.

Among those who appeared at this council, at which the Queen presided, was Valentina, the widowed Duchess of Orleans, attired in the deepest mourning, who on her knees demanded justice on the murderers of her husband, and the vindication of his memory from the slanders and calumny by which it had been attacked. In another assembly held at the Louvre, a few days after, the Abbé Serisy read a long discourse or sermon, replying point by point to the allegations of Jean Petit in his sermon, and either proving them false, or that the acts of Orleans which they impugned required no justification; and concluding with requiring the severe (but not capital) punishment of Burgundy, including the razing of his castles, fines and expiations, and his banishment from France. The council pronounced Orleans completely justified, but referred the punishment of Burgundy to the proper tribunals.

Preparations were accordingly directed to be made for his trial, and the princes of the blood had agreed with the Queen to assemble their vassals, and carry the war to extremities against Burgundy,

Sept. 1408. when news arrived, that the Duke had completely quelled the insurrection of the citizens of Liege, after a pitched battle and a horrible slaughter, and was again on his way to Paris, at the head of his army, breathing defiance to all his enemies. Terrified at the consequences which they might suffer from his vengeance, the princes instantly disbanded their forces, and gave up all thought of farther opposition to him; the Duchess of Orleans retired to Blois, where she died soon after, and the Queen precipitately quitted the capital for Tours, taking the King along with her although then in one of his frantic fits. The Duke of Burgundy made his entry into the capital, the populace of which were entirely devoted to him, on the 24th of November, and was received with all the honours usually paid only to the King himself. An apparent reconciliation, regulated by a formal treaty, took place at Chartres soon afterwards, and for a year and a half longer, Burgundy continued to retain the chief power in his hands. In the beginning of 1410, the young Duke of Orleans, then only nineteen years of age, married the daughter of the Count of Armagnac, a nobleman of great power and influence in the south of France, and who subsequently became the head and director of the Orleans party. A treaty was also soon after entered into between the princes of the blood hostile to Burgundy, with Orleans at the head, by which they agreed to raise an army of 10,000 men, to maintain the royal authority. Burgundy was no sooner apprised of this than he gave orders for the levy of troops throughout his vast dominions, and began to prepare for war.

The city of Paris, and the whole of France, were now split into two violent factions, espousing the cause of one or other of the two Dukes, and distinguishing themselves by badges, and by the designations of their parties. The Burgundians wore red sashes, with the cross of Saint Andrew, and after a time were called Cabochins, from Caboche, a butcher, one of their most active leaders; the Parisians were mostly of this party. The Orleanists, on the other hand, wore white sashes, with Saint George's cross, and termed themselves Armagnacs, after the father-in-law of the Duke of Orleans, who was made Constable of France by his son-in-law's interest, and looked upon as his principal partisan. The Armagnacs, in the first instance, consisted of the poor and needy Gascons, brought from the south by their leader, and who displayed a greediness and ferocity never surpassed by a foreign enemy. The capital and a circle of twenty leagues round it became a scene of the most horrible devastations. Towards the end of 1411, they advanced in force and threatened Paris with a siege. But the Duke of Burgundy threw himself into the city with a body of select troops, part of them English, whom he had obtained in consequence of a treaty with that nation. These English auxiliaries were commanded by the Earl of Arundel, conducted themselves with strict discipline, and were of great service to the cause of Burgundy.

The Orleans faction, seeing the advantage which this succour gave to the opposite party, felt no difficulty in entering into similar transactions, and opened a treaty with Henry IV. of England. The offers of the Armagnacs were too favourable to be neglected by that monarch, who was just obtaining a breathing time from the troubles and insurrections by which his reign had been successively disturbed,—by the Welsh, the Percys, and others who were dissatisfied with his title or his government. At this period of quiet, it was natural for him to look abroad to France, now engaged in a bloody civil war, and that he should support the party that would grant him the best terms. Or perhaps, in his heart, the English King desired, by assisting the one French party after the other, to prevent the civil war from drawing to a conclusion, as opening to England a fresh prospect of recovering her French dominions.

It is certain that, with whatever intention, Henry IV. listened favourably to the proposal of the Orleans or Armagnac faction, who offered to surrender all the provinces of Gascony to the English, with other advantages. Finally, tempted by their offers, he engaged, 18th May, 1412, to send to the assistance of the Armagnacs a thousand men-at-arms, and three thousand archers. A.D. 1412. To show himself more serious in their support, the King of England appointed his younger son, Thomas of Clarence, general of this auxiliary army.

Amid these preparations, in which the horrors of foreign invasion were to be added to those of civil war, Charles VI. awakened from a long fit of his malady, and became sensible, as he sometimes was at intervals, to the distresses of his subjects.

Isabella of Bavaria, the wife of the unfortunate King, had contrived to take a great share in the government, in the names of her lunatic husband and youthful son, whose station of next heir to the crown would have given him great authority had he known how to use it. The King's mandates

when his mind was strong enough to express them
were listened to with respect by the chiefs of both
parties; and, as the caprice of the queen threw her
into the arms of one or other of the contending
factions, he was alternately heard denouncing vengeance
for the death of Orleans, his only brother,
and vindicating or justifying the conduct of the
Duke of Burgundy, his brother's murderer.

Thus passively did the poor king follow the
views of the faction under whose charge he chanced
to be placed for the time, without expressing resentment
at his own treatment, although we have
one anecdote at least, tending to show that even
his means of living and support were strangely neglected
by those who had his person under their
control, even though these were at the time his
wife and eldest son.

So ill, we are assured, were the royal wants provided
for, that the governess of the royal household
once complained to the unfortunate King that
she had neither money nor the means of procuring
provisions or other necessaries for the service of
the royal children. "Alas!" said the King, "how
can I help you, who am myself reduced to the same
straits!" He gave her the golden cup out of which
he had recently drunk, as the means of meeting the
immediate necessity.

It appears that this unhappy prince, during the
rare intervals of his melancholy disease, had the
power of seeing, with some degree of precision, the
condition in which the country stood at one given
moment, and could then form a rational opinion,

though he was totally incapable of deducing any arguments founded on what had previously happened. His mind was like a mirror, which reflects with accuracy the objects presented to it for the time, though it retains no impression of such as formerly passed before it. He was therefore incapable of judging of affairs with a comprehensive reference to past events, or the actors in them, and his conduct was entirely decided by the light in which actual circumstances were represented by those interested in deceiving him.

Charles was therefore not a little indignant, on awaking from his illness in 1412, at finding the Armagnac party far advanced in a treaty, the principal article of which was the introduction of an English army into France; and while he felt natural resentment at a proceeding so unpatriotic, and so full of danger to his kingdom, he was kept ignorant of the fact, or could not draw the conclusion, that the Duke of Burgundy and his party had been guilty of exactly the same error when they accepted the assistance of the English, under the Earl of Arundel, who had formed the most effective part of the garrison of Paris.

Greatly displeased, therefore, with the Dukes of Berri and Bourbon, and with others included in the Armagnac party, Charles marched in person against them, and besieged the city of Bourges, which was one of their strongholds. They expressed the utmost deference for the King's person, but alleged that he had not undertaken the expedition of his own free will, protesting at the same time that, unless the King came, or rather was brought in company of that licensed murderer, John Duke of Burgundy, the gates of Bourges should fly open at the slightest summons in his name.

While making these fair pretences, the besieged organized a desperate sally, with the view of making prisoners of King Charles and his eldest son Louis. In this they were disappointed, and found themselves so hard pressed in their turn, that they were obliged to submit to conditions dictated by the King, in which both the parties of Armagnacs and Cabochins were obliged to renounce all their leagues with the English.

The English, in the mean time, under the Duke of Clarence, arrived, as appointed by the Armagnacs; and, as demonologists pretend of evil spirits, were much more easily brought into France than dismissed from it. The Orleans party, by a large sum of ready money, and a much larger in promise, for which hostages were granted, persuaded the English prince to withdraw, but not without doing much damage to the country.

The French nobles then assembled together in Paris, without distinction of parties, the very names of the factions being declared unlawful; so anxious did the leaders appear to be to bury the very memory of their dissensions, while secretly they were labouring to rouse and increase them.

Peace being thus concluded betwixt the factions, there seemed to be some chance of stopping the bleeding wounds of the distracted country; but the utter disregard to the ordinary bonds of faith be tween man and man threw all loose again within a short time.

A war with England began now to appear a likely event, and a meeting of the States-General was convoked, to find the means of meeting the emergencies of the country; but they were dissolved without having proposed any radical cure for the distresses and dangers under which the kingdom laboured.

Louis, Dauphin, and heir of the crown, was now beginning to take a decided part, independent of his mother, the Queen, and he naturally cast his eye on the Duke of Burgundy, as the party by whom so incurable a wound had been dealt to the domestic peace of France. In his secret enquiries into this prince's conduct, he learned, or perhaps pretended to learn, that the Duke had laid a plan for destroying the remaining branches of the house of Orleans. The informer was a certain Pierre des Essards, a creature of the Duke of Burgundy whom he had raised to the dignified and wealthy situation of minister of the finances, and who now, being threatened by the Dauphin with an examination of his accounts, changed sides, in the hope of eluding enquiries which he dared not meet. He received orders from the Dauphin to secure the Bastile, then in some degree considered as the citadel of Paris.

Burgundy, better accustomed to the management of plots than his young kinsman, counteracted so effectually this scheme of the Dauphin, that Des Essards had no sooner possessed himself of the

Bastile, than all Paris was in uproar. The mob, commanded by Caboche, the butcher, took up arms. Des Essards, obliged to surrender the Bastile, was seised, and put to death. Caboche and his followers also killed some persons in high office about the Dauphin's person, and compelled the King himself, with the Dukes of Berri and Bourbon, to go to the parliament, wearing white sashes, the emblem of the party of Burgundy,—at least of the Parisian mutineers,—and there register such edicts as the multitude were pleased to demand. The same rioters burst into the Dauphin's private apartments, having heard the sound of violins there, and behaved with the utmost insolence, putting those who were present in immediate danger of their lives.

Impatient of mob-tyranny, which is of all others the most difficult to endure, the Dauphin once more took measures for uniting and arranging the broken and dispersed party of the Duke of Orleans. At the call of the heir-apparent, in which he used the name of his father, the Orleans party entered Paris, while, by one of the changes common at the time, the Duke of Burgundy found he could not make his party good in the city, and retired, as was his wont, to his own territories of Flanders.

The Queen, the Dauphin, and the other lords, who had thus obtained power, were too jealous of each other to agree long, how much soever it was their interest to do so. Isabella of Bavaria had the art to induce most of them to join against the authority assumed by her son, as too absolate and peremptory to be engrossed by one whom she described as a giddy youth, liable to be seduced by evil counsel. The Queen even proceeded so far as to break into the Dauphin's apartments, and seize upon four attendants of his person, whom she described as agents of the Duke of Burgundy. The young Prince was so highly offended at this personal insult, that he wrote to the Duke of Burgundy that he was prisoner in his own capital, and invited him to come with his forces to his deliverance.

A slighter invitation would have brought the Duke to Paris. He instantly advanced, at the head of a large force of his own vassals.

Charles, however, had in the mean time a transitory interval of recovery, and assumed for a short time the reins of government. On this occasion, he sent forth an edict, charging the Duke with the murder of Orleans, and published the confutation of Doctor John Petit's abominable apology for that vile assassination. At the same moment, the Dauphin Louis, whose temper seems to have been fickle and uncertain, again changed his party, and invited the princes of the Orleans faction into the city. They came with so strong a body of horse (amounting, it is said, to eight thousand men), that they were able to disarm the whole citizens, save those of the better classes. He removed also the chains and barricades with which the Parisians were accustomed to block up their streets, and once more put it out of their power to disturb the public tranquillity. The Duke of Burgundy in the mean time advanced towards the walls of the city; but, dismayed at once by the royal edicts launched against him, by the Dauphin's desertion of his cause, and by the reduced state of the Parisians, who used to be his best friends, he retreated as formerly, after a vain attempt to obtain admission.

The King, surrounded with all the princes of the blood-royal, except the lineage of Burgundy, now marched into Artois, the territories of the Duke, took several of his towns, and laid siege to Arras. The citizens of the towns of Flanders declared, that although the Duke was their immediate prince, it was not their intention to assist him against the King, their lord paramount, or to shut their gates against their sovereign. The Duke of Burgundy, alarmed at the prospect of being deserted by his own immediate subjects of Burgundy and Flanders, saw the necessity of submission, and sued for a peace with more sincerity than hitherto.

Sept. 1414. It was concluded accordingly at Arras; but Orleans and some of his partisans refused to sign it. Charles and his son insisted on their doing so. "If you would have the peace lasting," said he, "you must sign it;" which was done accordingly. This pacification, being preceded by the humiliation of the Duke of Burgundy, might be accounted the most solid which had yet been attempted between the two factions, and appeared to possess a fair chance of being permanent.

But it was not the pleasure of Heaven to prolong the state of foreign peace, or truce at least, which France had enjoyed during her domestic divisions, and which prevented England from taking advantage of them. During some years, Henry IV. of England had reigned, an unpopular king, with a doubtful title, and could not, owing to disturbances at home, profit by the disunion of the French. In the year before this pacification between Charles and his subjects, that monarch died, and was succeeded by his son, the celebrated Henry V., a young hero, be- *March, 1413.* loved by the nation, and who breathed nothing at his accession save invasion against his neighbours, the scars of whose disunion were still rankling, though apparently closed.

And as the issue of the strife which ensued was remarkable, I shall here close my TALES for the present, not unwilling to continue them, if they shall be thought as useful as those from the History of Scotland.

GENERAL INDEX

TO THE

MISCELLANEOUS PROSE WORKS

OF

SIR WALTER SCOTT, BART.

IN TWENTY-EIGHT VOLUMES.

The Roman numerals refer to the volume, the figures to the page.

ABBOT OF UNREASON, vii. 202.
Abercorn, late Marquis of, xx. 182-184; his grounds at Duddingstone, xxi. 101, 102.
Abercrombie, General Sir Ralph, xi. 197, 198.
Aberdeen, George, Earl of, xv. 6, 92.
Abingdon, Countess of, Dryden's Elegy on, i. 320.
Aboukir, battle of, between the French and English fleets, x. 334-337.
———, between the Turks and French, x. 378.
Abou Taleb, Travels of, xviii. 392.
Absalom and Achitophel, by Dryden, i. 208, 230.
Acre, St John d', Siege of, by the Crusaders, xxvii. 246-248; Siege of, by Buonaparte, x. 355-367.
Actors, interest felt in the lives of, xx. 162-164.
Addison, Joseph, i. 315, note; ii. 70, note; 60, 83, 102, 126-138, note; 244 246.

Æneas Sylvius, Pope, vii. 79.
Agnew, Sir Andrew, xxvi. 295, 302-306.
Aikin's, Dr John, 'Collection of English Songs,' and 'Essay on Song writing,' xvii. 119, and 133-136.
Alaric, King of the Visigoths, xxvii. 58.
Albany, Robert Duke of, xxii. 246-248, 254, 255, 257.
———, Murdac, Duke of, xxii. 257, 261-2, 264-5.
———, Alexander, Duke of, xxii. 311, 314-318, 323-325; vii. 419-422.
———, John, Duke of, xxii. 379-389.
Albigenses, Crusade against the, xxvii. 283-285, 292-294.
'Albion and Albanius,' by Dryden, i. 257.
'Alexander's Feast,' by Dryden, i. 344.
Alexander I. King of Scotland, notices of, xxi. 160; xxii. 41
——— II. xxi. 164; xxii. 58-60.

Alexander III. King, xxi. 166, 171-173; xxii. 30-66.
—— III. Pope, xxvii. 223, 224.
—— I. Emperor of Russia, xii. 35, 36, 40, 43, 66, 73, 74, 79, 84-86, 160, 258-262, 265-276; xiii. 133-136, 356-358, 392-400; xiv. 34, 37, 55, 86, 87, 124, 125, 137, 276, 297, 347, 348, 352, 356, 386, 403, 417; xv. 66, 78, 83, 118, 119, 154, 167, 169, 182, 208, 217, 408.
Alexandria in Egypt, capture of, by Buonaparte, x. 318.
Alexius, Emperor of the East, xxvii. 161, 165, 168-173.
Allan a Sop. xxiii. 299-305.
'All for Love,' by Dryden, i. 156.
Alps, passage of the, by Buonaparte, x. 15; xi. 85, 86, 89-94.
Alquier, Baron, xiv. 3, 4.
Alsusieff, general, xv. 49, 56.
Alvinzi, Marshal, x. 131, 133, 134, 137, 140, 142, 143, 144, 146, 149, 154, 159.
'Amadis de Gaul,' vi. 196-199; Review of Mr Southey's edition, and Mr Stewart Rose's poem of, xviii. 1-43.
'Amboyna,' by Dryden, i. 146.
'Amelia,' by Fielding, remarks on, iii. 3.
America, U. S. of, x. 393; xi. 130.
Amherst, Lord, xvi. 262-264.
Amiens, treaty of, xi. 207.
Amphitryon,' by Dryden, i. 305.
Ancrem Moor, battle of, xxii. 58, 59.

Anderson, Dr Robert, 'Life of Dr Smollett,' iii. 117; his British Poets, iv. 149.
Andreossi, General, x. 37, 305, 382.
Angling, pleasures of, xx. 246-273.
Anglomania, in France before the revolution, viii. 66.
Angoulême, Duke of, xv. 84, 85, 90, 363-365.
——, Duchess of, xv. 364-365.
Angus, George (Douglas), Earl of, vii. 431; xxii. 296, 302 303, 306.
——, Archibald, Bell the Cat, Earl of, xxii. 320, 328, 364.
——, Archibald, Earl of, xxii. 378, 381-385; xxiii. 1-14, 45-52, 57-61, 72, 73.
Anjou, Louis, Duke of, Regent of France, xxviii. 202-204.
Anne, Queen, ii. 142, 378, 380; xxv. 51-225.
'*Annus Mirabilis*,' by Dryden, i. 49.
Antommarchi, Dr, xvi. 194, 195, 292, 300-306.
Anthony's, St. Chapel, near Edinburgh, description of, vii. 296.
Arbuthnot, Dr John, ii. 138, 305, *note*; 385.
Arcis sur Aube, battle of, xv. 122.
Arcola, three battles of, x. 140-146.
Arena, the Corsican deputy, xi. 23, 24, 28, 29.
Argyle, Earl and Marquis of, xxiii. 192, 193, 369-402; xxiv. 1-3, 12, 13, 16, 25.

INDEX.

56-60, 80, 83, 84, 101, 114, 179-183.
Argyle, Archibald, Earl of, xxiv. 186, 187, 261, 262, 272, 275-281.
——— Earl and Duke of, xxiv. 356.
———, John, Duke of, ii. 164, 167; xxv. 80, 162-166, 176, 180-185, 220, 229, 235-426.
Arish, El, convention of, xi. 192, 193.
Armies of the fourteenth century, xxviii. 34-45.
Armstrong, John, of Gilnockie, xxiii. 18.
———, William (or Kinmont Willie), xxiii. 196-199.
Arnott, Dr A., xvi. 269, 271, 302-305.
Arran, Sir Thomas Boyd, Earl of, xxii. 309, 310.
———, James Lord Hamilton, Earl of, xxii. 310, 381-383; xxiii. 1, 8. Duke of Chatelherault, 51-71.
———, Captain James Stewart, Earl of, xxii. 251-255; xxiii. 160-170.
Artavelde, Jacob Van, the brewer of Ghent, xxviii. 12, 47, 48.
———, Philip Van, xxviii. 208-212.
Arthur, Duke of Bretagne, xxvii. 258, 264-266.
'Arundel,' by Cumberland, remarks on, iii. 221.
Ascham, Roger, his censure of the *Morte d'Arthur*, vi. 187.
Aspromo, battle of, xiii. 200.
'Assignation, the,' by Dryden, i. 125.

'Astræa Redux,' by Dryden, i. 40.
Athole, Marquis and Duke of, xxiv. 337, 375-377; xxv. 88, 100, 136, 273, 274, 277; xxvi. 105, 107.
Attila, King of the Huns, xxvii. 49-53.
Auberoche, siege of, in 1344, xxviii. 29-34.
Audley, Lord, vi. 61; xxviii. 101, 102, 105-107, 160, 161.
Auerstadt, battle of, xii. 171-174.
Augereau, Marshal, Duke of Castiglione, x. 9, 20, 77, 104-108, 121, 125, 140, 146, 153, 268, 274, 413; xi. 4, 18, 24, 179; xii. 8, 176; xiv. 313, 314, 372, 382, 392; xv. 62, 74, 75, 134, 135, 232.
Aulderne, battle of, xxiv. 7.
Aulus Gellius, ii. 233, *note*.
Aurai, battle of, xxviii. 136.
'Aureng-Zebe,' by Dryden, i. 179.
Austen's, Miss Jane, 'Northanger Abbey, and Persuasion,' review of, and of her former works, ' Mansfield Park,' ' Pride and Prejudice,' &c. xviii. 209-249.
Austerlitz, battle of, xii. 75-81.

Baber, the emperor, Commentaries of, translated by Dr Leyden, iv. 195.
Babœuf, conspiracy of, x. 259
BAGE, ROBERT, BIOGRAPHICAL NOTICE OF, iii. 440; remarks on his novels, 451-464.

286 INDEX.

Bagration, General, Prince, xii. 237, 248; xiv. 43, 64-70, 73, 81, 103.
Baillie of Jerviswood, xix. 26, 236; xxiv. 263, 267.
——, General, xxiv. 3, 10, 11, 13, 14.
Balfour, John, of Burley, xix. 72-74, 275-280; xxiv. 233.
Ballangeich, Goodman of, and King of Kippen, xxiii. 22.
Ballantyne, James, printer, iv. 172; letter of Dr Leyden to, 173, 175, 178-185.
——, John, bookseller, iii. 1; life of Daniel Defoe by, 228-247.
Balmerino, Lord, xxvi. 142, 377, 380-388.
Bannatyne Club, account of the, xxi. 219 223.
Bannister, Jack, character of, xx. 243.
Bannockburn, battle of, xxii. 147.
Barharoux, the French revolutionist, viii. 321; ix. 39-124.
Barber, Alderman John, ii. 140, 166, 185, 337, 503.
——, Mrs. ii. 336-340.
Barclay de Tolly, general, commander of the Russian army, xii. 234, 238; xiv. 39-95, 307, 353, 392; xv. 151, 156, 408.
Bards, the, xxvii. 9.
'Barham Downs,' by Bage, remarks on, iii. 457.
Barncluth in Lanarkshire, description of, xxi. 89.
Barras, the French director, x. 260, 261, 279, 280, 312, 409, 410; xl. 6, 7, 14-16.
Bassano, battle of, x. 120.
Basseville, French Envoy at Rome, murder of, x. 12.
Bass Rock, description of, vii. 438. Siege of, xxiv. 399.
Battle of Chalons, xxvii. 52; of Poitiers, 58; of Tours, 68; of Hastings, 145; of Brenneville, 185; of Bouvines, 275; of Sluys, xxviii. 10; of Cressy, 57; of Poitiers, 97; of Aurai, 136; of Rosebeeque, 212; of Nicopolis, 255.
Battle of the Standard at Northallerton, xxii. 43; of Largs, 61; of Stirling, 85; of Falkirk, 90; of Bannockburn, 147-158; of Dupplin, 200; of Halidon Hill, 204; of Kilblene, 211; of Neville's Cross, 226; of Otterburn, 238; of Homildon, 249; of Shrewsbury, 250; of Harlaw, 256; of Sark, 283; of Flodden, 366-373; of Lillyard's Edge, xxiii. 59; of Pinkie, 68; of Langside, 131; of Tibbermuir, 390; of the Bridge of Dee, 397; of Inverlochy, xxiv. 3; of Aulderne, 7; of Alford, 10; of Kilsyth, 14; of Philiphaugh, 20; of Craigchonichen, 73; of Dunbar, 94; of Worcester, 163; of Rullion Green, 205; of Drumclog, 240; of Bothwell Bridge, 246; of Killiecrankie, 378-382; of Sheriffmuir, xxv. 353-363; of Glenshiel, 432; of Preston,

xxvi. 153-176; of Clifton, 239; of Falkirk, 261-276; of Culloden, 335-347.

Battles of Napoleon, &c.—Of Montenotte, x. 16; of Millesimo, 20; of Mondovi, 24; of Lodi, 40; of Borghetto, 77; of Lonato, 106; of Roveredo, 114; of Bassano, 120; of St George, 127; of the Brenta, 134; of Arcola, 140-146; of Rivoli, 153; of La Favorita, 159; of the Tagliamento, 203; of Alexandria, 318; of the Pyramids, 326; naval—of Aboukir, 333; land—of Aboukir, 376; of Montebello xi. 108; of Marengo, 110-119; of Hohenlinden, 128; of Alexandria, 197; of Austerlitz, xii. 75-81; of Trafalgar, 108-112; of Auerstadt and Jena, 172-179; of Pultusk, 231; of Eylau, 237; of Heilsberg, 249; of Friedland, 250; of Maida, 282; of Rio Seco, xiii. 64; of Baylen, 89; of Rorica, 113; of Vimeiro, 115; of Espinosa, 149; of Tudela, 151; of Corunna, 160; of Abensberg, 178; of Eckmuhl, ib; of Asperne, and Essling, 200-206; of Wagram, 212; of Oporto, 261; of Talavera, 263; of Ocana, 289; of Busaco, 300; of Fuentes d'Onoro, 383; of Barossa, ib; of Arroyo Molinos, 386; of Valoutina, xiv. 92; of Borodino, 96-104; of Malo Yaroslavets, 144; of Krasnoi, 186; of Lutzen, 297; of Bautzen, 307; of Vittoria, 335; of Dresden, 344; of Culm, 352; Gross-Beeren, 359; of Katzbach, 361; of Dennewitz, 365; of Leipsic, 380-403; of Hanau, 411; of Brienne, xv. 48; of La Rothiere, 51; of Champ Aubert, 56; of Nangis, 59; of Montereau, 60; of Mery, 62; of Orthez, 86; of Aire, 87; of Craonne, 110; of Laon, 112; of Bar-sur-Aube, 117, Arcis-sur-Aube, 122; Fère Champenoise, 139; o. Montmartre, 148; of Ligny, 428; of Quatre Bras, 431; of Waterloo, xvi. 1-40, 343-379.

Bautzen, Battle of, xiv. 306-308.

Bayes, nickname of Dryden, i. 118, 121, 216.

Beaton, Cardinal, xxii. 382; xxiii. 6, 42, 51, 61-66.

Beauharnais, Eugene, stepson of Napoleon, ix. 394; created Viceroy of Italy, xii. 29; married to the Princess Royal of Bavaria, 129; xiv. 42, 145, 156, 159-165, 170, 171, 183, 186-188, 272, 292, 293, 295, 339, 420; xv. 70, 325.

Beaulieu, General, Austrian commander in Italy in 1796, x. 15-51, 76-96.

Beaumont and Fletcher, dramas of, characterised, vi. 343.

Beddoes, Dr Thomas, ii. 21 note.

Becket, St Thomas à, Archbishop of Canterbury, xxvii. 222, 225-228, 231, 232.
Baker, General, xvi. 63, 64.
Belliard, General, xi. 196; xiii. 165; xiv. 82; xv. 176.
Bennigsen, General, Russian commander, xii. 223, 225, 230-245, 250, 255; xiv. 373; xv. 74.
Beresford, Marshal, now Viscount, xiii. 300, 383, 384; xv. 82.
———, Rev. James, 'Miseries of Human Life,' Review of, xix. 139-159.
Beresina, Passage of the, xiv. 203-211.
Bergen-op-Zoom, British attack on, v. 13-16; xv. 75, 76.
Berkeley, Thomas, Bishop of Cloyne, ii. 138, 210, 225-227.
———, Earl of, ii. 50-53.
Berlin Decrees of Napoleon against British commerce, xii. 205-215.
Bernadotte, Marshal, Prince of Ponte Corvo, now Charles John, King of Sweden, x. 205, 233, note, 311, 413; xi. 5, 6, 11, 18, 24 (Notice of, on the 18th Brumaire, App. 353-368); xii. 50, 52, 53, 72, 135, 169, 179, 181, 235, 236, 241; xiii. 203, 204, 341-352, 408-417; xiv. 2-6, 262-284, 292, 303, 340, 341, 358, 360, 364, 370, 375, 383, 393-395, 403; xv. 39-41.
Bernard, St, xxvii. 197.
Berners, John Bourchier, Lord, translation of Froissart's Chronicles by, xix. 114, 130, 131, comparison of, with Mr Johnes's version, 132-138, his romance, 'The Knight of the Swan,' vi. 212.
Berthier, General Alexander, Prince of Neufchatel, x. 44, 305, 382; xi. 37; xii. 9, 112, 135, 259; xiii. 177, 272; xiv. 74, 123, 215, 323; xv. 176, 199, 221.
Bertrand, General, xiv. 298, 299, 365, 373, 375, 378, 381, 403; xv. 200, 230; xvi. 100, 102, 149, 151, et seq.
Bessières, Marshal, Duke of Istria, x. 79, 382; xi. 121, 158; xii. 79, 259; xiii. 82-85; xiv. 41, 102, 123, 146, 296.
Bettesworth, Sergeant, Dean Swift's Satire upon, ii. 365; its consequences, 366, et seq.
Betty, Master, the Young Roscius, xx. 219.
Bianchi, General, xv. 63, 74, 134.
Bibliomaniacs, remarks on the pursuits of, xxi. 208-213.
Bickerstaff, Isaac, ii. 94, 96.
Binnock, William, surprise of the Castle of Linlithgow by, vii. 383; xxii. 138-141.
Bisset, William, remarkable case of, xxi. 235.
Black Agnes, Countess of Dunbar and March, heroic defence of Dunbar Castle by, vii. 414-417; xxii. 212, 215.

Black Dwarf,' Review of the, xix. 22-28.
Black, Dr John, the celebrated chemist, xix. 333-335.
Blackmore, Sir Richard, i. 354-358, 368.
Blair Athole Castle, blockade of, xxvi. 302-305.
Blake, General, xiii. 83, 143, 149, 385.
Blanche, Queen of France, mother of St Louis, xxvii. 300-306, 308, 310, 327-328.
Blucher, Marshal, Prince of Wahlstadt, xii. 180, 182; xiv. 280, 282, 297, 299, 306, 308. 340, 356, 363, 373, 375, 380, 382, 386, 393, 410; xv. 39. 46, 48, 53, 55, 58, 61, 63, 109, 114, 138, 157, 408, 423, 436; xvi. 5, 14, 16, 20, 21. 31, 39. See also v. 79, 88, 130.
Blount, Charles, i. 135, 152; notice of his *Religio Laici*, 268.
Boaden, James, 'Memoirs of the Life of John Philip Kemble,' Review of, xx. 152, 232. See Kemble.
Boccacio, first edition, the Duke of Roxburghe's copy of, xxi. 214.
Boece, or Boethius, Hector, History of Scotland by, xx 302. 304.
Bolingbroke, Henry St John, Viscount, ii. 109, 111, 117, 146, 156, 180, 186, 188, 189, 197, 279, 335, 386; xxv. 204. 224, 227, 236.
Boniface VIII. Pope, quarrels

of, with Philip the Fair, xxvii. 360, 362.
Booksellers, Publishing, discussion of authors' complaints against, xxi. 200, 205.
BORDER ANTIQUITIES, ESSAY ON, vii. 1; circumstances which give interest to the borders of Scotland and England, 3; British Antiquities, 5-17; Roman Antiquities, 18-25; invasion of the Saxons, 26; of the Danes, 31; settlement, of the present limits, 35; Saxon Antiquities, 37; the feudal system, 45; Celtic system of clanship, 47; effect of Edward I.'s invasion, 59; Scottish border castles, 64; the peels, 68; Scottish border towns, 71; magnificence of English castles, 75; English towns, 76; manners of the Scottish Borderers, 81, and 144; of the English, 83; their mutual relations. 87; the Wardens of the Marches, 98; English Border laws, 104; ancient rules of the Marches, 111; truces between the Wardens, 114; settlement of disputes by single combat, 118; days of truce, 120; retaliation of offences, 133; riding, 134; effect of Union of the crowns, 138; of the civil wars of Charles I., 139.
Borders of Scotland, state of, at the union of the kingdoms, xxiii. 272, 293.
Borodino, battle of, xiv. 98, 104, 157.

Borthwick castle, description of, vii. 190; notice of the family of Borthwick, 200-213; great hall of, 214.
Bossuet's 'Exposition,' and 'History of the Variations,' i. 271, 291.
Bothwell, James (Hepburn), Earl of, xxiii. 113-127.
——, Francis (Stewart), Earl of, xxiii. 190.
——, succession of Earls of, vii. 174-186.
—— Bridge, battle of, xxiv. 246.
Boulter, Archbishop, Primate of Ireland, vi. 274, 282, 374.
Bouvines, battle of, xxvii. 275-280.
Boyds, family of the, xxii. 308-310.
Bradshaigh, Lady, correspondence of, with Richardson, the novelist, iii. 22.
Breadalbane, John, Earl of xxiv. 393-395; xxv. 1-6, 252, 332.
Braemar, Hunting of, xxv. 250-254.
Braid, Fairly, the Laird of, a friend of Knox. vii. 247-8.
—— and Blackford hills, description of, vii. 249-50.
Braybrooke, Lord, Review of his edition of 'Memoirs of Samuel Pepys,' xx. 94-152.
Bretigny, treaty of, xxviii. 133.
Brienne, battle of, xv. 49.
Brothers, objects of the Society of, established by Swift, ii. 130.
Brown, Tom, i. 314, 361, 373.

Bruce, Edward, brother of King Robert, xxii. 145, 159, 162.
Brueys, Admiral, x. 305, 316, 332, 335.
Brumaire, Revolution of the 18th, 1799, xi. 10-30.
Brunswick, Duke of, Prussian Commander-in-chief, viii. 324, 363-368; xii. 164, 167, 179, 194, 197.
—— Oels, Duke of, xiii. 189, 215, 217; xiv. 418; xv. 421; xvi. 7.
Bubna, General, xiv. 286, 305; xv. 38, 74.
Buchan, Isabella, Countess of, sister of Robert Bruce, xxi. 194, 196; xxii. 102, 107-8.
Buccleuch, Sir Walter Scott, Lord of, xxii. 303; xxiii. 4, 6, 58, 197, 200.
——, Walter, first Earl of, vii. 184, 185; xxiii. 351; xxiv. 19.
—— and Monmouth, Anne Duchess of, i. 207, 244, 245; vii. 225.
——, Charles, Duke of, character of, iv. 297.
——, the present Duke of, his edition of the Chartulary of Melrose, xxi. 223.
Bucharest, treaty of, between Russia and Turkey, xiv. 87.
Buckingham, George Villiers, Duke of, i. 114, 121, 211.
Buenos Ayres, expedition to, in 1806, xii. 288, 280.
Bulow, General, xiv. 301, 305; xv. 41, 76, 109, 428; xvi. 14-16, 20.
Bunbury, General Sir Henry, xvi. 107, 114.
Bunyan, John, Review of Mr

Southey's edition of the 'Pilgrim's Progress,' and Life of,' xviii. 74; particulars of his life, 75-94; remarks on his 'Pilgrim's Progress,' 94; on his 'Holy War,' 110.

Buonaparte, Charles, father of Napoleon, ix. 320.

——, Letitia (Ramolini), mother of Napoleon, afterwards called Madame Mère, ix. 321, 323, 339, 398; xiii. 405, note; xvi. 249, 265.

——, Joseph, elder brother of Napoleon, ix. 321; afterwards King of Naples, and King of Spain, 339; marriage of, 366; x. 390, 412; xi. 8, 131, 174, 325; xii. 92, 121, 127; xiii. 55, 56, 72, 74, 84, 85, 94, 282, 285, 294, 295, 387; xv. 145, 147, 153, 155, 222.

BUONAPARTE, NAPOLEON, LIFE OF, viii.—xvi.

—— Birth and parentage, ix. 318; sent to the military school of Brienne, 326; removed to Paris, 331; appointed second lieutenant of artillery, 332; his first literary productions, 333, 401-420; becomes captain by seniority, 336; his first combat in Corsica, 338; his services at Marseilles and Avignon, 341; commands the artillery at the siege of Toulon, 344; appointed brigadier-general and chief of battalion, 360; his services in the Alps, 362; removed to the infantry, 365; commands the troops of the Convention against the insurgent sections of Paris, 387-390; appointed second in command of the army of the interior, 392; general in chief, 393; marriage to Madame Beauharnais, 398; commander of the army in Italy, ib.; his campaigns in Italy in 1796 and 1797, to the treaty of Campo Formio, x. 1-256; his arrival, reception in Paris, and character at that period, 268-295; preparations for invading England, 295-7; given up for an expedition to Egypt, 298, 303-312; departure from Toulon, 313; taking of Malta, 314; landing at Marabout, 318; his career in Egypt from the capture of Alexandria to the final defeat of the Turks at Aboukir, 322-378; departure from Egypt, 384; arrival at Frejus, 386; his reception and conduct at Paris, xi. 1-9; revolution of the 18th Brumaire (9th Nov. 1799), 10-31.

BUONAPARTE, FIRST CONSUL, 41, 47, 8; key note of his system of government, 64; his associate consuls, 67; his ministers, 68-72; overture of peace in England, 75; his plan of campaign against Austria in 1800, 84; his passage over the Great St Bernard, 89-94; short and brilliant campaign, ending with the battle of Marengo,

97-119; armistice with Austria. 120; peace of Luneville, with Austria, 130; friendship with the Russian Emperor Paul, 139; his politic conduct to the Pope, 142; treaty with Naples, 143; escapes assassination by the Jacobins, 151; and the infernal machine of the Royalists, 158; Special Commission Court, 163; law of suspected persons, 165; system of police, 165-170; his treatment of Madame de Staël, 172; Concordat with the Pope, 174; amnesty to the emigrants, 182; disappointment at the death of the Emperor Paul, 190; peace with England, 207; appointed First Consul for life, 212; interference with Switzerland, 223-231; angry discussions with England, 233-250; conferences with Lord Whitworth, 252-260; English declaration of war, 262; expedition to St Domingo, 263-271; establishment of the Legion of Honour, 275; retaliatory measure of detaining British travellers in France, 287; seizure of Hanover, 290; plans for the invasion of England, 294-304; conspiracy of Pichegru, Moreau, &c. 305-316; seizure and murder of Duke d'Enghien, 317-323; treatment of British diplomatists, 343-351.

NAPOLEON, EMPEROR OF THE FRENCH, xii. 8; coronation by the Pope, 13; crowned KING OF ITALY, 28; incorporates Genoa with France, 30; overture of peace to England, 33; fresh coalition against him between Russia, England, and Austria, 35-44; precipitate conduct of the latter, 45; campaign terminating with the battle of Austerlitz, and peace of Presburgh, 48-88; plans of invasion of England, baffled by the victory at Trafalgar, 93-114; Internal improvement of France, 115; elevation of his brothers and sisters, and other relations, to thrones, 118-134; his new nobility, 135; PROTECTOR OF THE CONFEDERATION OF THE RHINE, 140; negotiation with England on Fox's accession to power, 148-152; war with Prussia; rapid conquest of that country, 161-193; harsh treatment of the Duke of Brunswick, 195; vindictive conduct to Prussia, 198; Berlin decrees against British commerce, 206; Sequel of the Campaign against Russia—Battle of Friedland—armistice, 217-257; treaty of Tilsit, 264-274; disappointment at the success of the British expedition against Copenhagen, 297; internal government at this time, 301; new civil code, 316-337; system of taxation, 337; commerce, manufactures, &c., 338 public works, 345; his personal and family life, 348; his court, 351; management of the press, 359; system of education, 361; military system, 368; enforcement of the continental system by the treaty of Tilsit, xiii. 1-7; his relations with Spain and Portugal, 7; invasion of Portugal; departure of the royal family to Brasil, 13; his views on Spain, 21; her fortresses seized by his troops, 26; intrigue with the royal family and their renunciation of the crown, 28; appoints his brother Joseph king, 55; universal insurrection against him, 62-72; public feeling on his return to Paris, 75; early successes and reverses in the Spanish war, 78-98; meeting with the Portuguese nobles at Bayonne, 103; Portuguese insurrection, 105; British expedition to Portugal, 112; battle of Vimeiro, and evacuation of Portugal by the French, 115-121; Napoleon's conference at Erfurt with Alexander, 134; state of the Spanish insurgents and British auxiliary forces, 137-147; Napoleon's movements and triumphs, 148; advance and retreat of the British army to Corunna, 152-162; Napoleon's precipitate departure for France, 167; Austria determines to renew the contest, 172; mutual preparations, 174, 175; details of the campaign from the 9th of April to the battle of Wagram, July 6; armistice of Znaim, 175-213; minor circumstances till the treaty of Schoenbrunn, 213-256; Napoleon's divorce from Josephine, 257-270; his marriage to the Austrian Archduchess, Maria Louisa, 272; sends a fresh army into Spain under Massena, 297; Lord Wellington's retreat to Torres Vedras, 301; change in Napoleon's principles of government, 303; dismissal of Fouché, 313; increase of state prisons, 317; the license system of commerce, 323; differences with his brother Louis, 329; who abdicates the throne, 330; unites Holland to the French empire, 336; his conduct to Bernadotte, on being elected Crown Prince of Sweden, 340-352, and 402-417; his treatment of the clergy of Brabant, 352; seizure of the Valais, 355; and sea-coast of German ocean, 355; Russia protest against occupation of Oldenburg, 357; policy in refusing exchange of prisoners with England, 358 362; extent of power wielded by him at this time, 303; birth of his son, the king of Rome, 309; his treatment of the ex-queen of Etruria, 374; his brother Lucien received in England, 375; vicissitudes of the Peninsular War, 379-387; grounds of war with Russia, 388-405; political relations at this time, xiv. 1-18; force of the army, 19-22; overtures of peace to England, 25; meeting at Dresden with allied sovereigns, 30; campaign in Russia, 36-250; state of Paris on his return, 251; negotiations with the Pope, 264; preparations for the next campaign, 269; Prussian declaration of war, 277; Sweden also joins the coalition, 284-289; campaign of 1813, from battle of Lutzen to the armistice of June 4th, 297-312; Prince Metternich's interview with him, 327-332; Austria joins the allies, 334; resumption of hostilities, from the battle of Dresden to that of Leipsic, 337-405; effect of his late reverses on his political relations, 418-432; preparations for meeting the allied invasion, xv. 1; ineffectual negotiations for peace, 3-13; state of parties in France, 14; his speech to the Council of State, 22; to the Legislative Body, 26; his departure for the army, 31; events of the campaign of 1814, to the entrance of the allies into Paris, 33-170; Napoleon's subsequent operations, till his retreat to Fontainebleau, 171-180; decree of the Senate, declaring his forfeiture of the throne, 184-6; declarations of his marshals, 200; consents to abdicate conditionally, 202; unconditionally, 214; terms granted to him by the Treaty of Fontainebleau, 215; departure for Elba, 229; journey and voyage thither, 230-241; residence at Elba, 242-267; escape and landing at Cannes, 337; his progress from thence to Lyons, 338-345; decrees issued at Lyons, 346; advance from Lyons to Paris, 349-360; difficulties of his new position, 365; declaration of the Congress and Treaty of Vienna, 367-8; new Constitution, 397; dispute with the Representative Chamber, 403; preparations for the campaign, 408-413; departure for Flanders, 419; attacks and beats the Prussians at Charleroi, 425; and at Ligny, 428; attacks the English at Quatre Bras, 431; BATTLE OF WATERLOO, xvi. 8-40; and 343-379; (See also Vol v. 21-165, and 346-354;) his return to Paris, 42; his second abdication, 52; leaves Malmaison for Rochefort, 65; negotiations with Captain Maitland, 93 his surrender to that officer 102; arrival in Plymouth Sound, 107; removed to the Northumberland, 131; lands at St Helena, 136; residence there till his death, 146-307; his funeral, 309; character

INDEX. 295

311-342; last will and testament, 399-412.

Buonaparte, Lucien, younger brother of Napoleon, now Prince of Canino, ix. 321; x. 412; xi. 22, 30; xii. 119, 120; xiii. 55, 375; xv. 401; xvi. 45, 46, 48, 52, 53, 56.

——, Louis, King of Holland, younger brother of Napoleon, ix. 321, 334, note; x. 104, note; xii. 121, 123, 133, 202; xiii. 313, 314, 325, 332.

——, Jerome, King of Westphalia, younger brother of Napoleon, ix. 321; xii. 120, 121, 203; xiii. 4, 189; xiv. 42, 68, 69, 376, 419; xv. 222; xvi. 6, 9.

——, Eliza, eldest sister of Napoleon, Princess of Lucca, ix. 321; xii. 128.

—— Pauline, second sister of Napoleon, wife of General Leclerc, afterwards of Prince Borghese, ix. 322; xi. 267; xii. 128; xv. 249, 265; xvi. 292.

——, Caroline, youngest sister of Napoleon, afterwards Queen of Naples, ix. 322; xii. 128; xv. 378.

—— the Abbate Gregorio, x. 174.

Burke's, Edmund, ' Reflections on the French Revolution,' viii. 258-260.

Burlington, Countess of, anecdote of. ii. 420.

Burnet, Gilbert, Bishop of Salisbury, i. 280, 281, 287, 379; ii. 68, 159.

Burns, Robert, anecdote of. vii. 256; ' Reliques of, collected by Cromek,' Review of, xvii. 242-266.

Burt's, Captain, ' Letters from the North of Scotland,' xix. 177; xx. 21, 54, 78, 87, note.

Burton's, Robert, ' Anatomy of Melancholy,' iii. 292, note; his Verses to Melancholy, xviii. 302, 303.

Busaco, Battle of xiii. 300.

Bute, John, Earl of, relations of George III. with, iv. 326-7.

Butler, Samuel, the poet, i. 98, 105, 116.

Battafuoco, Matteo, a Corsican nobleman, Buonaparte's letter to, ix. 334; extracts from it, 401-412.

Button's Coffee-house, i. 315; ii. 71.

BYRON, LORD, censures the blank verse poets, i. 145, note; quotes ' Settle's Empress of Morocco.' 160, note; his estimate of Dryden and Pope, 403, note; DEATH OF, iv. 343; Review of the Third Canto of his ' Childe Harold,' 351, and of ' The Prisoner of Chillon,' 387; Lord Byron's acknowledgement of his obligations for this review, 399, note; Review of the ' Fourth Canto of Childe Harold's Pilgrimage,' xvii 337.

' Cadenus and Vanessa,' Swift's poem of, ii. 228-231.

Cæsar, Julius, conquests of, in Gaul, xxvii. 15-28.

Caffarelli, General, x. 314, 368.
Calais, siege of, by Edward III. xxvii. 58-79; plan for its recovery by treachery baffled, 79-84.
Calder, Admiral Sir Robert, xii 104, 105.
Cambacérès, minister of justice, x. 86; third consul, 67, 161; xv. 28, 32, 348.
Cambronne, General, xvi. 19, 20.
Cameron, Evan, of Lochiel, xxiv. 112-120, 380; xxv. 301, 330, 348; xxvi. 46.
———, Donald, of Lochiel, xxvi. 46-48, 63, 74-76, 86, 185-373.
Cameronians, sect of the, vii. 140; xix. 78-84; xxiv. 252-256; xxv. 125.
——— regiment, the, xxiv. 353, 366.
Campaign of 1815, v. 50-145, 346-354; xv. 413-438; xvi. 1-40, 343-379.
Campbell, Hon. A. C., a barrister, Dr. Smollett's letter to, iii. 182-187.
———, Colonel Sir Niel, xv. 230, 233, 236, 243, 252-257, 281, 282, 284, 286, 336-7.
———, Thomas, iii. 160, 232-236, 240, 249; Review of his 'Gertrude of Wyoming,' xvii. 167-221.
Caporal, Petit, nickname of endearment given to Buonaparte by the French soldiers, x. 49, 50.
Carlisle, siege of, xxvi. 207-209; retaking of, 257.

Carlyle, Rev Dr, minister of Inveresk, xix. 304.
Carnegie of Finhaven, remarkable trial of, xxi. 237-239.
Carnot, M. ix. 311-313, 387; x. 64, 99, 264, 276, 279; xi. 38; xii. 427; xv. 75, 312-317, 388, 401, 403, 410, 412-414; xvi. 45-47.
Caroline, Princess of Wales (afterwards Queen of England), ii. 285, 286, 305, 329, 337. See also xix. 190, et seq.; xxvi. 27.
Carr's, Sir John, ' Caledonian Sketches,' Review of, xix. 180-184.
Carmsies, Principal, xxiv. 359-361.
Cartaux, General, ix. 175, 346, 348, 350; x. 171, note.
Carteret, Lord, Viceroy of Ireland, ii. 262, 264, 327-332.
Cassilis, Earl of, and the Abbot of Crossraguel, xix. 224; xxiii. 154, 155.
Castanos, General, xiii. 143, 150, 151.
' Castle Dangerous,' germ of the novel of, vi. 36, 37; xxii. 133, 134.
' Castle of Otranto,' notice of, iii. 307, 318-324.
Castlemain, Lady, mistress of Charles II.; xx. 112-115.
Castlereagh, Robert Viscount, afterwards Marquis of Londonderry, xv. 8, 9, 119, 218, 219.
Caulaincourt, General, Duke of Vicenza, xii. 9, 259; xiv. 125, 215, 217, 311, 333-4; xv. 92-105, 172, 176,

178, 180, 199-209, 213, 215-222; xvi. 45, 46.

Caulincourt, General Augustus, xiv. 101, 104.

Celts in Gaul, manners of the, xxvii. 9; religion, 10; government, 11.

——, supposed inferiority of the, to the Goths, xx. 320, et seq.

Chabrol, Comte de, xiv. 260.

Chalmers, George, his edition of Sir David Lindsay's Works, vi. 272; his 'Caledonia,' vii. 5, 7, 19, 23, 25, 26, 27, 60, 388-390; his Apology for the believers in the forged Shakspeare MSS. xx. 218; his hypothesis respecting the ancient inhabitants of Scotland, 326, 335, 344.

Champagny, Duke of Cadore, xii. 115; xiii. 46, 47, 123, 126-128; xiv. 25, note.

Champ Aubert, battle of, xv. 56-58.

Chandos, Sir John, xxviii. 161-170.

Chantilly, description of, in 1815, v. 207-213; ancient state of, xxi. 93, 94.

Chantry Mr (now Sir Francis), the Sculptor, partiality of, for salmon fishing, xx. 277.

Charles Martel, Duke of Austrasia, xxvii. 66-70.

Charlemagne, the Emperor, xxvii. 72-77.

Charles the Fat, the Emperor, xxvii. 81-88.

—— the Simple, King of France, reign of, xxvii. 90-102.

Charles IV. (the Fair), King of France, xxvii. 378-382.

—— V. (the Wise), King of France, xxviii. 135-200.

—— VI. (the Well beloved), King of France, xxviii. 201-281.

—— of Anjou, brother of St Louis, xxvii. 311, 317, 325, 326, 331; becomes King of Naples and Sicily, 336-340, 348, 350.

—— the Bad, King of Navarre, xxviii. 93-96, 110, 111, 117, 125, 129, 197-199.

—— de Blois, xxvii. 16-25, 70, 71, 136, 138.

—— I. of England, i. 9; ix. 46-49; xxiii. 345; xxiv. 70.

—— II. of England, i. 36, 57, 58, 96, 173, 180, 205, 212, 215, 243, 249, 250; vii. 290, 309-313; xix. 256; xx. 110, 111, 135-142; xxiv. 170-270.

—— XII. of Sweden, scheme of, for invading Scotland, xxv. 428.

—— Edward, Prince (the Young Pretender), character of, xix. 353; his interview with Macdonald and Macleod, 355; with Lochiel, 356; vindication of him from the charge of cowardice preferred by the Chevalier Johnstone, 357-367; sketch of his campaign in 1745-6, xx. 3-9; his interview with Lord Lovat, 83; his early years, xxvi. 58-70; his expedition to Scotland in 1745-

1746, 74-375; his latter days, 415-424.
Charles IV. King of Spain, xiii. 19-57.
—— X. of France, residence of, at Holyrood House, vii. 294.
——. Archduke, of Austria, x. 98, 100. 198-207, 211-218; xi. 128; xii. 41, 68-71; xiii. 175, 176-183, 187, 195-198, 208-213.
Chateaubriand, Vicomte de, xv. 102.
Chatterton, Thomas, 'The Works of, with his Life by Dr Gregory,' edited by Messrs Southey and Cottle, Review of, xvii. 215-241.
Chaucer, Geoffrey, Review of Godwin's Life of, xvii. 55, 80.
——, indecency of his 'Canterbury Tales,' vi. 42.
'Chester Mysteries,' notice of, vi. 367, 371.
Chesterfield, Philip, Earl of, xix. 208.
Chevalier de St George (the old Pretender), xxiv. 314; xxv. 129, 269, 408-421; xxvi. 55-60.
CHIVALRY, Essay on, vi. 1; sense in which here treated of, 3; origin of, 6;—I. nature and spirit of the order, 10, 49;—II. its institutions; the Page, 50; the Squire, 55; Knighthood, 65; mode of conferring, 66; privileges, 74; duties, 79; distinctions, 88-94; associations, 98; mode of degradation, 104;—III. causes of decay and extinction of, 106, 126—See also, xxvii. 123-129.
'Chrysal, or Adventures of a Guinea,' remarks on, iii. 430-440.
Cibber, Colley, an extravagant admirer of Richardson's novels, iii. 18.
Cid, 'Chronicle of the, translated by Southey,' Review of, xviii. 44, 73.
Cintra, Convention of, xiii. 119, 121.
Cisalpine Republic, x. 178, 242, 247; xi. 208; converted into the kingdom of Italy, xii. 26.
Cispadane Republic, x. 177.
Ciudad Rodrigo, storming of, xiv. 23.
Civilisation, Progress of, xxiii. 215, 234.
Clan Act, xxv. 262-3.
Clanship, system of, on the Borders, vii. 47, 57; account of the Border clans, 148, 153; system of, in the Highlands, xx. 17, 51.
Clan Chattan and Clan Kay, conflict between, xxii. 243, 246.
Claret, epigram on, by John Home, xix. 331, note.
'Clarissa Harlowe,' remarks on, iii. 38, 49.
Clarke, General, Duke of Feltre, ix. 320; x. 168, 219-20; xv. 342.
——, Jeremiah, the original composer of the music to Dryden's Alexander's feast, i. 346.
Clausel, General, xv. 364, 365.

Claxton, Lawrence, a remarkable fanatic, xviii. 85, 89.
Clean the Causeway skirmish, xxii. 382-385.
Cleland, Colonel William, xxiv. 276, 353, 386.
' Cleomenes,' by Dryden, i. 308.
Clerk, John, of Eldin, ' Essay on Naval Tactics,' xii. 101.
Cleveland the poet, cause of death of, i. 35.
Clifford, Martin, Master of the Charter House, i. 116, 131.
Clifton, skirmish of, xxvi. 238.
Clisson, Oliver de, Constable of France, xxviii. 197, 230-232, 235-240, 246-249.
Clovis, King of the Franks, reign of, xxvii. 55-63.
Cobentzel, Count, x. 251, 252; xi. 129.
Cochran, Sir Robert, favourite of James III., xxii. 311, 315, 318-323.
Cochrane, Sir John, xxiv. 263, 273, 275-278.
——, Thomas, Lord, now Earl of Dundonald, xiii. 279.
Cockburn, Admiral Sir George, xvi. 108, 131-136, 145, 146, 176-182.
Cockups, a part of female head-dress in Scotland, xix. 217.
Code Napoleon (Civil Code), xi. 180, 181; xii. 316-336.
Collier, Jeremy, attack of, on the stage, i. 358-360; vi. 363.
Colman, George, the Younger, and John Kemble, quarrel between, xx. 215.
Coma Vigil, remarks on by D'Israeli, iii. 158, note.

Comedy, French, character of, i. 60; contrasted with the Spanish, 63.
' Complaynt of Scotland,' edited by Dr Leyden, iv. 166.
Comte, M., Editor of the *Censeur*, xv. 390, 391.
Concordat of Buonaparte with Pope Pius VII., xi. 174, 177.
Confederation of the Rhine, xii. 140-142.
Congress of Prague, xiv. 332-335; xv. 4, 5.
—— Mannheim, xv. 8.
—— Vienna, xv. 333-335 367-370.
—— Chatillon, xv. 45-55, 60, 64, 91-105.
Congreve, William, the dramatist, i. 314; Dryden's lines to, 322, 324; his character of Dryden, 375; Swift's relations with, ii. 136, 311.
' Conquest of Granada,' by Dryden, i. 94.
Conrad III., the Emperor, xxvii. 198, 200-202, 207-208.
Conscription, French system of, xii. 368-373.
Constable, Archibald, bookseller, iv. 154, 225; his ' Memoirs of George Heriot,' vii. 262, note.
Constant, Benjamin, xv. 342 398; xvi. 50.
Consular government established in France, xi. 30; outline of the system, 40-52.
Cope, General Sir John, xix. 298, 299 301; xxvi. 91, 92, 97-101, 118, 131-176.
Copenhagen, battle of, xi. 190;

British expedition against in 1807; xii. 289-297.

Copsewood, or *sylva caedua*, mode of cultivating, xxi. 54-60.

Casbineau, General, xiv. 353, 354.

Corneille, i. 101; vi. 294, *et seq.*

Coinuel, Archibald, remarkable case of, xxi. 246.

Corsica separated from France, ix. 337-339; reunited to it, x. 129.

Corunna, battle of, xiii. 160, 161.

Cossacks, the, xii. 226.

Coster, J. B. de, relation of what Napoleon did and said at the battle of Waterloo, v. 341-345.

'Count Robert of Paris,' foundation of the romance of, vi. 47; xxviii. 169, 171.

Covenant, National, xxiii. 358; Solemn League and, 381.

Coventry act, occasion of the, 176.

Craigmillar castle, description of, vii. 363.

Craon, Peter de, xxviii. 220, 235-240, 248.

Cravone, battle of, xv. 110.

Creech, William, 'Comparative View of Edinburgh,' by, vii. 231; xix. 176.

Creed, Mrs, i. 371; Dryden's lines on, 433.

Crichton, Captain John, ii. 346; xix. 30, 34, 46; xxiv. 218-220, 373, 374.

Cressy, battle of, xix. 132-138; xxviii. 57-66.

Crichton castle, description of, vii. 157; history of the family of Crichton, 158-173; and the subsequent owners of the castle, 173-195.

'Critical Review,' originally edited by Dr Smollett, iii. 142.

Criticism, anonymous, the advantages of, in England, iii. 219, 220.

Croker, Right Hon. John Wilson, character of Swift by, ii. 271; his explanation of Dr Johnson's dislike of Swift, 425; extracts from his edition of Boswell's Life of Johnson, iii. 262, *note, et passim*; Review of his 'Battle of Talavera, a poem,' xvii. 291-300; Review of the 'Countess of Suffolk's Correspondence,' edited by, xix. 185-212; his 'Stories from the History of England,' xxii. viii.; his answer to Malachi Malagrowther, xxi. 269, 332, *note.*

Cromarty, Earl of, xxvi. 311-315, 377, 380, 382, 384.

Cromek, R. H., 'Reliques of Robert Burns,' Review of, xvii. 242-266.

Cromwell, Oliver, vii. 210, xxiv. 38-147.

———, Richard, xxiv. 148-150

Crusades, origin of the, xxvii. 157; the First, 163-179; the Second, 197-209; the Third, 243-252; against the Albigenses, 282-285, 293, 294, 298, 299; against Egypt, 311-327; Eighth and last, against Tunis, 335, 336, 339-341

INDEX. 301

Caesta, General, xiii. 83, 138, 282, 283.
Culloden, battle of, xxvi. 337-347.
——— Papers, with an Introductory memoir of Lord President Forbes,' review of. xx. 1-93.
Calm, battle of, xiv. 353.
Cumberland, Frederick Duke of, xix. 8, 351, 352; xx. 87; xxvi. 224-240, 257-359.
CUMBERLAND, RICHARD, BIOGRAPHICAL NOTICE OF, iii. 191; remarks on his novels, 'Arundel,' 'Henry,' and 'John de Lancaster,' 221-225; Review of his 'John de Lancaster,' xviii. 138-157.
CURRENCY, LETTERS OF MALACHI MALAGROWTHER ON THE PROPOSED CHANGE OF THE, as affecting Scotland, xxi. 267-402.
Czernicheff, Prince, xiv. 176, 293, 302, 304, 305, 376, 410; xv. 137, 224.

Dalkeith, description of the town and palace of, vii. 216; the successive possessors of the palace; the Grahames, 217; the Douglasses, 218; the Scotts, 224.
Dalrymple. *See Stair.*
Dalziel, General Thomas, xxiv. 202-206, 209, 250, 251.
Damietta, capture of, by St Louis, xxvii. 312; restored to the Saracens, 325.
Danish ballad, translated by Mr Herbert, xvii. 110.

Danton, the French revolutionist, vii. 351; ix. 218, 230-239.
Dantzic, siege and capture of, by the French, xii. 245; made a free city, 266; surrendered by the French, xiv. 416, 417.
Danube, passage of the, xiii. 196.
Darien scheme, history of the, xxv. 26-47.
Darnley, Henry (Stewart) Lord, husband of Queen Mary, xxiii. 98-118.
Daru, Count, xii. 105, *note*, xiv. 135, 196.
Dauphin, the, title of the first-born male-heir to the crown of France, xxviii. 69.
Davenant, Sir William, i. 38, 50, 66, 98, 117; vi. 351, 352.
David I., King of Scotland, reign of, xxi. 180-182; xxii. 41-51.
——— II., xxii. 195, 202, 222-229.
Davidoff, Colonel, xiv. 129.
Davidowich, the Austrian general, x. 113-116, 134-147.
Davoust, Marshal, Duke of Auerstadt, Prince of Eckmuhl, xii. 51, 77, 79, 169, 172-174, 231, 241; xiii. 177, 178, 182, 207; xiv. 8, 11, 42, 100, 148, 156, 159, 161, 169, 188, 190, 194, 231, 294, 302, 378; xv. 346, 417, 418; xvi. 45, 48, 63, 64.
Davy's, Sir Humphry, 'Salmonia, or Days of Flyfishing,' Review of, xx. 245-300.

INDEX.

Day, Thomas, author of 'Sandford and Merton,' notice of, iv. 214, note.

DEFOE, DANIEL, BIOGRAPHICAL SKETCH OF, iv. 228-281; his account of the apparition of Mrs Veal, 288-296; his Dialogue between a soldier and countryman, xix. 41, 42.

Delany, Rev. Dr Patrick, ii. 241, 336-341, 401-403.

Dennewitz, battle of, xiv. 364-366.

Dennis, John, the critic, i. 157; ii. 163.

Denon, M. x. 382, 384; xv. 58; xvi. 251.

D'Erlon, General, xv. 418, 428, 432; xvi. 6.

Derwentwater, Earl of, xxv. 293-388.

Desaix, General, x. 305, 313, 374, 382; xi. 109-102, 115-117.

Desfontaine's, the Abbé, French translation of Gulliver's Travels, ii. 303; his continuation of them, 304.

Desgenettes, Dr, x. 369-372.

'Devil on two Sticks,' by Le Sage, remarks on, iii. 401-407.

Devonshire, William Duke of, author of the best poem on the death of Queen Mary, i. 344.

Diaries, private, more sincere than letters, xx. 97.

Dirleton Castle, description of, vii. 405.

Djezzar, Pasha of Syria, x. 355, 358, 359, 362-364; x. 246.

Dombrowsky, General, xii. 222; xiv. 175, 178.

Donald of the Hammer, xxiii. 312-321.

——— of the Isles, xxii. 235.

'Don Quixote,' English translations of, iii. 139-141.

'Don Sebastian,' by Dryden, i. 303.

Dorset, Thomas, Earl of, i. 96, 314.

———, Mrs, Memoir of Mrs Charlotte Smith by, iv. 20-58.

Douglas, the good Lord James of, xxii. 128-144, 164-176.

———, Sir William, Knight of Liddesdale, xxii. 203, 204, 210, 212, 218, 223-225.

———, William, Earl of, xxii. 231, 233.

———, James, Earl of, xxii. 236-240.

———, Archibald, Earl of, xxii. 247, 249-251, 259-261.

———, Archibald, Earl of, xxii. 278, 279.

———, William, Earl of, xxii. 279, 280.

———, James the Gross, Earl of, xxii. 281.

———, William, Earl of, xxii. 281, 293.

———, James, Earl of, xxii. 294-302.

———, Greatness of the ancient house of, vii. 428-430; elevation of the younger (Angus) branch on its ruins, 431-438; its fall, xxiii. 12 (See Angus—See Morton).

———, Archibald of Kilspindie, xxiii. 9, 13, 14.

Douglas, Marquis of, xxiv. 353.
——, Duke of, xxv. 362.
——, Rev. Robert, and Archbishop Sharp, anecdote of, xix. 239.
——,' first representation of the tragedy of, xix. 310-316; remarks on its merits, 342-348.
Doune Castle, imprisonment of John Home and his companions in, and escape from, xix. 305-7; xxvi. 273. *note.*
Drake, Francis, British Envoy at Munich, xi. 343-4.
DRAMA, ESSAY ON THE, vi. 217; the Grecian, 222; the Roman, 258; Modern, 266; the Mysteries and Moralities, 267; Historical Drama, 275; Romantic Drama, 278; Spanish Comedies of Intrigue, 280; Italian Operas. 286; Italian Comedies, 287; France, revival of the regular drama, 293; Corneille, 294; discussion of the three unities, 297-315; proscription of comic scenes in tragedy, 316; impertinent love scenes 319; Racine, 324; Voltaire, 325; French comedy —Molière, 328; English drama, *first period,* 332; Shakspeare, 336; Ben Jonson, 338; Massinger, 342; Beaumont and Fletcher, 343; *second period,* 352; Heroic plays, 353; Comedy —the 'Rehearsal,' 355; Tragedy—Otway, Lee, &c. 356; indecency of the drama at this period, 357; Comic authors, 360; effect of Collier's attack on the stage, 363; *third period*—effect of criticism—decay of the art, 365; domestic Tragedy —Lillo, 370; genteel comedy, 372; English opera, 374; *fourth period*—Garrick's revivals of Shakspeare's plays, 376; Horace Walpole—Home, 378; Sheridan—Goldsmith—Colman, 379; new impulse from Germany, 381; comparison of French and German dramas, 382-386; present state— Authors, 387; Actors, 388; evil influence of the monopoly of the two great theatres, 389.
'Dramatic Poetry, Essay on,' by Dryden, i. 77.
'Drapier's Letters,' by Dean Swift, ii. 237, 267, 268.
Dresden, battle of, xiv. 344-347.
Driden, John, of Chesterton, cousin to the poet, i. 313; Dryden's epistle to him, 362-364.
Drouet, General, xv. 230.
Druids, the, xxvii. 10.
Drumclog, battle of, xxiv. 240, 241.
Drummond, William, of Hawthornden, vindication of, from Mr Gifford's attack, on account of his character of Ben Jonson, vii. 374-382.
——, Sir John, xxiii. 390.
——, Lord, xxiii. 390.
——, James, Lord, xxv. 155, 252, 255, 356.

Drummond, Lord John, xxvi. 63, 228, 249-253, 264-266, 293, 295, 298, 299, 310, 310, 325, 335. See Perth.
———, Captain, afterwards Provost of Edinburgh, xxvi. 124, 137, 138.

DRYDEN, JOHN, LIFE OF, 1; the poet's ancestors, 16; his parents, 17; his brothers and sisters, 19; his birth, 20; early education, 21; studies at Cambridge, 22; patronized by Sir G. Pickering, 27, and Sir John Dryden, 29; his Elegy on the death of Cromwell, 31; his 'Astræa Redux,' a poem on Charles II.'s restoration, 40; reduced in circumstances, 43; connexion with Sir Robert Howard, 44; made a Fellow of the Royal Society, 46; his 'Annus Mirabilis,' 49; begins writing for the stage, 67; habits of life induced by his success, 73; his marriage with Lady Elizabeth Howard, 74; domestic unhappiness, 76; his 'Essay on Dramatic Poetry,' 77; and consequent quarrel with Sir R. Howard, 82; his contract with the players, 85; his 'Maiden Queen,' 88; 'Tempest,' 89; 'Sir Martin Mar-all,' 90; 'Mock Astrologer,' 91; 'Royal Martyr,' 93; 'Conquest of Granada,' 94; 'Essay on Heroic Plays,' 95; great change in his situation and fortunes, 96; created poet-laureat and royal historiographer, 98; ridiculed in 'The Rehearsal,' 114; Controversies in which he was engaged, 127; that with Clifford, 131; with Leigh and others, 133; with Ravenscroft, 137; his situation in 1674, 151; his quarrel with Lord Rochester, 154; and with Settle, Rochester's instrument, 171; waylaid and beaten by Lord Rochester's bravoes, 175; revolution in his dramatic taste, 181; his projected epic, 184; circumstances which led him to engage in politics, 204; 'Absalom and Achitophel,' 208; 'The Medal,' 215; 'Mac-Flecknoe,' 228; 'Absalom and Achitophel, Part II.,' 230; effect of these satires on English poetry, 238; influence of his political controversies on his fortune, 251; 'Threnodia Augustalis,' a poem on the accession of James II., 256; becomes a Roman Catholic, 260; receives an additional pension from the King, 278; his controversy with Stillingfleet, 277; 'the Hind and the Panther,' 278; his attack on Burnet, 280; answers to the 'Hind and Panther,' 282; storm raised against him at the Revolution of 1688, 297; deprived of his places, 300; resumes writing for the stage, 303; complete list of his plays, 312; his social connexions after the Revolution, 313; his friendship with Southerne and Congreve, 315; origin of Swift's enmity to, 318; his translation of 'Juvenal and Persius,' 319; Elegy on the Countess of Abingdon, 320; contributions to Tonson's 'third Miscellany,' 321; his translation of 'Virgil,' 325; his quarrel with Tonson, 329; attack upon his Virgil, by Milbourne, 336; his reply to Milbourne, 342; his version of Du Fresnoy's 'Art of Painting,' 343; his 'Alexander's Feast,' Ode for St Cecilia's Day, 344; his intended version of Homer, 350; his 'Fables,' 352; his controversies with Blackmore and Collier, 354; 'his Epistle to his cousin, Driden of Chesterton,' 362; his Secular Masque, 367; his last illness, 370; death and funeral, 371; his personal appearance, 373; Character of him by Congreve, 365; habits of life, 382; manners when in company, 385; his residence, 389; fate of his wife and three sons, 390; his collateral relations, 396; literary reputation at his death and afterwards, 397; Johnson's comparison of him and Pope, 402; characteristic of his genius, 406; his versification, 410; his character as a dramatist, 412; as a lyric poet, 415; as a satirist, 417; as a narrative poet, 420; as a philosophical and miscellaneous poet, 427; as a poetical translator, 434; as a prose writer, 444; as a critic, 447; Summary of his merits, 453.

Dryfe Sands, battle of, xxiii. 284-286.

Dubois, Edward, his 'My Pocket Book,' a Satire on Sir John Carr, xix. 160.

Dubois Crancé, French minister of war, xi. 37.

Ducos, Roger, third Consul of France, xi. 30, 41, 42.

Duffus, Lord, xxv. 252.

Dugommier, General, ix. 350, 354, 355, 360; xvi. 408.

'Duke of Guise,' by Dryden, i. 242.

Dumfries, loyalty of, to the government, in 1715, xxv. 290, 291; punished for it, by the rebel army in 1745, xxvi. 247.

Dumouriez, General, viii. 292-3, 299, 302. 384, 395; ix. 82-84, 96, 97, 100, 101.

Dunbar Castle, description of, vii. 410.

——, siege of, xxii. 212-215.

——, battle of, xxiv. 94.

Dunbarton Castle, surprise of, by Crawford of Jordan-hill, xxiii. 143-145.

Dundee, storming of, by General Monk, xxiv. 105.

——, capture of by the Pretender in 1745. xxvi. 110.

—— fidelity of, to the Government, 213.

——, Viscount. See Grahame.

Dunnotter castle, siege of, vii. 320-333; xxiv. 106-108; a prison for covenanters, 283-285.

806   INDEX.

Dunton, John, i. 332, *note*; li. 26, *note*.
Dupont, General, defeat and capitulation of, at Baylen, xiii. 86-94; minister of war to Louis XVIII., xv. 275.
Dupplin, battle of, xxii. 200.
Durand, Col., his weak defence of Carlisle, in 1745, xxvi. 209.
Duroc, Marshal, Duke of Friuli, xi. 121; xii. 8, 242, 259; xiv. 196, 215, 310, 311; xvi. 407.

Eckmuhl, battle of, xii. 178.
EDINBURGH, GENERAL Account of, vii. 236; High Street of, 243; view of from Braid Hills, 247; Castle from the Grassmarket, 257; Heriot's Hospital, 261; view of from the Glasgow road, 272; from Corstorphine hill, 275; from the Calton hill, 276; entrance to Leith harbour, 280; Holyrood house, 283; view of from St Anthony's chapel, 296.
Edmonstone, Miss Robina, of Cambuswallace, anecdote of, xxvi. 120, *note*.
Education, system of, in France under Napoleon, xii. 361.
Edward I. of England, a crusader, xxvii. 340; his first appearance in France, 346; his contests with Philip the Fair, and with the Scots, 354-361; his conduct towards, and proceedings in Scotland, to possess himself of that kingdom, xxii. 66-129.

Edward II. of England, contest of with Robert Bruce, xxii. 129-163; his connexion with France, xxvii. 380, 381.
—— III. of England, his contests with and invasions of Scotland, xxii. 163-228; his disputes with Philip de Valois and his successors, Kings of France, xxvii. 381, 382, and xxviii. 3-133.
—— the Black Prince, at the battle of Cressy, xxviii. 56, 63, 64; lieutenant of his father in Gascony, 95; great victory of, at Poitiers, 97-108; supports Don Pedro the Cruel, 144-147; cause of his unpopularity with the Gascons, 149; summoned to do homage, 155; commences war against France, 158; his death, 178.
—— IV. of England, xxiii. 319, 323.
—— Baliol, King of Scotland, xxii. 197.
Eguilles, Marquis d', xxvi. 193, 221, *et seq.*
Egypt, French expedition to under Buonaparte, x. 298, 304-388.
——, British expedition to, xi. 191-195.
——, in 1807, xii. 288.
Elba, isle of, assigned to Napoleon as his seat of empire, xv. 215; his residence there from May 4, 1814, to Feb. 26, 1815, 242-337.
Elcho, Lord, xxiii. 390, 391.
——, Lord, xxvi. 65, 139-141, 184-188, 190-191.

INDEX. 307

Eleanor of Aquitaine, Queen of Louis VII. of France, afterwards of Henry II. of England, xxvi. 195, 199, 207, 213, 216, 229, 264, 265.

Elgin, the Earl of, Buonaparte's conduct to, xi. 346-351.

Elibank, Patrick, Lord, anecdotes of, xix. 335-337; xxvi. 420, 421.

Elizabeth, Queen of England, transactions of her reign, in connexion with Scotland, xxiii. 74-208; anecdotes of her latter days, 237-241.

Elizabethan architecture, character of, xxi. 94, 95.

Ellis, George, the friend of Dr Leyden, iv. 175, 176; Review of his ' Specimens of the Early English Poets,' xvii. 1-15; Review of his ' Specimens of Early English Metrical Romances,' 16-54; his notes to Way's translation of the *Fabliaux*, xviii. 49.

———, Henry, interview of, with Buonaparte at St Helena in 1817, xvi. 262-265, and 387-393.

Empress of Morocco,' a play, by E. Settle, i. 159-161.

Enghien, the Duke of, seizure and execution of by Buonaparte's orders, xi. 317-332, 371-394.

England, Norman Conquest of, xxvii. 138-151.

———, views of parties in, with regard to the French Revolution, viii. 253-261; events by which war was excited between and France, 127-135; relative situation of the two countries in 1797, x. 285; French Government assembles an army for the invasion of, 287; idle demonstration against, 297; invasion of, postponed, 303; Napoleon's renewed plans for the invasion of, xii. 98-100.

English drama, state of, prior to the Restoration, i. 55; change produced by that event, 58; state of the theatres, 66; history of the, vi. 283, 284, 332-395.

——— language, Swift's proposal for establishing a standard for the, ii. 130-134; interest in tracing the rise and progress of, xvii. 1.

——— poetry, state of, during the first half of the 17th century, i. 4-16; changes in the public taste for, at the Restoration, 33-39.

——— Romances of Chivalry, notice of, vi. 203-209.

——— Satirists, Early, remarks on, i. 238.

Entraigues, the Count d', x. 272.

Erfurt, conferences between the Emperors Napoleon and Alexander at, xiii. 134.

Ericke, Abigail, mother of Dean Swift, ii. 5, 12.

Errol, Earl of, xxv. 155.

' Essay on Dramatic Poetry,' by Dryden, i. 77.

' ——— on Satire,' by Dryden, i. 319.

' ——— on Satire,' by Lord Mulgrave, i. 171; Dryden at first suspected to be the

author, 174; who is assaulted in consequence, by Lord Rochester's bravoes, 175.
'Essay on Chivalry,' vi. 1.
—— on the Drama,' vi. 217.
—— on Romance,' vi. 127.
—— on Border Antiquities,' vii. 1.
Eseling, battle of, xiii. 201.
Etherege, his poetry, i. 36.
Etruria, Queen of, treatment of by Buonaparte, xiii. 24, 373, 374.
Eudes, Count of Paris, xxvii. 83-85; elected King of France, 89.
Eugene, Prince, Viceroy of Italy. See Beauharnais.
Euphuism, influence of, on the English language, temp. Eliz. i. 5.
Europe, state of, after the peace of Versailles (1783), viii. 2-16.
Evans, Thomas, 'Old Ballads,' revised by his son, R. H. Evans,' Review of, xvii. 119-130.
Evelyn, John, contrast between the Memoirs of, and those of Samuel Pepys, xx. 107.
Evening's Love, a comedy,' by Dryden, i. 91.
'Examiner,' by Swift, ii. 113.
Excelmans, General, xv. 335, 339, 418, 434; xvi. 67.
Excommunication, danger of publishing letters of, against a feudal Baron, vii. 202-206.
'Eyrbiggia-Saga, Abstract of the, or Annals of a district of Iceland, &c. v. 355-413; remarks on an

incident in, vi. 25-6; xvii. 26.

Falkirk, battles of, xxii. 89, 92; xxvi. 261-276.
Faulkner, George, a Dublin bookseller, notice of, and his edition of Swift's works, ii. 362-370.
Farquhar, the dramatist, his ludicrous account of Dryden's funeral, i. 372, note.
Farquharson's of Deeside, cruel treatment of, by the Marquis of Huntly, xxii. 324-327.
Farquharson of Invercauld, xxv 250; xxvi. 292.
—— of Monaltry, xxvi. 254, 324.
Fast-castle, Description of, vii. 446.
Ferdinand IV, King of Naples, x. 84, 187, 188, 391, 392; xi. 133, 134, 139-141, 143, 144; xii. 91-94.
——, Prince of Asturias, afterwards Ferdinand VII, King of Spain, xiii. 9, 10, 19-54, 378, 379; xiv. 422-427.
——, Archduke of Austria, xii. 46, 56.
' —— Count Fathom,' remarks on, iii. 136.
Fergusson, Dr Adam, anecdotes of, xix. 331.
Ferriar, Dr. of Manchester, notice of his Illustrations on the writings of Sterne, iii. 292-298.
Fesch, Cardinal, ix. 323; xiii. 404, 405.
Feudal System, introduced into England by the Normans, vii. 40; xxii. 28-30; intro-

duction of, into Scotland, xxi. 178; establishment of, in France, xxvii. 91-96.

FIELDING, HENRY, BIOGRAPHICAL NOTICE OF, iii. 76-119; remarks on his 'Joseph Andrews,' 94; on 'Tom Jones,' 103-110; on 'Amelia,' 111; parallel between him and Richardson, 86; between him and Smollett, 171.

Findlater, Earl of. See Seafield.

Fisheries, Northern, importance of the, xxi. 352, 381, 382.

Flanders, Visit to, in 1815. first impressions of the country and people, v. 6-11; field of Waterloo, 146; agriculture, 166; forests, 169; political state, 170; religion, 173; commerce, 177; kind treatment of the English, 179; furniture and domestic implements, 181.

Flodden, battle of, xxii. 365-371.

Flecknoe, Richard, a wretched poet, i. 228.

Fly-fishing, picture of the delights of, xx. 231.

Forbes, Duncan, Lord President of the Court of Session, character of, xx. 60, 63, 64; his conduct in 1715 and subsequently, 69-72; services of, in the rebellion of 1745, 81; danger of his position, 82; most ungratefully rewarded, 85-87; xxvi. 94, 95, 194-201.

Forester's Guide. See *Planting*.

Forster, Thomas, a leader in the rebellion of 1715, xxv. 293-297, 310, 320-322-366, 370-384, 386.

Fouage, or tax on chimneys, xxviii. 149-173.

Fouché, Joseph, Duke of Otranto, xi. 9-16, 63-69, 166-171, 190; xiii. 22, 23, 263-266, 305-317, 400-403; xvi. 311-313, 323; xv. 18-29, 156-292, 318-322, 346, 350-352, 410-412; xvi. 28-43, 45, 46, 48-50, 52-58, 61-64, 88-90. See also v. 30-66, 310-314.

Fox, Charles James, xi. 146-152.

FRANCE, HISTORY OF, xxvii. Chap. I.—Gaul to Cæsar's conquest, 7-18.—Ch. ii. Roman Gaul, to the invasion of Rhadagaisus in 407, 26.—Ch. iii. Barbarian invasions including that of Attila, 40.—Ch. iv. Clovis, and his successors of the Merovingian race.—Pepin, and his successors of the Carlovingian dynasty, to Charles the Fat, 54. —Ch. v. Eudes, to Louis the Fainéant—extinction of the Carlovingian line, 89.—Ch. vi. Third Race: Hugo Capet; Robert, Henry I. 108.—Ch. vii. Minority of Philip I. 122.—Ch. viii. Norman conquest of England, 136.—Ch. ix. Philip I.; Louis VI. 152. —Ch. x. Louis VI. 160.— Ch. xi. Louis VII.—Ch. xii. Philip II.—Ch. xiii. Louis VIII. and IX. 296. —Ch. xiv. Louis IX.— Philip III. 330.—Ch. xv

310 INDEX.

Philip IV., Louis X., Philip V., Charles IV., 353.—Ch. xvi. xvii. xviii. Philip VI., xxviii. l. 46, 67.—Ch. xix. xx. John, 91.—Ch. xxi. xxii. xxiii. Charles V., 135, 151, 177.—Ch. xxiv. xxv. xxvi. Charles VI. 201, 233, 259.

Francis I. Emperor of Germany, afterwards of Austria, xii. 83, 84, 142; xiii. 186; xiv. 388, 403; xv. 64-84, 136-172, 409.

Francis Xavier, St. Life of, translated by Dryden, i. 290.

Franks, the, founders of the kingdom of France, xxvii. 37-44, 54; institutions of, 50-62.

Franck's, Richard, 'Northern Memoirs,' notice of, xx. 277.

Fraser of Gortuleg, xxvi. 93, et seq.

—— of Lovat. See Lovat.

——, General (Son of Lord Lovat), xxvi. 198, 199.

——, James Baillie, 'the Kuzzilbash,' a novel by, notice of, xviii. 393.

Frederick Prince of Wales, anecdote of, xxvi. 398.

—— William III. King of Prussia, xii. 166-171, 173, 174, 185-191, 192-215, 234, 235, 244-261, 274, 275; xiv. 7-12, 272-276, 297-334, 403-417; xv. 182, 318-408.

Free Companies, xxviii. 140, 221-224.

French drama, history of the, vi. 282, 293-331.

—— secondary actors, great superiority of, to the English, xx. 211.

French romances of chivalry, notice of, vi. 199-203.

—— Revolution, Preliminary View of, viii. and ix. 1-317; State of Europe, and of France previous to, viii. 1-72; proximate causes of, the deranged state of the finances, &c. 73-108; the meeting of the States General, 5th May 1789, the first day of the, 109; the National Assembly, 121; the Tennis-court oath, 124-127; parties in the assembly, 128-136; influence of the Duke of Orleans, 138; dismissal of Necker, 140; defection of the military, 141; taking of the Bastile, 148; departure of the Princes, 155; renunciations of the privileged classes, 158; abolition of tithes, 161; banquet of the body guard, 168; march of the Parisian mob to Versailles, 171; removal of the royal family to Paris, 181; Lafayette's firm conduct, 194; abolition of titles of honour, armorial bearings, &c., 200; confiscation of church property, 204; creation of the assignats, 206; constitution for the clergy, 208; abolition of the parliaments, 212; establishment of freedom of the press, and universal religious toleration, 213; limitation of the royal authority, 214-218; the King accepts the constitution, 219; his flight to Varennes, and recapture, 228-232; Lafayette's victory over the mob in the Champ de Mars, 234; dissolution of the assembly, 240; the LEGISLATIVE ASSEMBLY, 243; division of opinions in England and on the continent, 253-267; emigration of the French nobility, 268; motives of the different parties for desiring war, 276; the King refuses his assent to two decrees, 278; dissensions in the cabinet, 281; declaration of war against Austria, 287; Dumouriez minister at war, 293; his bold conduct in the assembly, 302; his resignation, 303; insurrection of June 1792, 305-312; the Girondists bring the Federates to Paris, 321; effect of the Duke of Brunswick's manifesto, 325; massacres of the 10th of August, 328-346; evasion of Lafayette and his companions, 348; the Jacobin triumvirate, Danton, Robespierre, and Marat, 351-355; the Revolutionary Tribunal, 357; timidity of the Legislative Assembly, 360; the September massacres in the prisons, 364-372; apathy and panic of the Girondists 375; dissolution of the Assembly, 377; the NATIONAL CONVENTION, 379; change of the monarchy into a republic, 382; unfortunate campaign of the Duke of Brunswick, 383-388; lamentable situation of the French emigrants, 389; successes of the republicans on the frontiers, 394-397; resumé of the King's past conduct—his universal unpopularity, ix. 1-8; remarks on the new form of government, 11-21; effects of the change, 22-27; state of parties in the Convention, 30; mutual jealousy of the triumvirs, 33; public measures of the Girondists, 35; report of committee on grounds for accusing the King, 42; resolution to bring him to trial, 53; treatment of the royal family in the Temple, 58-60; trial of the King, 64; his condemnation, 79; his execution, 87; trial and execution of the Queen, and the Princess Elizabeth, 89-92; death of the Dauphin, 93; projects of Dumouriez, 95; his escape to the Austrians, 100; ascendancy of the Jacobins; decree of accusation against the Girondists, 116; their fate, 121-126; sensation produced in England by the late events, 128; the Convention declares war against England, 134; state of the war on the different French frontiers, 136-140; the war in La Vendée, 1793-1796, 141-173; insurrections of the cities of the south of France, 173-187; the REIGN OF TERROR, 190, the Committee of Public Safety, 195; the law against suspected persons, 196; the Revolutionary Tribunal, 199; death of Marat, 217; public profession of Atheism, 221; marriage made a mere civil contract, 223; commencement of spirit of reaction, 227; execution of Hebert and others, 229; fall of Danton, 231-238; growing unpopularity of Robespierre, 247; symptoms of his approaching fall, 254; decree of arrest against him, 265; his death and that of his accomplices, 271; suspension of the law against the suspected, 281; deportation of four of the Jacobin chiefs, 291; dissolution of the Convention, 368; new constitution, 376; EXECUTIVE DIRECTORY, 377; revolt of the Paris sections, suppressed by Buonaparte, 382-390; conspiracy of 18th Fructidor, x. 275; Revolution of 18th Brumaire 1799, xi. 9-30; establishment of Consular government, 46.

Fresnoy's 'Art of Painting,' Dryden's translation of, i. 343.

Friedland, battle of, xii. 251.

Frochot, Compte, Prefect of the Seine, xiv. 257, 261.

Froissart, Sir John, life of, xix. 110-125; character and defects of his writings, 125-130; comparison of Mr Johnes's translation of his Chronicles with the old one by Lord Berners, 130-136; his account of Gaston de Foix's household, vi. 57-59; of Lord Audley's generosity to his squires, 62; his talent of describing battles, 79; adventure of an English knight, 80; the tournament in Scotland, 93; ceremony of Sir John Chandos being created knight-banneret by the Black Prince, 96.

Galt, John. 'The Omen,' a novel, review of, xviii. 333-353.

Gantheaume, Admiral, x. 332-333, 382-385; xi. 195; xii. 99.

Gardiner, Colonel James, xxvi. 127, 154-160, 163-165.

Garrick, David, relations of, with Dr Smollett, iii. 122, 126, 145, 146; his merits as an improver of the English stage, vi. 376; his relations with John Home, the author of Douglas, xix. 308, 309, 316, 348, 349; his merits as an actor, compared with those of Kemble, xx. 180, 181, 184-187.

Garth, Dr Samuel, his eulogy of Dryden, i. 291, 292, 371.

Gasparin, an early patron of Buonaparte, ix. 348; xvi. 408.

Gaston de Foix, Froissart's description of the household of, vi. 57; xix. 120, 121.

Gaudin, Duke of Geëta, xi. 34.

Gaul, state of, before the Romans, xxvii. 9; Cæsar's conquest of, 15-28; effect of Roman conquest of, 27; invasion of, by the Franks, 37.

Gay, John, the poet, ii. 138-285; his 'Beggars' Opera,' 310, 311; vi. 374; ill-treated by the Court, 320; his death, 385; Mrs Howard's patronage of, xix. 191-196; his letter to Mrs H., and her answer, 206, 207.

Geddes, Jenny, xxiii. 355; xxiv. 178.

Genoa, revolution of, x. 238-241; united to France, xii. 29-31.

George I., xxv. 232; state of parties at his accession, 233-238.

——— II., policy of, when Prince of Wales, ii. 285; behaviour of, on hearing of General Hawley's defeat, xxvi. 273.

——— III. King, Biographical Sketch of, iv. 322-342; his affection for John Home, the author of Douglas, xix. 318; his kindness to the Scottish Jacobites, xx. 68, 69; his partiality to the theatre, 160; his friendship for John, Duke of Roxburghe, xxi. 213; his conduct in 1760, contrasted with that of Louis XVI. in 1789. viii. 147; his munificence to the Cardinal York, xxvi. 425.

——— IV. residence of at Dalkeith in 1822, vii. 225; his levees at Holyrood house, 294; his warrant to open the Crown room and search for the regalia of Scotland, 344.

George, Cadoudal, the Vendean, xi. 39, 241, 311-316, 337, 338.

Gerard, Marshal, xv. 107, 116-118, 145, 416, 435.

Germaine, Lady Betty, a friend of Dean Swift, ii. 53, n., 338, 353; her letter to him in defence of Mrs Howard, xix. 205; her generosity to her brother George, ib.

German romances, notice of vi. 192-194.

——— drama, modern, remarks on, vi. 381-386.

Gibbon's, Edward, account of the arguments by which he was converted to Catholicism, l. 271, n.

'Gil Blas,' notice of, and remarks on, iii. 408-417.

Gillespie's Hospital, xxvi. 297.

Gilpin, Bernard, anecdotes of, vii. 96.

Gladsmuir, battle of Prestonpans, why so called, xxvi. 180.

Glasgow, riot at, on account of the Union, xxv. 84-86; and the Ale Tax, xxvi. 11.

———, contribution levied on by the Pretender, xxvi. 248, 249.

Glencairn, the Earl of, xxiv. 111-113.

Glencoe, Massacre of, xxv. 1-25.

Glenshiel, battle of, xxv. 431-433.

Godolphin, Earl of, Lord Treasurer, ii. 107; his conduct in effecting the Union, xxv. 97, 98.

Godoy, Manuel, Prince of the Peace, xiii. 8-10, 12, 19, 21, 29, 31, 48, 49, 82.

Godwin's, William, 'Life of Chaucer,' Review of, xvii. 55-80; Review of his 'Fleetwood,' xviii. 118-138.

GOLDSMITH, DR. OLIVER, BIOGRAPHICAL SKETCH OF, iii. 231-259; remarks on his 'Vicar of Wakefield,' 255.

Gordon Duke of, xxiv. 349, 355; xxv. 155, 277; xxvi. 184.

—— Lord, xxiv. 3, 6-9.

——, Lord Lewis (afterwards Marquis of Huntly), xxiii. 396, 397; xxiv. 4-8.

——, xxvi. 184, 214, 253-256.

—— of Glenbucket, General, xxv. 282, 302, 334, 358.

Goths, supposed superiority of the, to the Celts, xx. 320; origin of the, xxvii. 20; their settlement in Spain. 45.

Government of Scotland, xxii. 178-194.

Gourgaud, General, xiv. 346; xv. 431, 433; xvi. 100, 101, 151, 186-192.

Gower, Sir William Leveson, i. 326.

Gowrie conspiracy against James VI. account of the, xxiii. 200-207; references to, vii. 406, 449-456, xxi. 227.

Gracioso, or buffoon, in Spanish comedy, i. 65.

Grahame, Sir John, companion of Wallace, xxii. 112.

——, Sir Robert, xxiii. 268-274.

Grahame, John of Claverhouse, Viscount Dundee, xix. 68-72; xx. 56; xxiv. 214, 239-242, 247, 256-259, 332-335, 344, 349-353, 363-383.

'Grandison, Sir Charles,' remarks on, iii. 50-63.

Granger, Rev. James, minister of Kinneff, and his wife, share of, in preserving the regalia of Scotland, vii. 329-331, 398; xxiv. 106-108.

——, Rev. James, character of Dean Swift, by, ii. 443-446.

Grattans, the family of the, friends of Dean Swift, ii. 195.

Gray, Thomas, the poet, cause of his rupture with Horace Walpole, iii. 301, n.; his account of the Old Pretender and his family, xxvi. 60, n.

'Graves, Sir Launcelot,' remarks on, iii. 150.

Greek drama, history of the, vi. 221-258.

Gregor, Clan. See MacGregor.

Gross-Beeren, battle of, xiv. 359.

Grimeston Lord, i. 32.

Grouchy, Marshal, xiv. 42, 199, 401, n.; xv. 383, 433-434; xvi. 15, 17, 23, 32-36, 42, 54, 55.

Guer-clio, Bertrand de, xxviii. 138, 141-144, 147-8, 178, 182-186, 195 6.

Guerillas, Spanish, xiii. 287-291.

Guiche, the Duchess du, xi. 154-5.

Guiscard, the assassin of Lord Oxford, description, &c. of

INDEX.   315

the knife with which the crime was attempted, ii. 168, n.
'Gulliver's Travels,' remarks on, ii. 290-308, 479-489.
Gustavus Adolphus IV., King of Sweden, xii. 37, 89; xiii. 335-339.
Gwynn, Nell, Charles II.'s mistress, xx. 110; character of, as an actress, 115.

Hackston, David, of Rathillet, one of the murderers of Archbishop Sharpe. xix. 276-278; xxiv. 233-236, 245, 252-254.
Hailes, Sir David Dalrymple, Lord, 'Annals of Scotland,' by, xx. 314-316; vindication of, from the attacks of Mr Fraser Tytler, xxi. 185-196.
Halifax, Marquis of, i. 307.
Halidon Hill, battle of, xxii. 204-206.
Hall, Captain Basil, interview of, with Buonaparte, xvi. 259-262.
———. Bishop. Remarks on his Satires, i. 238.
Hallam, Henry, Esq., extracts from his criticism on 'the Life and Works of Dryden,' i. 47, n. 52, n. 73, n. 101, n. 304, n. 348, n. 343, n. 380, n. 406 n.
Hamburgh, French occupation of, in 1806, xii. 204; in 1813, xiv. 302-304.
Hamilton, Marquis of, xxiii. 360, 370.
———, James (first) Duke of xxiv. 56, 58-61, 81.
———, William (second) Duke of, xxiv. 83, 235.

Hamilton, William Douglas, (third) Duke of, xxiv. 348, 351, 357; xxv. 54, 57, 76, 78, 79, 84, 87-92, 136-209.
———, Sir James, of Cadyow, xxii. 292, 299-301, 303.
———, Sir James, of Draphane, xxii. 384; xxiii. 8, 45, 49.
———, General, xxv. 278, 282, 325, 326.
———, Captain, anecdote of, and Dyan Swift, ii. 346.
Hamlet, remarks on, and on Kemble's personification of, xx. 176-180.
Handel's music to Dryden's 'Ode to St Cecilia,' i. 347.
Hanover seized by Prussia, xi. 189, by France, 289-291; exchanged with Prussia for Anspach and Bareuth, xii. 125, 153, re-occupied by the French, 203; retaken by the allies, xiv. 418.
Harcourt, Sir Godfrey de, xxvii. 49, 88, 112-114.
Hardwick Castle, in Derbyshire, description of, by Mrs Radcliff. iii. 381.
Harispe, General, xv. 77.
Harlaw, battle of, xxii. 256.
Hastings, battle of, xxvii. 145.
Hatsfeld, Prince of, xii. 199-201.
Haugwitz, Count, Prussian minister, xii. 72, 82, 124-5.
Hawkesbury, Lord. See Liverpool.
Hawley, General Henry, the cause of burning Linlithgow palace, vii. 394; his conduct

at the battle of Falkirk, xix. 303; xx. 7; xxvi. 259-278.
Hawthornden, description of, vii. 372.
Heber, Richard, visit of, to Edinburgh in 1799-1800, iv. 154; co-executor of Dr Leyden, 195-6.
Hebrides, or Western Isles. *See* Isles.
Henley, Antony, ii. 79, n. his satire against Lord Oxford's ministry, 127.
Henry I., King of France, reign of, xxvii. 115-121.
—— of Transtamar, King of Castille, xxviii. 144-148, 152-3.
—— I., of England, xxvii. 182-194.
—— II., of England, xxvii. 213-243.
——, III., of England, xxvii. 292, 296-298, 306-308, 311, 330.
—— IV., of England, xxii. 218, 250, 251; xxviii.
—— V., of England, xxii. 258; xxviii. 281.
—— VI., of England, xxii. 260.
—— VII., of England, xxii. 337, 348-350, 353, 358.
—— VIII., of England, xxii. 40-66.
——, Prince of Wales, son of James I., vii. 184, n.
'——,' by Cumberland, remarks on, iii. 221-224.
Hepburn of Keith, xxv. 286-289, 387; xxvi. 142-144.
Hepburns, Earls of Bothwell, vii. 174-183.
Herbert, Hon. William, Miscellaneous Poetry by, Review of, xvii. 102-118.
Heriot's Hospital, Edinburgh, account of, vii. 261-270.
'Herrnsprong,' by Bage, remarks on, iii. 458.
Herodotus, Dean Swift's character of, ii. 233, n.
Hesse Cassel, the elector of, xii. 156, 201, 202; xiv. 416.
——, Prince Frederick of, xxvi. 295-297.
——, Philipsthal, Prince of, xii. 93, 94.
Highlands of Scotland, present interest of the, compared with former indifference and ignorance respecting, xx. 1; the rebellion of 1745 awakens attention to their state, 3-9; parallelism between the Afghauns and the Highland clans, 10; points in which they differ, 15; the people, 16; their country and government, 17; authority of the chiefs, 18; division of the clans, 19; consequences of the over-population, 26; artisans, 29; the tenants and commoners, 30; hereditary right not always observed in the chief's succession, 32; junction of small clans with larger, 34; resistance to the law, 37; former subjection to the Lords of the Isles, 38; extinction of that dynasty, 40; the various branches of the clan MacDonald, *ib.*; other powerful clans, 42; effect of the statute of Mary 1587, 44; the clan Gregor, 45

their outrages, and the vengeance they incurred, 46-50; military superiority of the Highlanders in the civil wars, 51; bridled by Cromwell, 53; favoured by Charles II. and James II., 54; pacified by Lord Breadalbane, and how, 57; address of the Highland chiefs to George I., 58; rise against him in 1715, 59; battle of Sheriffmuir, 60; history of Lord Lovat, 61-69, 76-85; effect of the acts of 1715, 72; military roads, 73; the independent companies, 75; severities of the Duke of Cumberland in 1746, 87; abolition of clanship by the acts of 1748, 91.

Highlands, state of, and changes produced in, by the union of the crowns, xxiii. 311-330.

Hill, General Lord, xv. 423; xvi. 2.

——, Abigail. *See* Masham.

'Hind and Panther, The,' by Dryden, i. 278; reprinted at Holyrood-house, 286; parodied by Montague and Prior, 283, 284.

Hobbes, Thomas, his opinion of 'Gondibert,' i. 47, n.

Hofer, Andrew, the Tyrolese chief, xiii. 220.

Hohenlinden, battle of, xi. 128.

Holland converted into a kingdom by Napoleon, xii. 121-122, 133; becomes a province of France, xiii. 333; restored to independence, xiv. 429-432.

Holland, Lord, 'Life of Lope de Vega,' vi. 279-282; his speech in favour of Buonaparte, xii. 276-283.

——, Lady, Napoleon's bequest to, xvi. 400.

Home, Lord, xxii. 326, 328, 331, 360, 368, 370, 379, 380.

—— Sir David, of Wedderburn, xxii. 380, 381, 385, 388.

—— John, author of Douglas, 'The Life and Works of,' edited by Henry Mackenzie, Review of, xix. 283-367.

Homer, Dryden's intended translation of, i. 351; Pope's account of the time he took in his translation, 334, n.

Honours to departed, denied to living genius, reflections upon, i. 371.

Hooke, Col. negotiations of, with the Scotch Jacobites, xxv. 135-140, 152, n.

Horte, Dr Joseph, bishop of Kilmore, unhandsome conduct of, to Faulkner, the Dublin bookseller, ii. 369, 370.

Hortense (Beauharnais), Queen of Holland, now Duchess of St Leu, xii. 122, 123; xiii. 328, 331; xv. 328, 352; two French romances by, v. 163, 164; translations of, 159, 160.

Hotham, Admiral Sir Henry, xvi. 89-92, 103.

Howard, Sir Robert, the friend and patron, and afterwards brother-in-law of Dryden, i. 44, 68, 69; his 'Indian

Queen,' 70 ; his controversy
with Dryden, 80-84 ; his
'Conquest of China,' 349.
Howard, Hon. Edward, brother-
in-law of Dryden, i. 82, 84,
115, 391.
—— Lady Elizabeth, daughter
of the Earl of Berkshire, the
wife of Dryden, i. 75; her
letter days, 391.
——, Mrs (afterwards Coun-
tess of Suffolk), ii. 285,
312, 313 ; Review of her
Correspondence, edited by
Mr Croker, xix. 185-212.
Howie's ' Lives of the Scottish
Worthies,' xix. 49, 50, 72,
73 ; his ' History of the
Rising at Bothwell Bridge,'
49, 52-3.
Howell, James, i. 98.
Howison, John, of Braehead,
adventure of James V. with,
xxiii. 23-26.
Hudibras, Butler's, i. 37, et
passim ; compared with
Dryden's MacFleckoe, 240,
283.
Hudson and Donat, Mistresses,
'The New Practice of
Cookery' by, Review of,
xix. 100-107.
Hugh the Great, Duke of
France, xxvii. 101; thrice
refuses the crown, 102-103.
Hugo Capet, elected King of
France, becomes founder of
the third dynasty, xxvii.
110-112.
Hulin, General, xi. 320 ; xiv.
257 ; xv. 145.
Hume, David, the historian,
anecdotes of, xix. 287, 327-
331.

Hume, Sir Patrick, of Polwarth
Earl of Marchmont, xxiv.
265-268.
' Humphrey Clinker,' remarks
on, iii. 160.
Hundred Days, The, of Napoleon, xv. 346, to xvi. 52.
Huns, description of the, and
their invasion of Europe,
xxvii. 46 ; fresh invasion of,
under Attila, 49 ; defeated
at Chalons, 51.
Hunt, Thomas, an antagonist
of Dryden, i. 247 ; Dryden's
character of him, 249.
Hunter's, Dr, A. ' Calton
Famulatrix Medicinæ,' Re-
view of, xix. 107-111.
Huntly (Gordon), Earl of,
xxiii. 92-96, 191-194.
——, Marquis of, xxiii. 309,
322-326, 369, 343, 387 ;
xxiv. 81.
——, xxv. 154, 252, 298-
300, 328, 329, 348, 352,
353, 354, 365, 400, 407.
Huske, General, xxvi. 260-
265, 271, 278, 337.
Hutton, Dr James, the geo-
logist, anecdotes of, xix.
334, 335.
——, W. of Birmingham, iii.
441 ; Letters of R. Bage to,
445.

Iceland. See Eyrbiggia.
Icelandic Poetry, translations
of, xvii. 102-110
Imperial government of France
under Napoleon, xii. 301-
348.
Income-tax commissioners, and
Michael Kelly, characteristic
dialogue between, xx. 237.

Independents, sect of, xxiv. 35-39.
India, British, Russian plan of invading, xi. 187, 188.
'Indian Emperor,' by Dryden, i. 71, 162-3.
'Indian Queen,' a tragedy by Dryden and Howard, i. 70.
Indulgence, the, xxiv. 209-210.
Infernal machine, plot for assassinating Buonaparte, xi. 158-160.
Inoerwick (or Aoderwick) Castle, attack and defence of, in 1544, vii. 142; description of, 407.
Innes's, Father, 'Essay on the early inhabitants of Scotland,' xx. 307, 313, 344.
Ireland's Shakspeare forgeries, xx. 216-218.
Ireland, unsuccessful attempt of Robert and Edward Bruce to conquer, xxii. 159-162.
Iron Crown, order of the, xii. 29.
Isles of Scotland (Western or Hebrides), state of, at the Union of the crowns, xxiii. 294-310.
'Italian, The,' by Mrs Radcliffe, remarks on, iii. 347.
—— Drama, history of the, vi. 284-293.
—— romances, notice of, vi. 194.
Italy, Norman conquests in, xxvii. 131-135.
——, state of, at the French invasion of 1796, x. 53-55; Buonaparte's conduct to the inhabitants of, 170; the north of, erected into a kingdom, xii. 26.

Jacobin Club, origin of the, viii. 135-137.
Jacquerie, The, or peasant insurrection in France, xxviii. 121.
Jaffa captured by Buonaparte, x. 350; massacre of the garrison, 351-354; poisoning of the sick at, 368-372.
James I. of Scotland, reign of, xxii. 264-276.
—— II. xxii. 277-306. See i. 2.
—— III. xxii. 307-334.
—— IV. xxii. 335-373; vii. 385.
—— V. xxiii. 1-60; iv. 82, 87; vii. 285, 290.
—— VI. (and I. of England), xxiii. 159-209; after the Union, 216-344; vii. 287, 392, 393; xix. 226; xxi. 245-247.
—— VII. (and II. of England), xxiv. 271-324; xxv. 50, 130; his profession of Catholicism, i. 125; cause of his unpopularity when heir to the throne, 204; offended by Dryden's 'Spanish Friar,' 202, 206; his partiality for the Duchess of Monmouth, 245; hopes excited on his accession to the throne, 256; supposed to have influenced Dryden in his change of religion, 274, 276; rigid economy of his administration, 294; birth of his son, 295; his residence at Holyrood-house, vii. 291; his praiseworthy conduct when at the head of the admiralty, xx. 130-132.

INDEX.

Jamieson, Rev. Dr John, opinion of, respecting the ancient language of Scotland, xx. 345.

—— Robert, 'Northern Antiquities,' edited by, v. 358; vi. 193; his collection of 'Scottish Ballads,' xvii. 115; his reprint of 'Burt's Letters from the North of Scotland,' xix. 177.

Janssens, General, bold march of, xv. 115.

Jedburgh, storming of, xxii. 367.

Jefferies, Judge, xxiv. 274, 323, n.

Jeffrey, Francis, now Lord, Editor of Edinburgh Review, critiques by, on Swift, ii. 443; on Scott's edition of Swift, 446; his house at Craigcrook, vii. 278; his 'Reviewer's Groans,' xix. 156.

Jena, battle of, xii. 175-179.

Jerusalem, siege of, by the first crusaders, xxvii. 174; erected into a kingdom for Godfrey of Boulogne, 176; retaken, and the kingdom extinguished, by Saladin, 245.

Jews, persecution of the, under Philip the Long, xxvii. 375-377.

John, King of England, xxvii. 240, 242, 252, 254, 256; succeeds to the crown on his brother Richard's death, 258; banishes his wife and takes another, 262; war with, and murder of his nephew Arthur of Bretagne, 264-266; loses his French dominions, 267; excommunicated, 270; resigns his kingdom to the Pope, 272; wars with his barons and Prince Louis of France, 286; death, 290.

John Balliol, King of Scotland, xxii. 71-73.

—— the Good, King of France, xxviii. 27, 50, 68, 69, 91-134.

—— of Gaunt, Duke of Lancaster, xxviii. 170, 171, 181, 187-189, 193, 194.

—— the Fearless, Duke of Burgundy, xxviii. 254, 265 280.

—— of Lorn. See Lorn.

——, Prince Regent, afterwards John VI., King of Portugal, xi. 144, 145; xiii. 11-15.

Johnes', Thomas, translation of Froissart's Chronicles, Review of, xix. 112-136.

Johnson, Miss Esther (Stella), origin of Dean Swift's connexion with, ii. 46-48; goes to Ireland, 60; rejects Dr Tisdal's proposals of marriage, 62; Swift's correspondence with her from London, 105; her secret marriage to Swift, 210; doubts as to this marriage, ib. n.; and 468; her personal appearance, 215; her last illness and death, 314-317.

——, Dr Samuel, Biographical sketch of, iii. 260; remarks on his 'Rasselas,' 270; his supposed prejudice against Swift, ii. 424, 441, 442; his intimacy with Richardson, iii. 12, 14-16;

his preference of Richardson to Fielding, 66; his opinion of Fielding's Amelia 112; his black servant, Barber, 154; his corrections on Smollett's epitaph, 165; his interview with Adam Smith, 269. Extracts from his works, on Ben Jonson, vol. i. 3; the wits of Charles's reign, 62; Dryden's dislike to the clergy, 191; Parallel of Pope and Dryden, 402; on the critical prefaces of Dryden, 443.

Johnstone, the Chevalier, notice of his 'Memoirs,' and his charge of cowardice against the young Pretender, xix. 357-367; quotations from, xxvi. 169, 218, 223, 225, et passim.

———, Charles, Biographical Notice of, iii. 427; remarks on his 'Chrysal, or the Adventures of a Guinea,' 430-440.

———, Jack (or Irish), iii. 200; xx. 244.

———, the Smuggler, xvi. 294, 295.

Jones, Inigo, i. 56.

Jonson, Ben, his saying of Charles I., i. 9, n.; manners and habits of, 227; character of, as a dramatist, compared with Shakspeare, vi. 338-342; his visit to Hawthornden, and Drummond's character of him, vii. 373-382; doggrel verses imputed to, xix. 160. See also, i. 56, 79, 127, 192, 223, n. 435, 450.

'Joseph Andrews', remarks on iii. 94.

Josephine, the Empress, ix. 395, 398; x. 234-236, 417-423; xi. 3, 29, 155, 157, 169; xii. 348, 349, 355, 356; xiii. 176, 259-271; xv. 223.

Joubert, General, x. 9, 21, 152-155, 207-208, 411.

Jougs, the Earl of Strathmore's, xxi. 280.

Jourdan, Marshal, x. 99, 100, 397, 413; xi. 4, 5, 120; xii. 6; xiii. 205.

——— Coupe-tête, viii. 179.

'Julia de Roubigné,' remarks on, iv. 15.

Junot, Marshal, Duke of Abrantes, ix. 351; x. 224; xiii. 12-19, 107-120; xiv. 42, 92.

Jury trial, origin of, xxvi. 81.

Juvenal and Persius, Dryden's translation of, i. 318.

Kaminskoy, Marshal, the Russian general in 1806, xii 225, 231, 235.

Katzbach, battle of, xiv. 361.

Keies, Robert, a Gunpowderplot conspirator, anecdotes of, i. 18.

Keith, Sir Robert, mareschal of the Scottish army at Bannockburn, xxii. 130.

———, Earl Marischal, part of, in preserving the regalia of Scotland during the Civil Wars, vii. 315, 335.

———, Earl Marischal, a leading actor in the Jacobite rebellions of 1715 and 1745, xxv. 155, 252, 273, 298, 421, 430-433; xxvi. 64, 67,

Keith, Earl of Kintore, xxiv. 108.
———, Sir Alexander, of Ravelston, Knight Marischal of Scotland, vii. 276, 335.
———, Anne, Lady Methven, xix. 270-272; xxiv. 216.
———, Admiral Lord, xi. 99, 102, 193; xvi. 88, 107-116, 121-126, 130.
Kellermann, Marshal, Duke of Valmy, x. 10, 71; xi. 112, 116; xiv. 385; xv. 418.
Kelp, manufacture of, in the Highlands, xxi. 353, 381, 382.
Kelly, Michael, of the King's and Drury Lane theatres, 'Reminiscences of,' Review of, xx. 152, 164, 233-244.
Kemble, John Philip, I. 160, n.; traditional anecdote related by, of ancient indelicacy in conversation, ii. 343; his admirable performance of Penruddock, iii. 214, n.; sketch of his life, xx. 167-232.
Kenmure, William, Viscount, xxv. 155, 252, 269-388.
Kennedy, Archbishop of St Andrews, xxii. 295, 299-308.
Kennet, Bishop, his account of Swift's behaviour at Court, ii. 121.
Kenneth I. victory of, over the Picts, xx. 313, 353-357, 359; extent of his conquest, xxi. 154; his successors to the time of Duncan, 156.
Kent's system of landscape gardening, xxi. 96-102.
Ker of Fairnieherst, xxii. 357, 387; xxiii. 17, 142.

Ker of Crawford, xxiii. 5, 6.
——— of Graden, Col., xxvi. 153, 224.
———, Lord Mark, xxvi. 168.
Keralio, M. de, report of, on the conduct of Buonaparte at the school of Brienne, ix. 330.
Kilblene, battle of, xxii. 211.
Killiecrankie, battle of, xxiv. 378-383.
Killigrew, Thomas, theatrical manager at the Restoration, i. 66; contract of, with Dryden, 85.
———, Mrs Anne, i. 293.
Kilmarnock, Earl of, xxvi. 184, 185, 271, 283, 377, 380-387.
Kilpont, Lord xxiii. 390, 394.
Kilsyth, battle of, xxiv. 14, 15.
———, Viscount, xxv. 155, 252.
'King Arthur,' by Dryden, ? 306.
King, Dr., Archbishop of Dublin, a correspondent of Dean Swift, ii. 82; employs Swift to solicit the remission of the first fruits on behalf of the Irish clergy, 84; recalls his commission, 115; coolness between him and Swift, ib. n.; his sarcastic hint to Swift, and the latter's vindication, 192, 193; supposed communication made to him by Swift, 213.
———, Dr William (of Oxford), friend of Swift, ii. 361, n.; his connexion with the Pretender, xix. 354; xxvi. 419, 420.
———, Tom, the actor, character of, xx. 201.

King's, the, company of players, their contract with Dryden, I. 85, 68, 124, n.
Kirkton's, Rev. James, 'Secret and true history of the Church of Scotland,' Review of, xix. 213-262.
Kit-cat Club, i. 330.
Kleber, General, x. 302, 305, 359, 362, 378, 382; xi. 192-194.
Kleist, General, xiv. 354, 384; xv. 113, 151, 420.
Knighthood. See Chivalry.
Kneller, Sir Godfrey, i. 343.
Knight-Banneret, ceremony of creating a, iv. 101; vi. 96.
Knights Templars. See Templars.
—— Hospitallers, origin of the order of, xxvii. 178.
—— of Malta surrender the island to Buonaparte, x. 313, 314.
Knolles, Sir Robert, xxviii. 127, 174.
Knox, John, deathbed scene of, vii. 249; his original plan of church policy, xix. 222; object of his 'Book of Discipline,' 223, 225. See also xxiii. 79, 80, 84, 85, 91, 150.
Kohler, General, xv. 230, 231, 236, 250-252.
Kolli, Baron, plan of for liberating Ferdinand VII. of Spain, xiii. 377.
Kourakin, Prince, xiv. 28, 30.
Koutousoff, Prince, General of the Russians, xiv. 95, 104, 128, 131, 144-146, 150, 161-163, 164-189, 201, 202, 296.

Krasnoi, battle of, xiv. 187-191.
Kray, the Austrian General, xi. 82, 83.
Kremlin, destruction of the, at Moscow, xiv. 151-153.
Kynaston, the actor, i. 180.

Labedoyère, Colonel, xv. 340, 341, 402, n., 418; xvi. 56, 57.
Laborde, the French banker, magnificent residence of, xix. 211.
Lafayette, the Marquis de, popular opinions of, formed in America, viii. 71; commands the Parisian national guards on their march to Versailles, 172; his doubtful conduct there, 177; returns with the King to Paris, 181; supposed motives of his conduct, 188; enforces the law against rioters, 194, 225; the national guard refuse to obey him, 226; puts down the rioters in the Champ de Mars, 234; decline of his influence, 274; why desirous of foreign war, 275; intercedes in favour of the King, 312; is obliged to return to the army, 315; failure of attempt to impeach him, 320; escapes from France, and made prisoner by the Prussians, 349; exchanged for the Princess Royal of France, ix. 94; returns to France, xi. 37; his conduct on the fall of Napoleon, xvi. 44, 49.
Lafleur, Sterne's French valet

324   INDEX.

notice of, iii. 284; his anecdotes of Sterne, 285-288.
Laing's, Malcolm, 'History of Scotland,' extracts from, xxiii. 336, n. et seq.
Lallemand, General, xv. 336, 343, 344; xvi. 95, 102, 127.
Lamarque, General, xv. 412.
LANDSCAPE GARDENING, On, xxi. 77; Horace Walpole's essay on the subject, 79; old fashioned system of gardening, 80; Italian and Dutch styles, 87; the chase or park, 91; system of Kent, 96; of Brown, 100; of Payne Knight, and Sir Uvedale Price, 102; higher requisites now required for the profession, 105; materials for rural design, earth, water, trees, 108; difficulty to get the immediate command of the latter, 109; now removed by Sir Henry Stewart, 113; his park of Allanton, ib; report of committee on his mode of transplantation, 117; principles on which it proceeds, 118; mode of preparing trees for, 128; size of subjects, 131; process of removing and replanting, 132; expense of, 144; obstacles to the general introduction of the system, 149.
Langeron, General, xv. 109, 110, 113, 161, 408.
Lanjuinais, M. xv. 402-3; xvi. 50, 53.
Lannes, Marshal, Duke of Montebello, x. 23, 37, 141, 296, 305, 323, 362, 382; xi. 89, 97, 104, 108, 112, 114, 115, 158, 179; xii. 57, 78, 80, 170, 176, 231, 332; xiii. 179, 199, 205, 328.
Le Noue, the Mareschal de, condemns the institutions of Chivalry, vi. 115; his censure of the romances of Chivalry, 187-8.
Lansdowne, Granville, Lord, his vindication of Dryden's private character, i. 378.
Laon, battle of, xv. 112-114.
Laplace, the Astronomer, xi. 71.
Larch tree, qualities and merits, and best mode of cultivation of the, xxi. 31-36, 50-54.
Larochejacquelin, M. de, xv. 17,79, 83, 86, 412, 413.
Las Cases, Count, xvi. 64, n., 93, et. seq. 276.
Latouche, Treville, Admiral, xii. 113.
Latour, Maubourg, Count, xi. 37; xiv. 175, 199, 385.
Laud, Archbishop, and Archie Armstrong, xxiii. 357.
Lauderdale, Earl (Duke) of, xix. 238, 245, 250; xxiv. 56, 173, 194-5, 211, 223-229, 248, 256.
———, James, Earl of, xii. 149-151.
Lauriston, General Law of, xi. 206; xii. 86; xiii. 212; xiv. 34, 125-6, 130, 131, 134, 297, 360-363, 382, 384, 385.
Lavalette, General, xv. 358; xvi. 55.
Lawburrows, writ of xxiv 217

Leadhills, mines of, xxiii. 28.

Lebrun, Third Consul, Arch-treasurer and Duke of Placentia, xi. 12, 67, 154; xiv. 431.

Lee, Nath., assists Dryden in the composition of 'Œdipus,' i. 189; and in 'The Duke of Guise,' 242.

Lesslie Anderson, anecdote of the, xxl. 288.

Leclerc, General, brother-in-law to Napoleon, xi. 266-270.

Lefebvre, Marshal, Duke of Dantzic, xi. 11, 13, 14; xii. 137, 245; xiv. 41; xvi. 69.

—— Desnouettes, General, xiii. 82, 95-97, 158; xv. 50, 329, 343-4.

Leghorn seized by Buonaparte, x. 87, 129.

'Legion Club,' Swift's satire on the Irish House of Commons, ii. 373.

Legion of Honour, xi. 275-281.

Leigh, Richard, his controversy with Dryden, i. 134, 164.

Leipsic, battle of, xiv. 384-405.

Lennox, Earl of, xxiii. 3, 6-8, 61-98, 110-120, 143-147.

——, Esmé, Duke of, xxiii. 159-160, 166.

Le Noir, Richard, xv. 329.

Leoben, treaty of, between France and Austria, x. 220.

Le Sage, Alain René. Biographical Sketch of, iii. 390-426; remarks on his 'Diable Boiteux,' 401; on his 'Gil Blas,' 408; on his

'Bachelier de Salamanque, 418.

Lesley, Alexander, Earl of Leven xxiii. 360-367, 382; xxiv. 19, 43, 44.

——, General David, xxiii. 362; xxiv. 19-23, 57-74, 91-98.

——'s, Bishop, account of the manners of the Scottish Borderers, vii. 61, 144 148; character of his History of Scotland, xx. 384.

Leslie, Norman, of Rothes, xx. iii. 58-64.

Letourneur de la Blanche, the French director, x. 264.

Letter writers, causes for placing little reliance on the sincerity of, xx. 95-97.

Leveson, Gower, Sir William, a patron of Dryden, i. 306.

LEYDEN, JOHN, M.D. BIOGRAPHICAL MEMOIR OF, iv. 137.

License System of Commerce xiii. 323-325.

Ligny. Battle of, v. 79-88; xv. 428-430.

Lillie, John, 'Euphues and his England,' notice of, i. 8.

Lillo, John, the introducer of domestic tragedies on the English Stage, vi. 370.

Lima, Count de, xiii. 103, 104.

'Limberham,' by Dryden, i. 188.

Lindsay, Lord David, of the Byres, xxii. 338-342.

——, Lord Patrick, xxii. 339 342, 364.

——, Sir David, his 'Satire of the Three Estaites,' vii. 390; xxiii. 41.

Linlithgow, Description of the Palace of, vii. 362; burning of, xxvi. 271, n.

Liston, the Comic Actor, xx. 243.

Liverpool, Robert, Lord, xi. 242, 243.

Livingstone, Sir Alexander, xxii. 277, 279, 280.

Lloyd's, Bishop, correction of the errors of Boece, xx. 306.

Loban, General Count, xvi. 6; Lloyd Dr. 16, 17, n.

Lockhart, Sir Simon, of Lee, xxii. 175.

—— Sir George, murder of, xxiv. 358.

—— of Carnwath, memoirs of, quoted, xxv. 78, 84, 91, et passim.

——, John Hugh, Dedication of 'Tales of a Grandfather' to, xxii. vii. xxiii. 213; xxv. 109; xxvii. i.

Lockier, Dr. Dean of Peterborough, his account of his first acquaintance with Dryden, i. 383, n.

Lodi, battle of, x. 41.

Logan, Robert, of Restalrig, vii. 406, 449-456.

Loison, General, xiii. 106-7, 112-115; xiv. 214, 225, 229.

Lonato, battle o', x. 106-7.

Lorn, John (MacDugal) Lord of, xxii. 104, 105, 119-122, 144, 145.

Loudon, Earl of, xxiii. 361; Lord Chancellor, xxiv. 55.

——, xxv. 362; xxvi. 91, 98, 254, 284, 288-293, 310, 311.

Lothian, Earl of, xxiii. 400, 401.

——, Marquis of, xxiv. 279, n

Louis the Debonnaire, the Emperor, reign of, xxvii. 77.

——. IV. (Outremer) King of France, xxvii. 107.

—— V., (the Faintant), xvii. 107.

—— VI., (the Fat), xxvii. 137, 184-195.

—— VII., (the Young), xxvii. 196; leads the second crusade, 198; accompanied by his wife Eleanor, 199; disasters attending it; 200-206; becomes jealous of his wife, 207; returns home, 209; divorced, 215; disputes with Henry II. of England 216-223.

Louis VIII., (the Lion), xxvii. 296-300.

—— IX., (Saint), xxvii. 300; his unfortunate crusade to Egypt, 311-328; his second crusade to Tunis, and death, 335-6.

—— X., (Hutin), xxvii. 367, 369, 371-2.

—— XVI. King of France, opposes the war with England in favour of America, viii. 69; restores the parliaments, 76; economises the revenue, 78; his excellent qualities, 80; defects of his character, 81; his want of decision on the 14th of July, 1789, 147-152; conduct at Versailles to the Paris mob, 175; carried to Paris with his family, 183; accepts the new constitution, 219; corresponds with Bouillé to effect his escape, 223; his escape and re-capture at Varennes, 228, 229; brought back to Paris, 232; petition for his dethronement, 233; re-accepts the Constitution, with farther clogs on his authority, 235; refuses his assent to two decrees against the emigrants and clergy, 278, 279; declares war against Austria, 286; puts his veto on the decree for a departmental army, 299; afterwards assents to it, 301; his conduct during the attack on the palace, June 20, 1792, 310; his part in the ceremony of the Champ de Mars, 319; his want of firmness on the 10th of August, 331, 334, 335; claims the protection of the Legislative Assembly, 337-339; agony in that situation, 345; deposed and committed to prison, 378; progress and reasons of his unpopularity, ix 1-8; both parties prepared to sacrifice him, 9; report on grounds for his accusation, 42; absence of all criminality in his conduct, 51; motion carried to try him, 53; his trial, sentence, and execution, 64-94; Buonaparte's saying of him, xi. 73.

Louis XVIII. decree of National Assembly against, viii. 277; residence of, at Verona, x. 61; at Warsaw, xi. 135, 241; correspondence of, with Buonaparte, 154, 281-284; called to the throne, xv. 271; conduct of his government till Buonaparte's return to Paris, 272-358; his second restoration, xvi. 89. *See also* vol. v. 21-49, and 253-284.

Louisa, Queen of Prussia, xii. 157, 168, 198, 254, 261-264.

Louvre, Gallery of the, xvi. 82.

Lovat, Simon Fraser, Lord, xx. 61-85; xxv. 394-399, xxvi. 48-52, 92-95, 102, 103, 113, 194-201, 245, 246, 360, 361, 388-391.

'Love Triumphant,' by Dryden, i. 310.

Lowe, General Sir Hudson, Governor of St Helena, relations of, with Buonaparte, during the confinement of the latter on that island, xvi. 162, 307.

—— Mr. notice of his essay 'On the Ancient History of the Kingdom of the Gaelic,' ix. 374.

Lucian, Dryden's Life of, i. 342.

Luneville, treaty of, between France and Austria, xi. 129, 130.

Lutzen, battle of, xiv. 207-300.

Lynch, Count, mayor of Bourdeaux, xv. 78, 89, 364.

Lynedoch, Sir Thomas Graham, afterwards Lord, ix 358; xlii. 286, 363; xiv 432; xv. 41, 76.

Lyon. Rev. Dr John, guardian of Dean Swift's person during his last years, ii. 400, extracts from his 'Additions to Hawkesworth's Life of Swift,' 396, 469-473; his letter to Mr Dean Swift on Guiscard's penknife, 169, n.

Lyons, revolt and siege of, ix. 175-184.

Lyttl-ton, George, Lord, iii. 134.

Macbeth, Story of, xxii. 11-26; tragedy of, as performed in by Kemble and Siddons, xx, 189-192.

MacCrie, Rev. Dr Thomas, his attack on the 'Tales of my Landlord,' xix. i. n.; the use of ridicule on points of religion justified by his own example, 76-77.

Macdonald, the various branches of the clan, ix. 40; xxiii. 295.
———, Alaster, Lord of the Isles, xxii. 265.
——— of Barrisdale, xxvi. 311, 313, 322, 327.
——— of Boisdale, xxvi. 71, 72.
——— of Clanranald, xxv. 300, 348, 357, 362, 303; xxvi. 71, 73, 76, 81, 158, 184, 190, 206, 281-270, 284-285, 324, 338-342, 364.
——— of Colkitto, xxiii. 388; xxiv. 7-9, 57.
———, of Eigg, xxiii. 296-299.
——— of Glenaladale, xxvi. 67, n.
——— of Glencoe, xxv. 4-25,

348; xxvi. 89, 158, 190, 401.
——— of Glengarry, xxv. 241, n.; 252, 300 342-343, 348, 357, 402, xxvi. 89, 158, 206, 236-240, 261-270, 282, 354-355, 361.
——— of Keppoch, xxiv. 385-372 : xxv. 348; xxvi. 45, n., 84. 89, 148, 158, 190, 206. 261-278, 274, 284-285, 298, 324, 338-342
——— of Kinloch Moidart, xxv. 73. 301; xxvi. 73, 79, 81, 252, 394.
——— of. Kingsburgh, xxvi. 366, 397.
——— of Lochgarry, xxvi. 98, 190, 284, 285, 421.
——— of Skye, Sir Donald, xxv. 330, 348; xxvi. 288, 365.
———, of Sleat, Sir Alexander, xxvi. 71, 72, 76, 88, 93, 95, 195-198.
——— Lady Margaret, xxvi. 366, 367.
———, Flora, xxvi. 365-367, 397, 398.
———, Marshal, Duke of Tarentum, x. 397; xi. 10 132; xiii. 212; xiv. 41 88, 233-237, 298, 339, 342, 359-362, 382, 385, 392, 397, 401 ; xv. 47, 107, 116-118, 121, 174, 175, 199-215, 228, 344, 345, 356-358 ; xvi. 69 ; xxvi. 74.

'Mac Flecknoe,' by Dryden, i. 228; compared with the Dunciad, 231, n.; and with Hudibras, 240, 383.

MacGillivray of Drumnaglas, xxvi. 214, 289, 346.

MacGregor, clan of, xx. 45.
—— of Dubaldie, xxvi. 63, 120.
—— of Glengyle, xxvi. 215, 127.
—— See Rob Roy.
MacIntosh of Borlum, Brigadier, xxv. 273, 302, 307, 309-322, 368, 376-381, 386, 387.
—— of MacIntosh, xxiii. 322-324; xxv. 376; xxvi. 288-292, 324, 346.
—— of Muy, and MacDonald of Keppoch, feud between, xxiv. 365-371.
Mackintosh, Sir James, xl. 244; xv. 361, 369.
Mack, General, x. 391; xii. 42, 45-47, 50-61.
MacKay General, xxiii. 336, 371-388.
—— the clan, xxvi. 310, 311.
Mackenzie, Sir George, his 'Defence of the Royal Line of Scotland,' xx. 306; his conduct on a trial for witchcraft, xxiv. 137; his severities against the Covenanters, 302.
——, Henry, Biographical Notice of, iv. 1; remarks on his character as a Novelist, 9; his 'Man of Feeling,' 13; his 'Man of the World,' 14; his 'Julia de Roubigné,' 15; Review of his edition of 'The Life and Works of John Home, author of Douglas,' xix. 283-367.
——, Sir John, of Coull, xxv. 302, 398-399.
—— of Kintail, xxiii. 307.

Mackenzie, Capt. of Saddie, xxiv. 366-369.
MacLauchlan, Colonel, xxvi. 215, 256, 324, 346.
MacLean of Duart, xxiii. 299.
—— of Torloisk, xxiii. 300, 305.
—— Sir John, xxv. 241, n. 301, 349, 356, 401; xxvi. 324, 346.
MacLellan of Bomby, xxii. 289, 290.
MacLeod, Lord, xxvi. 314, 315.
—— of MacLeod, xxiii. 295-297; xxvi. 71, 72, 76, 88, 93, 95, 195-198, 254, 255, 290-291, 365.
MacPherson of Cluny, xxiii. 388; xxiv. 370; xxv. 298-299.
——, xxvi. 93, 103, 104, 194, 196, 237-239, 261, 300-304, 323, 361, 372-374.
MacQuarrie of Ulva, xxiii. 302-305.
MacVicar, Rev. Mr, and the Pretender, xxvi. 178, 179.
'Maid's Tragedy, the,' of Fletcher, prohibited, i. 60. n.
Maida, battle of, xii. 281-293.
Maiden, the, instrument of capital executions, xxiii. 164; xxiv. 280.
'Maiden Queen,' by Dryden, i. 88.
Maimbourg's 'History of the League,' translated by Dryden, i. 249.
Maison, General, xiv. 213, 214.
Maitland of Lethington, xxiii. 90-149.
——, Sir John, Chancellor of James VI.; xxiii. 187, 243.

INDEX.

Maitland, Captain Frederick, xvi. 86-90, 93-106, 111, 112, 120-125, 129-131, 380-385.
—— Club, account of the, xxi. 223.
MALAGROWTHER, MALACHI, LETTERS FROM, ON THE PROPOSED CHANGE OF CURRENCY, &c. xxi. 267-402.
Malcolm Canmore, King of Scotland, reign of, xxi. 157-160; xxii. 37-40.
—— IV., reign of, xxi. 162; xxii. 51, 52.
——, General Sir John, his account of Dr Leyden, iv. 187-191; his anecdote of Leyden's father, 196.
—— Admiral Sir Pulteney, xvi. 254-256.
Mallet, General, conspiracy of, xiv. 166-7, 254-258.
Malo-Yaroslawetz, battle of, xiv. 144-146.
Malta, taken by Buonaparte, x. 313-315; taken by the English, xi. 147, 186, 205, 246-7, 252, 260.
Malt-tax in Scotland, xxv. 176-177.
Mamelukes of Egypt, x. 319, 326; xxvii. 318.
'Man of Feeling,' by Mackenzie, remarks on, iv. 13.
'Man of the World,' by Mackenzie, remarks on, iv. 14.
Manon L'Escaut,' by Prevost, remarks on, by George Steevens, iv. 43, n.
Mantua, siege of, by Buonaparte, x. 79, 80, 96, 103, 111-114, 126, 127, 147-149, 162-5.

Mar, Donald, Earl of, regent of Scotland, xxii. 199, 200.
——, Earl of, xxii. 256.
——, brother of James III., xxii. 311, 315.
——, Robert Cochran, Earl of, xxii. 318.
——, James Stewart, Earl of, xxiii. 90.
——, Earl of, regent, xxiii. 146-148.
——, John (Erskine), eleventh Earl of, xxiv. 350; xxv. 75, 186, 219, 239-241, 250-423.
Marat, the French revolutionist, character of, viii. 354; ix. 34; threatened with impeachment by the Girondists, 36; decree of accusation against him, 105; acquitted, 106; killed by Charlotte Corday, 217, 218.
March, Patrick, Earl of, xxii. 158, 200, 210, 226.
——, George, Earl of, xxii. 247, 249, 261.
——, Black Agnes, Countess of, her defence of Dunbar castle, vi. 38; vii. 414; xxii. 212.
Marchmont, Earl of, xxv. 80-100, n. See Hume.
Marengo, battle of, xi. 109, et seq.
Maret, H., Duke of Bassano, xiv. 25, 213, 327; xv. 8, 199, 203, 231, 328; xvi. 47, 49, 50.
Margaret of Provence, Queen of St Louis, miseries of, when shut up in Damietta, xxvii. 320, 323-325.
——, Queen of Scotland (wife

of Malcolm Canmore), xxii. 37, 40.
——, (wife of James IV.), xxii. 349-351; her second marriage to the Earl of Angus, 378; her third marriage to Henry Stewart, xxiii. 2.
Marie Antoinette, Queen of France, behaviour of, when attacked by the Paris mob at Versailles, viii. 178-181; escape with the King, and recapture at Varennes, 228, 229; escapes assassination in the attack on the Tuileries, 309; her energetic conduct on the 10th of August, 337, 338, 345; her captivity in the Temple, ix. 56, 58, 59, 85, n.; her trial and execution, 89-91.
Maria Louisa, Archduchess, afterwards Empress of the French, xiii. 166, 274, 275, 368, 369; xiv. 32; xv. 13, 14, 16, 146, 222, 223, 249-251, 384.
Marischal, Earl. See Keith.
Marlborough, John, Duke of, ii. 426; xxiv. 320; xxv. 190, 192, 424.
——, Sarah, Duchess of, i. 32, n.; ii. 488; xxv. 190-195, 198.
Marmont, Marshal, Duke of Ragusa, x. 127, 382; xii. 51; xiii. 383; xiv. 23-25, 297, 299, 382, 384, 386, 387, 412; xv. 47, 108, 113, 115, 138-141, 144, 146, 150, 152, 155, 156, 199, 204-212; xvi. 69.
'Marriage-a-la-Mode,' by Dryden, i. 122.

Marriages, ill-assorted, reflections on, i. 76, 77.
Marston, the dramatist, i. 3.
'Martin Mar-all, Sir,' by Dryden, i. 90.
Marvel, Andrew, and the Duke of Monmouth, i. 42.
Mary Queen of England, xxiii. 74.
—— of Guise, Queen-Regent of Scotland, xxiii. 71-82.
——, Queen of Scotland, xxiii. 51-186
—— of Este, Queen of James VII., xxiv. 260, 314.
——, Queen of England, spouse of William III. xxiv. 226-7.
Masham, Lady, favourite of Queen Anne, ii. 144, 149, 187; death of, xxv. 193, 195, 386.
Mason, W. Monck, Historian of St Patrick's Cathedral, Dublin, ii. 23, n. 31, n. 210, 414-417, 468-479.
'Massacre of Amboyna,' by Dryden, i. 140.
Massena, Marshal, Duke of Rivoli, Prince of Essling, x. 9, 20, 21, 24, 35, 36, 78, 104-108, 115, 121, 125, 134, 137, 154, 158, 202, 204, 414; xi. 80, 98-103, 120; xii. 56-71; xiii. 178, 184, 185, 204, 297, 300-302, 380-383, 418.
Massenbach, General, xiv. 234-236.
Massinger, characterised as a dramatist, i. 2, et. seq.; vi. 342.
Matilda, the Empress, daughter

of Henry I. of England, xxvii. 188, 192, 214.

Matthews, Charles, the actor, xx. 243.

Maturin, Rev. Charles, of Dublin, iii. 358; remarks on the supernatural machinery of his romance, 370, n.; Review of his 'Fatal Revenge' xviii. 157-172; Review of his novel, 'Women, or Pour et Contre,' 172-203; remarks on a suppressed scene in his tragedy of 'Bertram,' 204-208.

Maximilian, King of Bavaria, xii. 44, 51.

Maxwells and Johnstones, feud between the, xxiii. 280-288.

Maxwell, Lord, xxiii. 17, 48.

—— and Hawley, fray between, xxiii. 251.

'Medal, The,' by Dryden, i. 315.

Mehrfeldt, General, of Austria, xiv. 384, 387-389.

Melas, the Austrian General, x. 96, 102-103; xi. 79, 96-116, 119, 120.

Melfort, Lord, Secretary of State to James II, xxiv 363.

Melville, Lord, xxiv. 264, 357, 359.

——, Henry Dundas, Viscount, the planner of the expedition to Egypt, iv. 336-337; xi. 196-197, n.

——, Sir Andrew, xxii. 184.

——, n. the two preachers, xxiii. 272-3.

——, General, xxvi. 304, n. 308, n.

Menteith, Sir John, betrayal of Sir W. Wallace by, xxi. 191; xxii. 94, 95.

Menou, General, viii. 263; ix. 386-387; x. 305, 365, 382-384; xi. 194-195, 199, 204.

Merchiston Tower, description of, vii. 358.

Merovingian dynasty of Frankish kings, xxvii. 46, 51, 54-71.

Metaphysical poetry in England, character of, i. 7; causes of its decline after the restoration, 36.

Metternich, Prince, Austrian Prime-minister, xiv. 328-335; xv. 411-412. n.

Mickle, William Julius, seventeen ballads supposed to be written by, xvii. 123-128.

Middleton, General, afterwards Earl of, xix. 238, 245, 249, 250, 256; xxiv. 111-113, 174-176, 178, 185-188, 194.

——, Earl of, Secretary to the Old Pretender, xxv. 90.

Milan, Buonaparte's triumphant entrance into, in 1796, x. 52; in 1800, xi. 105.

—— decree against British commerce, xiii. 5-7.

Milbourne, Rev. Luke, notice of, and his attack on Dryden's Virgil, i. 336-342, 360-364.

Mildmay, Sir Henry, xxiv. 67.

Miloradovitch, General, xiv. 160, 186, 192, 299, 308-309.

Milton, John, his 'Paradise Lost,' converted by Dryden, into a dramatic poem, i. 141; Milton's opinion of it, 152; Lord Byron's opinion of, 145, n.; an Independent in religious principle, xxiv. 38.

Mincio, Passage of the, x. 77.

Miot, M., historian of the French Egyptian expedition, x. 312, 351, 352, 360.

Minstrels, the, claim of, to the authorship of the Metrical Romances, vi. 154-162; condition of, 162-169; their degraded state when put down, 209-212; notice of, by Mr Ellis, xvii. 33.

'Minstrelsy of the Scottish Border,' contributions of Dr Leyden to. iv 165.

Mirabeau, the Count de. viii. 153-161, n.; 162-173, 174, n.; his opinion of the Duke of Orleans, 191; his rage at being called Riquetti, 202, n.; his intrigues with the king for the restoration of royalty, 220; his death, 222.

Mirabelle de Gordon, M., xxvi. 281.

Miseries of Human Life, by the Rev. James Beresford, Review of, xix. 139-159.

Mitchell the preacher, remarkable case of, xxiv. 230-232.

Modena, Duke of, treatment of by Buonaparte, in 1796, x. 57, 8; his States revolutionized by Buonaparte, 176, 177; plundered by the Venetians, 233; xiv. 32.

Moir of Stonywood, xxvi. 214, 324, 325.

'Mock Astrologer,' by Dryden, i. 91.

Molière, Review of his Life and Works, xvii. 137-215; character of, as a Comic Dramatist, vi. 328.

Moncey, Marshal, Duke of Conegliano, xi. 104-106; xiii. 86; xv. 155; xvi. 69.

Monge, member of the Institute, x. 288-293, 316-382; xi. 183.

Monk, General, afterwards Duke of Albemarle, xxiv. 104, 105, 152-158, 181.

Monluc's observation on soldiers, xxvi. 354.

Monmouth, Duke of, his intercourse with the Corporation of Hull, i. 42; character of, 204; his return from Holland, 205; satirised by Dryden in 'Absalom and Achitophel,' 208; Charles II.'s affection for him, 243; his landing at Lyme, in arms against James II., 259; See also, xxiv. 244, 248, 273-275.

Mons Meg, an ancient piece of ordnance in Edinburgh castle, vii. 321, n. 342.

Montague, Charles, Earl of Halifax, an antagonist of Dryden, i. 283; well pensioned for his labours by king William, 284, n.; subscribes for a funeral to Dryden, 371; projects, but never executes, a monument to his memory, 399-400; his courtier-like letter to Swift, ii. 103, n.

———, Lady Mary Wortley, remarks of, on 'Clarissa Harlowe,' iii. 59; on the character of Fielding, 80.

Montbrun, General, xiv. 42-104; xv. 60.

Montebello, the residence of Buonaparte in Italy in 1796-7, x. 236.

———, Battle of, xi. 108.

Monteith (Graham), Earl of, xviii. 317-319.

———, Robert, 'Forester's Guide and Profitable Planter,' Review of, xxi. 1-76. See *Planting*.

Montfort, Simon de, leader of the crusade against the Albigenses, xxvii. 285, 293; his son, Amaury, 294.

———, John de, pretensions of, to the duchy of Bretagne, xxviii. 15-17, 48.

———, Jane, Countess de, xxviii. 18, 21-23, 25, 26, 29, 70, 71.

———, John de (son of the two preceding), Duke of Bretagne, xxviii. 18, 136, 138, 192-195, 206-7.

Montgomery, Sir James, xxiv. 401, 402.

Moniteur, The, xi. 240.

Monro of Culcairn, xxv. 432; xxvi. 254, 355.

Montholon, Count, xvi. 124, et seq.

Montrose, James (Graham), Earl and Marquis of, xxiii. 368-370, 383-402; xxiv. 1-24, 72-80.

———, Duke of, xxv. 100, n.

Moore, Dr John, the friend and biographer of Smollett, ii. 117; letters of Smollett to

x. 148; his character of Smollett, 170, n.

Moore, General Sir John (son of the preceding), xiii. 144, 147, 152-162.

———, Admiral Sir Graham (idem), xii. 97.

More, Sir Antonio, his picture of the Seton family, vii. 398.

Moreau, General, campaign of in Germany, in 1796, x. 90; his retreat, 101; denounces Pichegru's intrigues, 277; his army of the Rhine, 301, 302; xi. 10, 81-84, 128, 307-310, 312-315, 339, 340; xiv. 341, 346, 347.

Morier, James, 'Hajji Baba in England,' a novel, Review of, xviii. 354-391.

Morrison, Valet to the Pretender, xxvi. 371, n.

Mortier, Marshal, Duke of Treviso, xii. 202-206; xiv. 41, 113, 141, 142, 151, 152, 188, 190, 191, 412; xv. 108, 114, 138-140, 199, 344-358.

Morton, James (Douglas), Earl of, Regent, xxiii. 106, 108, 109, 115, 116, 121, 123, 127, 131, 146-165.

Moscow, conflagration of, xiv. 113-120.

Moy, the Rout of, xxvi. 291.

Mozart's advice to Michael Kelly, xx. 234-5.

Muiron, aide-de-campte Buonaparte, x. 141, n.; xvi. 408.

Mulgrave, John Sheffield, Earl of (afterwards Duke of Buckingham), i. 154; his account of Lord Rochester's

cowardly conduct in a duel, 155, n.; his 'Essay upon Satire,' 171; character of Rochester, from this poem, ib. n.; his flippant lines on Dryden, 177; for a time in opposition to the court, 200; reconciled to it, 206.
Munro, Sir Robert, of Foulis, xxvi. 272, n.
Murat, Joachim, brother-in-law of Napoleon, Grand Duke of Berg, King of Naples, x. 25, 158, 305, 323, 359, 360, 374, 377, 382: xi. 18, 20, 105, 140, 141, 143, 320; xii. 51, 78-80, 126, 177, 181, 222; xiii. 32, 39, 43, 48, 62-68, 78; xiv. 42, 77, 82, 83, 105, 111, 112, 130-134, 139-141, 148, 204, 215, 225, 231, 271-2, 339, 385, 407, 421, 429; xv. 71, 72, 334, 335, 374-381.
Mure of Auchindrane, remarkable trial of, xxi. 228-230.
Murray, Sir Andrew, of Bothwell, Regent of Scotland, xxii. 203, 204, 210, 215.
——, Archibald (Douglas), Earl of, xxii. 301.
——, James (Stewart), Earl of, Regent, xxiii. 76, 90-96, 102-104, 109, 110, 121, 127-142.
——, the bonny Earl of, xxiii. 191, 192.
——, Earl of, xxv. 155, 405.
——, Lord, xxiv. 376, 377.
——, Lord Charles, xxv. 278, 306, 376, 382.
——, Lord George, xxvi. 106-377.

Murray, Sir Gideon, of Elibank, xxiii. 278.
——, Sir David, xxvi. 67, 142.
——, John, of Broughton, Secretary to the Pretender, xxvi. 67-360, *passim.*
——, Rev. Professor, the orientalist, iv. 149.
' My Pocket Book,' a burlesque on Sir John Carr, xix. 160-165.
' Mysteries of Udolpho,' remarks on, iii. 345.

Nairne, Lord, xxv. 155, 252, 278; xxvi. 104, 146, 155, 157-8, 190-304, n.
Names of characters in fictitious composition, xviii. 111-114.
Nansouty, General, xiv. 104.
Napier of Merchiston, notice of the family of, vii. 358-363.
Naples. *See* Ferdinand.
Napoleon. *See* Buonaparte.
——, Saint, ix. 323.
Narbonne, Comte de, viii. 281, n.; xiv. 34, 35, 316.
Necker, minister of Finance in France, viii. 79, 82, 84, 102-107, 123, 140, 154, 204, 206; xi. 89.
Nelson, Lord, anecdote of, after the battle of Copenhagen, xx. 278, n.; his pursuit of Buonaparte to Egypt, x. 315; victory of Aboukir over the French fleet, 333-337; honours paid to him by the Turkish Sultan, 347; victory of Trafalgar, and death, xii. 104-111. *See* Southey.

Neutrality, armed, xi. 188-190.
Newcastle, Duke of, a patron of Dryden, i. 92, 96.
Newburn, battle of, xxiii. 364.
Newton, Sir Isaac, Swift's character of, ii. 293-4.
Ney, Marshal, Duke of Elchingen, Prince of the Moskwa, xi. 228, 228; xii. 51, 176, 177, 236, 242, 247. 253; xiv. 42, 159. 169-171. 190-194, 204, 231, 297, 306-308, 342, 345, 364-366, 369, 373-4, 393-395; xv. 47, 110, 120, 199-211, 353-355. 417, 426, 428, 431, 432, 436; xvi. 17-19, 54, 55.
Niemen, passage of the, xiv. 43, 44.
Nithsdale, Earl of, xxv. 155, 252, 289, 388-390.
Nokes, the player, characterized by Cibber, i. 90. n.
Norfolk, Duke of xxiii. 138.
Normans, invasions of France by the, xxvii. 80-87; their invasion of Neustria under Rollo, and settlements in Normandy, 96-100; their invasions of and settlements in Italy, 129-135; their invasion and conquest of England under Duke William, 139-151; See also xxii. 32-35.
Northampton, treaty of, xxii. 170.
'Northern Antiquities,' by Jamieson and Weber, v. 358; vi. 193.
Northumberland, Percy, Earl of, xxii. 237, 250, 282-284, 329.

Northumberland, xxiii. 138, 150, 151, 240.
—— Hugh, Duke of, generosity of, to John Kemble, xx. 171.
NOVELISTS, BRITISH, BIOGRAPHICAL AND CRITICAL NOTICES OF, iii. and iv.
—— causes of their want of success as dramatists, iii. 87-88.

Obscenity, the disgrace of French literature, xviii. 27.
October club, of whom consisting. ii. 123.
'Œdipus,' by Dryden. i. 189.
O'Flaherty's, Roderick, Ogygia, notice of, xx. 305.
Ogilvie, Sir Walter, sheriff of Angus. xxii. 242.
—— Lord, xxvi. 183, 190, 266, 325, 416.
——, Lady, xxvi. 192.
—— of Boyne, xxv. 339, 340.
Ogilvy of Barras, Sir George, gallant defence of Dunotter castle by vii 320-337.
O'Hara, General, British commander at Toulon in 1793, ix. 347, 353.
Oldbuck, Jonathan, xxvi. 141, n.
Oldenburg, Dukedom of, xiii. 356.
'Old English Baron,' remarks on, iii. 328-336.
Oldham, the Satirist, i. 239.
'Old Mortality,' review of the story of, with historical illustrations, xix. 28-85; origin of the character of, xxiv. 222.
Oldisworth, Mr, the supposed

author of 'The Examiner,'
ii. 128, 129, n.
Oliphant of Gask, xxvi. 105-
213, 351.
O'Meara, Barry, British sur-
geon to Napoleon, xvi. 129,
192, 288.
Oneyers and Moneyers, xix.
391; xxvi. 125.
O. P. Row, notice of the,
xx. 226-229.
Oporto, storming of, by the
French, under Soult, in
1809, xiii. 280.
Orange, William, Prince of,
afterwards William III., xxiv.
271, 272, 314, 316-327.
See William III.
—— Prince of, xv. 421-423;
xvi. 7.
Orford, Sir Robert Walpole,
Earl of. See Walpole.
—— Horace Walpole, Earl of.
See Walpole.
Orkney, Patrick Stewart, Earl
of, the model of a real feudal
tyrant, xxi. 230-233; xxiii.
327-329.
Orleans, Philip, Duke of, Regent, fatal influence of the
licentiousness of, on society
in France, viii. 50.
—— Philip, Duke of, (Egа-
lité), viii. 138, 139, 190,
191; ix. 8, 79.
—— Louis Philippe, Duke of,
now King of France, xv.
324, 325, 342, 344.
Ormond, Hugh (Douglas) Earl
of, xxii. 283-301.
—— James, Duke of, a patron
of Dryden, i. 90; characterized in Dryden's Absalom and
Achitophel, 212; Dryden's

dedication of his 'Fables' to
his grandson, 365.
Ormond, Duke of, xxiv. 320, n.;
xxv. 227, 235, 236, 238,
343, 344, 430; xxvi. 66.
—— Duchess of, Introduc-
tory Verses to, in Dryden's
Fables, i. 365; her liberal
donation to the poet, 366.
Orrery, Earl of, his remarks on
Swift's Love of Domination
Controverted, ii. 121; mistaken in his account of Swift's
first reception as Dean of St
Patrick's, 152; character of,
and of his 'Remarks on
Swift's Life and Writings,'
393-395.
Orthez, battle of, xv. 66-68.
Ostermann, General, Count,
xiv. 352, 353.
O'Sullivan, Col. xxvi. 134-
136, 190, 331.
Otterburn, battle of, xxii. 238.
Otway, Thomas, patronised by
Lord Rochester, i. 166;
lampooned by him, 167; his
lines on Lord Rochester,
178.
Oudinot, Marshal, Duke of
Reggio, xii. 78, 250; xiv.
42, 163, 164, 173, 174,
198-201, 213, 308, 339,
358-360; xv. 107, 116-
118, 121, 199, 200, 214;
xvi. 69.
Oughton, Sir Adolphus, xxvi.
362, n.
Ouvrard, M. xiii. 313-315.
Oxburgh, Col. xxv. 379.
Oxford University, loyal character of, xxiv. 309; conduct
of James VII. to, 310; its
return for it, 320, n.

Oxford, Thomas (Harley), Earl of, head of the Tory ministry in 1710, ii. 108; Swift's first intimacy with, 109, 117; his treatment of Swift's friends, 136, 137; fails in introducing Swift to the Queen, 143, n.; makes Swift Dean of St Patrick's, 148; dissension between him and St John, 156; partly allayed by Swift, 159; wounded by Guiscard, 168; saved by Swift from another attempt on his life, 170; marries his son to the Duke of Newcastle's daughter, 171; loses his daughter, ib.; Swift's great attachment to him, 172; member of the Scriblerus club, 179; increased discord between him and St John, ib.; Swift's censures upon him, 183; his summons to Swift on leaving office, 187; imprisoned in the Tower, 196; declines Swift's offer of sharing his captivity, 197. See also xxv. 194-195, 198, 205-6, 221-224, 235-237.

'Palamon and Arcite,' by Dryden, i. 403, 424.
Palafox, General, xiii. 94, 143, 150, 151.
Palm, the Bookseller of Nuremberg, xii. 158, 159.
'Pamela,' remarks on, iii. 27-38.
Panmure, Earl of, xxv. 273, 279, 359.
Paoli, General, return of, to Corsica, ix. 337; Buonaparte's letter to him, 389, 399; his opinion of Napoleon when a boy, 331.
Parallel roads of Glenroy, xxiv. 365.
Paris in 1815, Visit to, v. 214-283.
Parliament, the Long, xxiii 365; xxiv. 61, 62, 156-162.
Parma, Duke of, how treated by Buonaparte in 1796, x. 56.
Parnell, Dr Thomas, introduced to Lord Oxford by Swift, ii. 137.
Partouneaux, General, xiv. 205, 209.
Partridge, John, the almanack-maker, notice of, ii. 93, n.
Pass of Corryarrack, xxvi. 97.
—— of Killycrankie, xxiv. 378.
—— of Cockburn's path, xxiv. 93.
Paterson, William, founder of the Bank of England, xiv. 27-48.
Patrick's, Bishop, 'Parable of the Pilgrim,' notice of, xviii. 95.
Patronage, lay, arguments in favour of, xxiv. 403, 404; act of Queen Anne respecting, xxv. 215.
Patten, Rev. Robert, historian of the rebellion in 1715, xxv. 314-319, n. et seq.
Patten's, William, account of the attack and defence of two Scottish Border strongholds, vii. 142-144; his account of Somerset's expedition to Scotland, xxiii. 69.

Pattison, Mayor of Carlisle, xxvi. 208.

Paul, Emperor of Russia, x. 395; xi. 78, 134-144, 146, 184-191.

———, Rev. William, execution of, xxv. 391-2.

'PAUL's LETTERS TO HIS KINSFOLK,' during his Tour on the Continent in 1815; v. Letter I. Passage to Flanders—First impressions of the country and the people, 1.—II. Bergen-op-Zoom—British attack on it in 1814, 12.—III. and IV., Retrospect of French history and politics from the surrender of Paris in 1814, to Buonaparte's return, 21.—V. Buonaparte's plan and preparations for the approaching campaign, 50.—VI. His advance into Belgium—Battle of Quatre Bras with the English, 64.—VII. Battle of Ligny—defeat and retreat of the Prussians, 79.—VIII. Battle of Waterloo, 99, and 346-354.—IX. Visit to the field of Waterloo, 146.—X. Agriculture, Statistics, &c. of Belgium, 160.—XI. Country between Brussels and Paris, 183.—XII. and XIII. Paris in 1815 during the occupation by the allies, 214. —XIV. Political events in Paris after the battle of Waterloo—conduct of the allied troops, 253.—XV. State of religion in France, 285.—XVI. Continuation of the political state of France,

and negotiations with the allies, 309.

Pavia, insurrection of, x. 72.

Pease-weep (green-plover), cause of dislike to, among the Scottish peasants, xxiv. 221.

Pedro, Don, the Cruel, King of Castile, xxviii. 143-147, 152-153.

Peltier, John, xi. 237, 244-245.

Peninsular war, sketch of the, xiii. chap. xli. xlv. li. liv.

Pepin the Elder, mayor of the palace, xxvii. 65.

——— Bref, founder of the Carlovingian dynasty, xxvii. 70.

'Pepys, Samuel, Secretary to Admiralty, in the reign of Charles II., and James II., Memoirs of,' Review of, xx. 94-152; founder of the Pepysian library at Cambridge, i. 352.

Percival's, Dean, satire on Dean Swift, ii. 242-245.

Percy, origin of the family of, xxii. 40.

———, Sir Henry (Hotspur), xxii. 237-240, 250, 251.

———, Sir Ralph, xxii. 237.

———'s, Bishop, 'Reliques of Ancient English Poetry,' characterised, xvii. 18, 25, 26, 119-122.

'Peregrine Pickle,' remarks on, iii. 130.

PERIODICAL CRITICISM, Vols. xvii. xviii. xix. xx., xxi.

Perkin Warbeck, xxii. 347, 348.

Perth, James (Drummond), Earl and Duke of, xxiii.

338; xxiv. 299, 302, 331, 338; xxv. 255-260.
Perth, James, Duke of, xxvi. 63, 69, 77, 78, 106, 139, 161, 190, 208-212, 228, 249, 250, 335, 340.
Peter the Hermit, xxvii. 160, 163, 172.
Peterborough, Earl of, i. 283; ii. 309, n., 320, n.
Philadelphes, Secret Society of, in the French army, xvi. 258.
Philip I., King of France, xxvii. 121, 152-157.
—— II. (Augustus), xxvii. 237; early measures of his reign, ib. 239; disputes with Henry II. of England, 241-243; engages in the Third Crusade, 243; details of its events, 244-250; returns home, 251; intrigues against Richard, 254; marries and divorces his second wife, 259; marries a third wife, 260; excommunicated 261; takes Normandy from King John, 266; prepares to invade England, 271; league against him, 272; defeats his foes at Bouvines, 275-279; supports his son Louis when offered the crown of England, 287-292; sends him against the Albigenses, 293; death, 294.
—— III. (The Hardy), xxvii. 336, 341-346, 349-352.
—— IV. (the Fair), disputes of, with Edward I. of England, xxvii. with Pope Boniface, 361; wars with Flanders, 362; destruction of the order of Templars, 364; death, 368.
Philip V. (the Long), xxvii. 367, 372-377.
—— VI. (of Valois), xxvii. 382; makes Edward III. of England do homage for his French possessions, xxviii. 2; banishes Robert of Artois, 8; his fleet defeated by Edward at Sluys, 11; supports Charles de Blois as Duke of Bretagne, 16; his troops defeated in Guienne, 29-33; collects an army to meet Edward in Normandy, 50; defeated by Edward at Cressy, 56-68; fails to relieve Calais, 74; his death, 89.
—— the Hardy, Duke of Burgundy, xxviii. 104, 170, 171, 202, 211-213.
——, Ambrose, his account of Dean Swift's first appearance at Button's, ii. 71, n.
Phillips, Sir Richard, bookseller, xvii. 64; xix. 164, 165.
——, Mrs, i. 111.
Philiphaugh, battle of, xxiv. 20-22.
Pichegru, General, ix. 330; x. 266, 267, 272-278; xi. 79, 308, 311-316, 332-334.
Pickering, Sir Gilbert, one of the intended victims of the Gunpowder Plot, i. 17.
—— cousin and patron of Dryden, notice of, l. 27; character of, 28, n.; his fate at the Restoration, 39.

Picton, General Sir Thomas, xv. 423; xvi. 7, 10, 11.
Picts, the, when first mentioned in Scottish history, xx. 309; their contests with the Scots of Ireland, 312, 313; hypotheses of Pinkerton and Chalmers as to their origin, 324-339; their language, 340; remains of it a single word, 342; list of their kings, 344; their inroads on the Roman provinces, 347; their round towers, 348; renewed contests with the Scots of Argyle, 352; finally and completely conquered by the latter, 353-356; unanimity of evidence to this fact, death-blow to Pinkerton's hypothesis, 357-365; conclusions arrived at respecting them, 365; notices of them after their dispersion, 370-373.
Pignatelli, Prince Belmonte, x. 187, 188, 191.
Pilkington, Rev. Thomas, and his wife, unworthy protegés of Dean Swift, ii. 335-341.
Pinkerton, John, character of, xx. 319; his 'Essay on the Early History of Scotland,' 320; his theory of the Gothic origin of the Picts, and controversies to which it has given rise, 324-358; rich gleanings which he has left of ancient Scottish history, xxi. 197-198.
Pinkie, battle of, iv. 99, 100; xxiii. 67.
Pitcairn's, Robert, 'Trials and other proceedings in matters criminal, before the High Court of Justiciary in Scotland,' Review of, xxii. 199-265.
Pitsligo, Lord (the original of the Baron of Bradwardine), xxvi. 183, 190, 222, 261, 322, 399.
Pitt, William, xi. 126, 203; xii. 145.
Pius VI., Pope, x. 11, 66, 86, 87, 112, 180, 182-190, 390: xi. 36.
—— VII., Pope, xi. 141, 142, 174-177; xii. 12-15, 28; xiii. 236-249; xiv. 263-265, 427-429.
PLANTING WASTE LANDS, on, xxi. 1; importance of the subject, 4; division of it, profitable and ornamental, 6; requisites for planting on a large scale, 13; choice of ground, 15; shape of plantations, 19; inclosures, 26; draining marshy ground, 28; formation of paths through plantations, 28; preparation of soil, 30; choice of trees, 31; manner and time of planting, 36; distance between the plants, 45; nurses, 48; the Athol mode of planting, 50; pruning, 61; thinning, 64; sowing seeds, 69; supposed tardy returns of plantations, 75.
Platoff, Hetman of the Cossacks, xii. 247, 248; xiv. 43, 161, 163.
Plutarch's Lives, preface to, by Dryden, i. 249.
Po, passage of the, x. 37.

Port Squob, or *Squab*, a nickname given by Lord Rochester to Dryden, i. 169, n.; 221, 374.
Poitiers, battle of, xxviii. 97-108.
Poker Club, anecdotes of the, xix. 336-338.
Poland, policy of Napoleon towards, xii. 217-232.
Police, French system of, under Buonaparte, xi. 165-171.
Polignac, Armand and Jules de, xi. 318; xv. 17, 78, 120.
Polytechnic School, xi. 183; xv. 150.
Poniatowski, Marshal Prince, xiv. 42, 140, 361, 384, 386, 397, 401, 402.
Pope, Alexander, reviews Lord Mulgrave's ' Essay on Satire,' i. 173; his lines on the fate of Elkanah Settle, 235; his epitaph on Rowe, 400; friendship between, and Swift, ii. 137; his anecdote of Swift's manner, 239, n.; Swift's visit to him at Twickenham in 1726, 279; character of, 280; liberality of Swift to, 307.
—— and Dryden, the poetical merits of, contrasted by Dr Johnson, i. 402; Lord Byron's remarks on, 403, n.
Popish plot, the, Dryden's lines on, i. 201, n.
Purdage, Samuel, an obscure adversary of Dryden, i. 219, 220, n.
Portalis, minister of religion under Buonaparte, xi. 178.

Porteous mob, history of the, vii. 258; xxvi. 17-33.
Portsmouth, Duchess of, i. 173.
Pozzo di Borgo, General, xv. 182.
Pradt, the Abbé de, Archbishop of Malines, xiii. 167, 168; xiv. 93, 56-58, 217-222; xv. 162, 182, 183.
Praise-God-Barebone, xxiv. 158.
Presburg, Treaty of, xii. 87-89.
Presbytery, established in Scotland, xviii. 83, 84; attempts of James I. to introduce episcopacy, 269-275; followed up by Charles I., 353-357; ' National Covenant' to support, 358-360; state of, under Cromwell, xxiv. 123, 124; subverted by Charles II. xxiv. 176; finally restored by King William III., 388, 402.
Preston, defence and surrender of, by the rebels in 1715, xxv. 375-382.
—— General, of Valleyfield, xxvi. 166, 188, 189.
Prestonpans, battle of, xxvi. 153-176.
Pretender, the Old. See Chevalier de St George.
—— the Young. See Charles Edward.
Preuss-Eylau, battle of, xii. 237-242.
Price, Sir Uvedale, xxi. 102-105.
Pride's Purge, xxiv. 61, 62.
' Prince Arthur,' an Epic

INDEX. 343

Poem,' by Sir Richard Blackmore, i. 335.

Pringle, Captain J. W., 'Remarks on the campaign of 1815' by, xvi. 343-379.

Prior and Montague, their parody of the 'Hind and Panther' of Dryden, i. 283, 284.

———, Matthew, i. 283, 284; ii. 125, 138.

Projectors, Dean Swift's enmity to, ii. 4, 295.

Provera, the Austrian General, x. 20, 21, 152, 158, 159.

Prussia, fall of, in 1806, xii. 185-193.

Publishers, an author's opinion of, i. 332 n.

Pyramids, battle of the, x. 326-329.

Quasdonowich, the Austrian general, x. 102, 103, 106, 107, 109, 128, 131, 154, 155.

Quatre Bras, battle of, v. 64-78; xv. 431-433.

Queensberry, Duke of, xxiv. 302, 332; xxv. 57, 75, 77, 87, 88, 91, 118, 131, 174.

———, Duchess of, letters and character of, xix. 208.

Rabelais, Swift's admiration of, ii. 72, n.; 417, n.

Radagaisus, invasion of the Roman Empire by, xxvii. 40.

RADCLIFFE, MRS ANNE, BIOGRAPHICAL SKETCH OF, iii. 337; details of her history and literary career, 337-358; character and peculiarities of her romances, 359-384; of her poetical compositions, 385-389.

Raid of the Redswair, xxiii. 151-153.

Raleigh, Sir Walter, i. 13, n.

Ramorgny, Sir John, xxii. 247.

Ramsay, Sir Alexander, xxii. 210, 211, 218-220, 222, 223.

———, Sir John, Lord Bothwell, a minion of James III. of Scotland, vii. 169, 173; xxii. 322, 325.

———, Sir John, page of James VI., 23, 203, 249.

Randolph, Thomas, Earl of Murray, surprise of Edinburgh castle by, vii. 258-260; various exploits of xxii. 135-138, 164-170, 195-199.

Rapin, M., i. 397.

Rapp, General, xi. 226; xii. 80; xiv. 92, 98, 142, 155, 191, 203, 204, 416.

Ratcliffe, Lord, i. 321, 322, n.

———, Charles, Earl of Derwentwater, xxvi. 395, 396.

Ravenscroft, Edward, dramatist, notice of, and his controversies with Dryden, i. 197; specimen of his satire, 199, n.

Read, Thomas, Alderman of London, xxiii. 60.

Reay, Lord, xxvi. 197.

Rebellion, Jacobite, in 1715, history of, xxv. 269-426.

———, in 1719, history of, xxv. 430-433.

———, in 1745, history of, xxvi. 83-436.

Reding, Aloys, xi. 224, 229.

REEVE, CLARA, BIOGRAPHICAL SKETCH OF, iii.; particulars of her life, 325-328; remarks on her 'Old English Baron,' 328-336.
Reeves, Mrs, the actress, her intimacy with Dryden, i. 74.
Reformation. See Religion.
Regalia of Scotland, history and description of the, vii. 295-357.
Regnier, General, xii. 281-283, 285; xiv. 42, 89, 174, 175, 178, 179, 233, 308, 359, 365, 382, 394.
'Rehearsal, The,' a satire upon the heroic plays, notice of, i. 114; authors of, 116, 126, n. 389, n.
Reille, General Count, xvi. 6.
'Religio Laici,' by Dryden, i. 263; by Blount. See Blount.
Religion, state of, in France, in 1815, v. 285-308.
——, Reformation of, in England and Scotland, xxiii. 31-36, 43, 44, 73-80, 83-85, 267, 268.
Rentallers, or kindly tenants in Scotland, vii. 403, 404.
Rents of land, great increase of, in the neighbourhood of Edinburgh, vii. 251.
Restoration of Charles II., xxiv. 168.
—— of the Bourbons, xv. 271; Second Restoration, xvi. 69.
Reubel, the French director, x. 264, 403.
Reveillère Lepaux, the French director, x. 262.
Reviews, Sir Walter Scott's contributions to the *Edinburgh*, *Quarterly*, and *Foreign Quarterly*, xvii.—xxi.
'Reviewers' Groans,' a jeu d'Esprit, xix. 158.
Rhine, the river, German veneration for, xiv. 418.
Rhyme, in tragedy, vindicated by Dryden as the most legitimate style for that species of drama, i. 75; afterwards regarded by him as unnatural and unfit for it, 181; and more fit for the Epic, 183.
Ribeaumont, Sir Eustace de, and Edward III. xxvii. 83-85, 98.
Richard I. (Cœur de Lion), King of England, rebels against his father, xxvii. 240-242; succeeds to the crown, and engages in the Crusade, 243; his exploits in Palestine, 246-252; captivity on his way home, 253; release, 255; subsequent events till his death, 256-258.
—— notice of the romance of, xvii. 43-50.
—— II. of England, xxiii. 231.
—— III. of England, xxiii. 323-325.
RICHARDSON, SAMUEL, his letter regarding Swift, ii. 18-20; BIOGRAPHICAL NOTICE OF, iii.; details of his life and character 1-27; remarks on Pamela, 27-38; on 'Clarissa Harlowe,' 38-49; on 'Sir Charles Grandison,' 50-64; on his general merits as an author, 65-76

Ridicule the test of truth, how far a just axiom, xvii. 171-177.
Ritson, Joseph, character of, iv. 166, 167; anecdote of, vii. 21, n.; Review of his 'Ancient English Metrical Romances,' xvii. 16-54; Review of his 'Annals of the Caledonians, Picts and Scots.' xx. 301-374; his abstinence from animal food, 349; his 'North Country Chorister,' xxiii. 248.
Rival Ladies, The,' by Dryden, i. 69.
Rizzio, David, xxiii. 100-109.
Rob Roy (MacGregor), xxv. 264, 360, 361; xxvi. 164.
Robert Bruce, King, xxi. 180-184; history of his reign, xxii. 97-177.
—— II. (Stewart) xxii. 230-240.
—— III. xxii. 241-252.
—— the Wise. King of France, reign of, xxvii. 112.
—— the Devil, Duke of Normandy, xxvii. 115-118.
—— Curthose, Duke of Normandy, son of William the Conqueror, xxvii. 152; one of the leaders in the first crusade, 167, 176; his adventures after his return to Europe, 180-184.
——, Count of Artois, xxviii. 5-8, 12, 25-27.
—— of Paris, Count, xxvii. 169-171.
Robespierre, Maximilian the French Revolutionist, viii. 352-354, 380; ix. 33-36, 52, 73, 218, 225-229, 231, 232, 240-244, 251, 252, 259-275.
' Robinson Crusoe,' remarks on, iv. 274-281; Swift probably indebted to it for the incidents of his ' Gulliver's Travels,' ii. 481.
Roche d'Arien, siege of, xxvii. 70.
Rochester, John, (Wilmot) Earl of, i. 30, 53, 96; his patronage of Dryden, 124; cause of his subsequent enmity to the poet, 154; his cowardice, 155, n.; sets up Settle against Dryden, 158; and afterwards Crowne, 165, and Otway, 166; his criticism on Dryden, 169, n.; Dryden's retort, 170; character of, in Lord Mulgrave's Essay on Satire, 171, n.; his base and cowardly revenge on Dryden, as the supposed author, 174; Otway's lines upon him, 178; Hyde, Earl of, one of Dryden's patrons, i. 254, 309.
Rochfort, Lord Chief Baron, ii. 242.
' Roderick Random,' remarks on, iii. 127.
Rodrigo de Bivar, the Cid, abstract of the history of, xviii 45-66.
Roland, Madame, indelicate details of her Memoirs, viii. 51, 52; her Salon, 250; her husband appointed minister, 292-294; her letter to the king, 300; her husband dismissed, 301; her portrait of Barbaroux, 322, n.; of

Robespierre, 352, n.; her efforts to save the king's life, ix. 31, 32; her death and that of her husband, 124, 125.

Rollo, the Norman, invasion of France by, xxvii. 96; becomes a vassal of the crown and Duke of Normandy, 98-100.

Roman Border Antiquities, notice of, vii. 18-25.

—— Catholic Hymns, 1-293, n.

—— Drama, Antient, notice of, vi. 258 264.

—— civilization, influence of, upon the conquered countries, xxvii. 27-33.

Romans, General, xiii. 141-158, 280-286.

ROMANCE, ESSAY ON, vi. 127: definition; distinction between and *Novel*, 129; derivation of the word, 131.—I. General history and origin of, 133; Metrical Romances, 154; Prose Romances, 178.—II. Characteristics of the different European Romances; Scandinavian, 189; German, 192; Italian, 195; Spanish, 196; French, 199; English, 203; Scottish, 209.—III. Romances subsequent to those of Chivalry, 213-216. See *Novelists*. See *Ellis*. See *Ritson*. See *Amadis*.

'Romance of the Forest,' by Mrs Radcliffe, remarks on, iii. 342.

Roscommon, Earl of, 1-84, v.

Rose, William Stewart, 'Amadis de Gaul, a Poem,' Review of, xviii. 1, 40-43; his lives on Mrs Bankes' defence of Corfe castle, vii. 415, 416.

Rosebecque, battle of, xxviii. 212.

Roslin Glen and Hawthornden, description of, vii. 366.

Rostopchin, Count, Governor of Moscow, xiv. 107-109, 119-128.

Ruthen (Lesley). Earl of, xxv. 274, 315, 323-362.

Rothsay. Duke of, xxii. 246-248.

Roundheads and Cavaliers, party nicknames in the time of Charles I., xxiii. 272, 273; superseded by those of Whigs and Tories, during James VII's reign, xxiv. 2&c.

Roveredo, battle of, x. 114.

Roxburgh Castle, capture of, by Lord James Douglas, xxii. 141; siege of, by James II., xxii. 305; taken and destroyed, 308.

Roxburghe, Duke of, xxv. 100, n. 362, 413.

——, John. Duke of, the great bibliomaniac. iv. 325; vii. 213-215; sale of his books, and the establishment of the Roxburgh Club. 215-219.

'Royal Martyr,' by Dryden, i 93.

Rule. Elspeth, trial of, for witchcraft, xxiv. 143, n.

Rumbold, Richard, the Rye-House plot conspirator, xxiv. 281, 2.

Rump Parliament, xxiv. 158-162.

Run-about-Raid, the, xxiii. 103, 104.
Russell, James, one of the assassins of Archbishop Sharp, his account of the murder, xix. 274-281. See also, xxiv. 236.
Russia, Napoleon's invasion of, and campaign in, in 1812, xiv. 36-250.
Ruthven, Lord, xxiii. 106-108, 110-112.
———, Raid of, xxiii. 165-167.
———, See Gowrie Conspiracy.
Rymer, Thomas, an unsuccessful dramatist. i. 322; Dryden's lines on his being made historiographer, ib.; his dramatic criticism, 366; vi. 356.

Sacheverall, Dr., explosion to which he gave rise against the Whig ministry, ii. 100; cause of his obtaining the living of St Andrew's, Holborn, 101, n.
Sacken, General, xiv. 178, 179; xv. 55-57, 408.
SADLER, Sir RALPH, Biographical Memoir of, iv. 71.
Saint Aignan, Baron de, xv. 3.
Saint Cyr, Gouvion, Marshal, xiv. 88. 172, 173, 339, 343, 344, 374, 415; xvi. 69.
St Domingo, French expedition to, xi. 263-271.
St Francis Xavier, Life of, by Dryden, i. 288-291.
St Helena, residence of Napoleon in the island of, xvi. See Napoleon.
St Napoleon, ix. 923.
St Patrick's Hospital for lunatics, founded by Dean Swift, ii. 388-390; present state of, 500.
St Pierre, Eustace de, the patriotic burgher of Calais, xxviii. 76-78.
Saint Priest, General, xv. 114.
Saladin, Soltan, xxvii. 244-247, 252.
Salamanca, battle of, xiv. 99.
Salic Law, the, xxvii. 60, 373.
Salisbury, Montague, Earl of, xxii. 213.
Salmon, fear of their deserting the Scottish rivers, ix. 287; ancient Scottish legislation on the subject, ib.; causes threatening the destruction of the fish every where, 291; suggestions for redeeming the fisheries from ruin, 299.
Salmon-fishing, superiority of, to all others, ix. 273.
Sanctuary, privilege of, in Holyrood-house, vii. 295.
Sandford, the actor, i. 81, n.
San Marino, Buonaparte's conduct to the republic of, x. 193.
Sanquhar (Crichton), Lord, case of, xxiii. 258, 259.
Saracen invasion of France, defeated by Charles Martel, xxvii. 67-69.
Saragossa, siege of. See Zaragossa.
Sardinia, Victor Amadeus III. king of, Buonaparte's first campaign against, x. 16-25; terms of treaty of Cherasco, with, 28; treaty with the Directory, 241, 242; despoiled of his continental states, 389, 390.

Satire of Dryden, on the Dutch, extract from, i. 45, n.; of Dryden and Pope compared, 231, n.; First introduced into English poetry by Bishop Hall, 238; its effect upon English poetry, ib. et seq. 'Essay on,' by Dryden, 319. Estimate of his merits in, 417.

Satirists, the minor, Dryden's contempt of, i. 221, n.; 228, n.; 251.

Savary, General, Duke of Rovigo, x. 372; xi. 117-121, 321, 322, 336; xii. 73; xiii. 35, 36, 40-43, 79, 315; xiv. 257; xvi. 93, 94, 102, 108, 127.

Saxe, Marshal, xxvi. 65.

Saxony, Augustus, king of, xiv. 224-294, 300-348, 374, 397-399, 403.

Scandinavian Romances, notice of, vi. 189-191.

'Scenes of Infancy,' by Dr Leyden, notice of, iv. 168, 173-175.

Schill, Colonel, xii. 255; xiii. 188-190, 214, 215.

Schoenbrunn, treaty of, xiii. 254.

Schomberg, Duke of, circumstances connected with Dean Swift's monument to, li. 321.

Schwartzenberg, Prince, xiv. 41-89, 174-176, 178-180, 232-233, 339, 343, 346, 348, 367; xv. 37-39, 43, 59, 63, 64, 67, 107, 117-121, 138-157, 182, 408, 416.

Scotchmen of former days, ferocious and vindictive temper of, xxi. 256-259.

Scotchmen in London, after king James's accession, xxiii. 245-250.

SCOTLAND, HISTORY OF. Story of Macbeth, xxii. 11-26; Reign of Malcolm Canmore, 36; Alexander I. and David I. 41; Malcolm IV. 51; William the Lion, 52; Alexander II. 58; Alexander III. 60; John Baliol, 71; usurpation of Edward I. 73; Story of Sir William Wallace, 77-96; Robert (I.) Bruce, 97-177; David II. 195; Edward Baliol, 201; Robert (II.) Stewart, 230; Robert III. 241; James I. 262; James II. 277; James III. 306; James IV., 335; James V. xxiii. 1; Mary, 81; Regency of Murray, 127; of Lennox, 143; of Mar, 147; of Morton, 148; James VI. 159; union of the Crowns, 200; Charles I. 345; Charles II. xxiv. 72; James VII. 271; William and Mary, 356; Anne, xxv. 50; union of the kingdoms, 93; George I. 226; George II. xxvi.

————, PROVINCIAL ANTIQUITIES OF, vii. 155-457.

————, REGALIA OF, HISTORY AND DESCRIPTION OF THE, vii. 298-357; details of their preservation during the Siege of Dunottar, xxiv. 105-108.

————, Review of the Ancient History of, xx 301-376.

Scotland, Review of Mr Fraser Tytler's History of, xxi. 154-198.

——, —— of Thornton's Sporting Tour in the Highlands of, xix. 87-111.

——, —— of Sir John Carr's Tour in, in 1807, xix. 160-184.

——, Kirkton's Secret and True History of the Church of, xix. 213-282.

—— Highlands of. See Highlands.

Scott of Buccleuch, xxiii. 17, 70, 142, 297-299.

—— of Thirlstane, John, xxiii. 48.

——, Captain, afterwards General John, xxvi. 83-86.

——, Sir William of Harden, xxiii. 280, n.; xxiv. 268, 269.

——, Thomas, the author's brother, reported to be the author of Waverley, xix. 86, n.

Scottish Banking system, xxi. 282-296, 336, 338-342, 344, 345.

—— Criminal Trials, Review of Mr Pitcairn's collection of, xxi. 199-265.

Scrope, Lord, xxiii. 197, 198.

Seafield, Earl of, Chancellor of Scotland, xxv. 100, 101, 178, 181.

Seaforth, Earl of, xxv. 154, 252, 301, 302, 330, 399, 407, 430-433.

——, Lord, xxvi. 197.

Sea-sickness, miseries of, v. 4-6.

Sebastiani, General Count, xi. 248, 253; xiv. 199, 361, 362, 385.

Sedley, Sir Charles, i. 36, 53, 96, 170.

Segur's, Count Philip de, 'History of the Russian Expedition,' xiv. 49, n. et passim.

Selkirk, Alexander, account of, iv. 282.

Serrurier, General, x. 9, 24, 80, 102, 110, 162, 164, 205.

Setons, Earls of Winton, notice of the family of, vii. 397-401; description of Seton chapel, 402. See Winton.

Settle, Elkanah, dramatic poet, i. 153; his plays, 'Cambyses, King of Persia,' and 'The Empress of Morocco,' 158; character of the latter, 160; attacked by Dryden, Crowne, and Shadwell, 164; satirised by Dryden, 230; his lamentable fate, 233; Pope's lines on it, 235.

Severn, Well of, vii. 20-22.

SEWARD, MISS ANNA, BIOGRAPHICAL SKETCH OF, iv. 199-227.

Shadwell, Thomas, dramatic poet, i. 43, n.; 83, n.; 112, 164; controversy between him and Dryden, 222-228, 230, 237; succeeds to Dryden's places at the Revolution, 300, 322; his 'Bury Fair,' an imitation of Molière, xvii. 152.

Shaftesbury, Antony, Earl of, the 'Achitophel,' of Dryden's satire, i. 208; again satirised by him in 'The Medal,' 215; his grandson's retaliation on Dryden, 216, n.

Shakspeare, dramatic genius of, characterized, vi. 336-338; compared with Ben Jonson, 341, 342.

Sharpe, Archbishop of York, prejudices Queen Anne against Swift, ii. 142; repents and apologizes for it, 150, n.

——, Dr, Rector of St Giles, anecdote of, xxiv. 307, n.

——, James, Archbishop of St Andrews, xix. 274-278; xxiv. 172, 176; murder of, 230-238.

——, Charles Kirkpatrick, Review of his edition of Kirkton's History of the Church of Scotland, xix. 213-282; his account of Lady Warriston, the murderess, xxi. 260; his edition of Law's Memorials, vii. 182, n.

Sheale, Richard, one of the last minstrels, notice of, vi. 210-212.

Shelley's, Mrs, 'Frankenstein,' Review of, xvii. 250-269.

Shenstone's ballad of 'Jemmy Dawson,' xxvi. 392, n.

Sheridan, Sir Thomas, the Pretender's tutor, xxvi. 72, 73, 108, 190, 211.

——, Rev. Dr, friend of Dean Swift, ii. 241; character of, 273; his unfortunate sermon at Cork, 276; anecdotes of, 277, n.; his latter years and death, 396-398; droll anecdote of, 422, n.

—— Richard Brinsley, proprietor of Drury-lane Theatre, conduct of, to his managers, King and Kemble, xx. 201, 202, 213; anecdotes of, by Michael Kelly, 236-241.

Sheriffmuir, battle of, xxv. 353-363.

Shrewsbury, Earl of, xxiii. 174.

'Sicilian Romance,' by Mrs Radcliffe, remarks on, iii. 341.

—— Vespers, the, xxvii. 348.

Siege of Lochleven, xxii. 209; of Dunbar, 212-214; of Roxburgh, 304-308; of the Bass, xxiv. 399; of Carlisle, xxvi. 207; of Stirling, 256.

Siege of Lyons, ix. 179-182; of Toulon, 186, 187, 343-357; of Mantua, x. 96, 103, 127, 147, 158-164; of Acre, 355-365; of Genoa, xi. 99-103; of Zaragossa, xiii. 94-97, 151, 285.

Sièyes, Abbe, viii. 105, 109, 204, n., 211; x. 403, 405; xi. 7, 8, 13, 16, 30, 33, 41-47; xv. 388, 401.

Sinclair, Oliver, xxiii. 48, 168.

—— Lord, xxiii. 192; xxv. 155.

—— the Master of, a leader in the rebellion of 1715, xxv. 275, 276, 280, 281, 348, 401, 406, 407.

'Sir Martin Mar-all,' a comedy by Dryden, i. 90.

Skirving, Mr, Ballad of 'Battle of Prestonpans' by, xxvi. 172-176.

shuys, naval victory of, xxviii. 10-11.
Smedley, Rev. Jonathan, Dean of Clogher, verses by, on Dean Swift's instalment, ii. 193; notice of his 'Gulliveriana,' 333.
Smith, Dr Adam, meeting of, with Dr Johnson, iii. 269, n. anecdotes of, xix. 338-342.
—— Mrs Charlotte, Biographical Notice of, iv. 20; critical remarks on her novels and poetry, 58-70
—— Admiral Sir Sydney, conduct of, at Acre, x. 355-357, 361-365, 381; convention with Kleber for evacuating Egypt, xi. 192, 193.
Smolensk, battle of, xiv 83.
Smollett, Tobias, M.D., Biographical Notice of, iii. 117; parallel between his genius and literary character and those of Fielding, 171-181; letter of, to the Hon. A. C. Campbell, 182; his literary controversies with Grainger and Shibbeau, 187; his 'Tears of Scotland,' xxvi. 353, n.
Sobieski, Princess Clementina, wife of the Chevalier de St George, xxv. 55-58.
Soissons, battle of, xv. 108.
Solan goose, description of, by Defoe, vii. 445
Somers, Lord, relations of Swift with, and supposed ingratitude of the latter to, discussed, ii. 86-91; Swift's quarrel with him on the ground of his duplicity, 107.

Somerset, Duke of, expedition of, into Scotland, xxiii. 68.
——, Duchess of, favourite of Queen Anne II. 144; Swift's Satire upon her, ib.; revenges herself by preventing his being made a bishop, 146, n.
Somerville, John, Loan, Character of, iv. 309-321; notice of Sir A. More's picture of the Seton family in his possession, vii. 398 his ancestor's marriage, xix 240; conduct of one of his ancestors to James III. xxii. 312-314; of another to the Earl of Morton, xxiii. 157, 158.
'Somerville, Memoirs of the, xxii. 314, n.; xxiii. 379, n.; et passim.
Sonham, General, xiv. 382-384, 386; xv. 208-210.
Soult, Marshal, Duke of Dalmatia, xi. 102; xii. 51-81 176-181; xiii. 155, 156 179-282, 286; xiv. 308-335, 422; xv. 77, 86-88 339-340, 243, 417; xvi. 6, 42.
Southerne, Thomas, the dramatist, i. 241; Dryden's friendship for, 253, 315-316; great success of his plays, 203, n.; 384, n.; 433, n.
Southesk, Earl of, xxv. 252, 273, 278, 350.
Southey, Robert, his edition of the Morte d'Arthur, vi. 175; of Amadis and Palmerin, 198; Review of his edition of Chatterton's Works, xvii

215-241; Review of his 'Curse of Kehama,' 301-337; Review of his edition of 'Amadis de Gaul,' xviii. 1; of his 'Chronicle of the Cid,' 44; of his edition of the 'Pilgrim's Progress and Life of Bunyan,' 74; his Life of Nelson, x. 333, n.; and xii. 111, n.

Spain, war declared by, against England in 1804, xii. 98.

———, invasion of, by Buonaparte, xiii. 20; insurrection of the people against him, 62, et seq; renewed alliance with England, 101. See Peninsular War.

Spanish comedy, the model of the English comedies at the Restoration, i. 63; notice of vi. 279-282.

' ———— Friar,' by Dryden, i. 194, 303, 314.

———— and Portuguese Romances, notice of, vi. 196-199.

Spenser, Edmund, ' Works of, edited by the Rev. H. J. Todd,' Review of, xvii. 80-101.

Spottiswood, Sir Robert, Lord President of the Court of Session, xxiv. 18, 29, 30.

Sprat, Thomas, Bishop of Rochester, one of the authors of the ' Rehearsal,' i. 115.

Sprot, notary public, xxiii. 205-207.

Stair, John (Dalrymple) first Earl of, xxiv. 344-359; xxv. 2-4, 6, 8-11, 20-22, 30-34, 75, 230.

———— John, second Earl of, xxv. 230-232, 340.

Staël, Madame de, relations of, with Buonaparte, x. 291, 292; xi. 53, 74, 89, 172, 173.

Stanley, Sir Edward, xxii. 369, 370.

Stapleton, General, xxvi. 298, 322, 344.

Stapps, the intended assassin of Buonaparte, xiii. 251, 252.

' State of Innocence,' altered from Milton's Paradise Lost, by Dryden. i. 141; extract from, 148.

Steele, Sir Richard, offence given by, to the Tory ministry, ii. 127; feud between him and Swift, ib.; their controversy, 168-163; expelled the House of Commons, 164. See also xiv.

Steevens, George, commentator on Shakspeare, traits of, iv. 43, 45-47.

Stephen, King of England, xxviii. 196, 214, 215, 217-219.

STERNE, REV. LAWRENCE, i. 40; BIOGRAPHICAL SKETCH OF, iii. 273-298.

Stewart, of Ardshiel, xxvi. 190, 237-239, 261, 284, 325, 346.

———— of Ardvoirlich, xx. 46-48; xxiii. 393-395.

———— of Balloch, xxvi. 273, n.

———— of Invernahyle, anecdotes of, xix. 7-10; xxiii. 312.

———— Sir James, and Sir George Wharton, duel between, xxiii. 254.

————'s, Sir Henry, ' Planler's Guide,' review of, xxi. 77, 151.

Stewart's, General David, 'Sketches of the Highlands,' xxvi. 375, n. et passim.

—— Provost of Edinburgh in 1745. xxvi. 127-132, 136-138.

——, Colonel John Roy, xxvi. 105, 152, 237-240.

—— fate of the royal race of, xxiii. 342, 343.

—— Walter, High Steward of Scotland, xxii. 230.

—— of Appin, xxiii. 312; xxvi. 80.

Stillingfleet, Edward, controversy of, with Dryden, i. 276, 277.

Stirling of Keir, xxii. 333; xxv. 151, 153, 154.

Stokoe, Dr, xvi. 289.

Stolberg, Princess Louisa of, wife of Charles Edward, xxvi. 433.

Strathallan, Lord, xxvi. 105, 158, 206, n; 253, 256.

Stratherne, Malise, Earl of, xxii. 44.

Strathmore, Earl of, xxv. 275, 306, 308, 359-367.

Suchet, Marshal, Duke of Albufera, xi. 99, 100, 101, 109, 110; xiv. 422; xv. 418.

Suffolk, Henrietta, Countess of. See Howard, Mrs.

Sunday, remarks on the observance of, xx. 279, 280.

Sunderland, Earl of, xxiv. 299, 300.

Supernatural in fiction, remarks on the use of the, in the 'Castle of Otranto,' iii. 317-321; in the 'Old English Baron,' 328-331; in Mrs Radcliffe's, Mr Maturin's, and other romances, 370-376; in Mrs Shelley's 'Frankenstein,' xviii. 250-254; in Hoffmann's novels, 270-293.

Superstition, various kinds of, cherished even by superior minds, xviii. 337-339.

'Supper of Beaucaire,' a pamphlet by Buonaparte, ix. 412-420.

Surrey, Earl of, afterwards Duke of Norfolk, xxii. 350, 351, 359-363, 370, 380, 387.

Sutherland, Earl of, xxv. 280, 301, 302, 399, 406, 431; xxvi. 197.

Suwarrow, Marshal, x. 396, 397; xi. 135-137.

Swandlingbar iron manufactory, origin of the singular name of, ii. 4, n.

Swearing, profane, prevalence of, in Scotland, xix. 217, 218.

Sweetenham, Captain, xxvi. 99.

Swift, Rev. Thomas, vicar of Goodrich, grandfather of Dean Swift, ii. 3; Appendix, 453-455.

—— family anecdotes of, by Dean Swift, ii. Appendix, 452-461.

——, Rev. Thomas, cousin of Dean Swift, ii. 74; claims the original authorship of the 'Tale of a Tub,' 75, n. 77, n.

——, Deane, Esq., nephew of Dean Swift, ii. 391, 441, n

354   INDEX.

Swift, Jonathan, Dean of St Patrick's, Dublin, Life of, ii.; his parentage, 3; (pedigree and anecdotes of the family, *Appendix*, 451;) remarkable circumstances of his early years, 8; admitted into Trinity College, Dublin, 10; his studies and reading at that period, 11; academical irregularities, 14, 16; received into Sir William Temple's family, 19; his first poetical pieces, 24, 28; takes orders and obtains a living in Ireland, 30; returns to Sir William Temple, 32; his character of Sir William, 35; his 'Battle of the Books', 37; his first acquaintance with Miss Johnson (Stella), 41-46; with Miss Waryng (Varina), 44; goes to Ireland with Lord Berkeley, 50; his residence at Laracor, 54; his political and religious opinions, 65; his 'Tale of a Tub,' 71; disappointed in his hopes of preferment from the Whigs, 85; his satire on Partridge the astrologer, and its consequences, 93; death of his mother, 98; objects of his journey to London in 1710, 105; his 'Journal to Stella,' *ib*; attaches himself to Harley and St John, the new ministers, 108, 117; his 'Conduct of the Allies,' 125; controversy between him and Steele, 127; his assistance to men of letters, 138; and to others, 140; circumstances under which he was made Dean of St Patrick's, 148; reception on his return to Dublin, 152; return to England to reconcile the ministers, 157; new controversy with Steele, 159; gives offence to the Scottish peers, 165; his vain attempts to reconcile Oxford and Bolingbroke, 160; his retreat to Letcombe, 181; his prospects from Lord Bolingbroke's ministry, 186; his conduct at Queen Anne's death, 188; unpopular reception on returning to Ireland, 190; his defence against the charge of Jacobitism, 193; his companions at this time, 195; his noble conduct to Lord Oxford, 195; his acquaintance with Miss Vanhomrigh (Vanessa), 200; his marriage to Stella, in 1716, 210; (doubts as to this marriage, *ib. note*, and Appendix, 468); death of Vanessa, 225; his poem of 'Cadenus and Vanessa,' 228; his mode of life from 1714 to 1723, 232; his parsimonious hospitality, 238; his friends Sheridan and Delany, 240; resumes political writing in 1720, 249; his pamphlet recommending the use of Irish manufactures, prosecuted as a libel, 250; reprobates the scheme of a National Bank, 251; his 'Drapier's Letters' against Wood's copper coinage, 254; consequences of the publication of his fourth letter, 263; his bold conduct on the occasion of, 264; successful termination of the struggle, 268; honours paid to him in consequence, ib; revisits London in 1726, 279; his interview with Sir Robert Walpole, 281; introduced to the Prince of Wales, 285; publication of 'Gulliver's Travels,' 288; (remarks on them, Appendix. 479); Swift's last visit to England in 1727, 308; death of George I., 311; disappointment of his hopes on that event, 312; death of Stella, 317; his final rupture with the court, his 'Rhapsody on Poetry,' ib.; other tracts of that period, 323; relations between him and Lord Carteret, 327; quarrel with Dean Smedley, 332; offence given to Queen Caroline by three forged letters in his name, 337; his 'Verses to a Lady,' &c. 340; 'Essay on Polite Conversation,' 341; his indelicate poems, 342; his intimacy with Sir Arthur Acheson, 345; anecdotes of that period, 348, note; his conduct as a dignified clergyman, 357; his zealous opposition to the dissenters, 356; his controversy with the Irish bishops, 357; his Verses on his own death,' 360; Paulkner's edition of his Works, 362; quarrel with Sergeant Bettesworth, 365; the 'Legion Club,'

a satire on the Irish House of Commons, 373; opposes the lowering of the gold coin, 374; retires from public life in 1736, 376; his 'Instructions to Servants, 381; his private life after 1732, 385; his anticipation of his own fate, 387; resolves to found a Lunatic Asylum, 388; his treatment of his relations—Mrs Whiteway, 390; Mr Deane Swift, 391; his acquaintance with Lord Orrery, 393; separation from Dr Sheridan, 396; dispute and reconciliation with Mrs Whiteway, 399; becomes furiously mad, 400; details as to his last five years, 401, n.; his death, 403; funeral and epitaph, 405; his personal appearance, 407; manners and conversation, 410, personal habits, 412; learning, 412; paradoxes in his character and history, 418; his antipathy to soldiers and lawyers, 421; his economy and liberality, 423; his patriotism and regard for literature, 427; openness to criticism, 429; his three peculiarities as an author, 431-433, character of his poetry, ib.; of his prose writings, 436; summary of his character, by Granger, 443; his last will and codicil, 489.

Swift, Dean, his repeated attacks of the literary reputation of Dryden, i. 317; in-

stances of, 317, n. 318, n. 360, n.; and in the 'Translation of Virgil,' 334.
Swinton, Sir John, xxii. 249, 250.
—— John, of Swinton, xxiv. 183-185.
Swiss Guards, massacre of, on 10th August, 1792. viii. 329-345.
Switzerland attacked by the French Directory, and her constitution remodelled, x. 288, 369; Buonaparte's conduct to, xi. 225-232; violation of its neutrality, by the allies, xv. 36.
Syria, Buonaparte's campaign in, x. 349-373

Tacitus, remarks of, on the early inhabitants of Scotland, xx. 330-333.
Tactics, Buonaparte's system of, x. 4-8.
Tagliamento, passage of the, x. 203.
Talavera, battle of, xiii. 283.
'Tale of a Tub,' by Swift, ii. 71.
'Tales of My Landlord,' first series, Review of, xix. 1-86.
TALES OF A GRANDFATHER, HISTORY OF SCOTLAND, *first series* to 1604. xxii. and xxiii. 1-209; *second series*, 1604-1707, xxiii. 211-409; xxiv. xxv. 1-105; *third series*, 1707-1760, xxv. 107-433; and xxvi. *See* Scotland.
—— HISTORY OF FRANCE, xxvii. and xxviii. *See* France.

Talleyrand de Perigord, Cardinal, xxviii. 99.
—— C. M. de, Bishop of Autun, afterwards minister of State, and Prince of Beneventum, viii. 204, n.; x. 298, 347, 394; xi. 8, 9, 68, 250, 255, 259, (369, 370), 388, 384. 320; xii. 86, 135, 258; xiii. 21, 47, 306, 308; xiv. 311, 323; xv. 31, 81, 120, 160-162, 182, 184, 274, 334, 357.
Talma, the actor, early relations of, with Buonaparte, ix. 356, n.
Tantallon Castle, description of, vii. 427.
Tarras, Walter Scott, Earl of, xxiii. 240, n.; xxiv. 263, 269, 337.
Tarbat, Lord, xxiv. 337.
Taschereau, Jules, 'Histoire de la Vie et des Ouvrages de Molière,' Review of, xvii. 137-215.
Tate, General, descent of, on Wales, x. 297, 424, 425.
——, Nahum, author of the second part of Absalom and Achitophel, i. 230; succeeds Shadwell as poet-laureat, 329.
'Tatler,' origin of the, ii. 96.
Tchitchagoff, Admiral, xiv. 89, 175-180, 202-206.
'Tempest, The,' altered from Shakspeare by Dryden, i. 89.
Templars, Knights, origin of the order of, xxvii. 178; dissolution of, by Philip the Fair, 364-367.
Temple, Sir William, the first

patron of Dean Swift, ii. 19.
20, n., 28, 29, 33; visits of
King William to him, 22,
462; his death and character,
35; controversy of with Wotton, *ib.*; his legacy and bequest to Swift, 48, 464;
tigment of Swift being his natural son disproved, 213, n.
395, n.
Tencin, Cardinal, xxvi. 64, 69, 70.
Test Act, plan of James II.
for annulling the, in favour
of Roman Catholics, xxiv.
294-299.
Texier, M., a celebrated reader
of French plays, xviii. 112;
xx. 232.
Theatres, in London, in the time
of Queen Elisabeth, i. 3;
at the Restoration, i. 68; sequence of fires of the great
London ones, xx. 220; evil
consequences of their being
rebuilt on too large a scale,
221-225.
Theatrical monopoly, great evils
of, in London, vi. 389-395.
—— amusements, vindication
of, xx. 152-161.
—— speculations, great hazard
of, xx. 220, 221.
Thiebault, Count of Champagne, the Troubadour, xxvii.
302-306.
Thielman, General, xvi. 15, 34, 35.
Thornton's, Colonel Thomas,
'Sporting Tour through the
North of England and Highlands of Scotland,' Review
of, xix. 87-99.

'*Threnodia Augustalis*,' a
poem, by Dryden, on the accession of James II., i. 256.
Thriepland, Sir Robert, xxvi. 142.
Thumbikins, the, an instrument
of torture, xxiv. 206, 359, 360.
Tibbermuir, battle of, xxiii. 90, 91.
Tickell, Thomas, the poet, and
friend of Swift, ii. 246.
Tibit, conference at and treaty
of, xii. 258-278.
Tithes in Scotland, settlement
of, xxiii. 349-351.
Todd, Rev. Henry John, Review of his edition of 'The
Works of Edmund Spenser,'
xvii. 80-101.
'Tom Jones,' remarks on, iii. 103-109.
Tone, Theobald Wolfe, interview of the widow of, with
Napoleon, xvi. 396-398.
Tonson, Jacob, the bookseller,
quarrel between him and
Dryden, i. 328-334.
Tories and Whigs, xxiv. 285-289.
Tormasoff, General, xiv. 88, 89, 174, 175.
Torres Vedras, the lines of, xiii. 118, 289, 301.
Torture, methods of, practised
on the Scottish Covenanters;
the *boot* and *thumbikins*,
xxiv. 206; final abolition of,
in Scotland, xxv. 156.
Toulon, royalist insurrection of,
ix. 186; surrendered to the
English, 342; siege and recapture of, by the French,
343-359.

Touran Shah, Sultan of Egypt, xxvii. 318-421.
Toussaint L'Ouverture, xi. 267-270.
Town and Country Mouse,' i. 282.
Townley, Mr, xxvi. 232, 257.
Trafalgar, battle of, xii. 108-111.
Tragedy, Rhyming or Heroic, introduced on the English Stage at the Restoration, i. 58; vindicated by Dryden, 78; his controversy with Sir R. Howard on the subject, 80-84; composition of these plays, and reasons for their great popularity, 100-114; Dryden's change of opinion respecting them, 181.
Transpadane Republic, formation of the, x. 178.
Transplantation. *See* Landscape Gardening.
Traquair (Stewart), Earl of, xxvi. 63.
Treason, change in the law of, in Scotland, xxv. 159.
Treaty of Charasco, x. 28. —of Tolentino, 191.—of Leoben, 220.—of Campo Formio, 253.—of Luneville, xi. 129.—of Amiens, 218. of Presburg, xii. 87-89.—of Tilsit, 264-275.—of Fontainebleau, xiii. 12.—of Schoenbrunn, 254.—of Fontainebleau, xv. 213.—of Vienna, 369.—of Paris, xvi. 82-83.
Tressan, Count de, his account of the latter years of Le Sage, the novelist, iii. 423;

his specimens of the Romances of Chivalry, vi. 186; xvii. 53; xviii. 27.
'Tristram Shandy,' remarks on, iii. 294.
'Troilus and Cressida, altered from Shakspeare by Dryden, i. 190; Prologue to, 193.
Truchsess Waldbourg, Baron, xv. 230, 236.
Tschaplitz, General, xiv. 203-207.
Tugendbund, the German, xii. 132.
Tuite, Killbuck, anecdote of and Dean Swift, ii. 348, n.
Tullibardine, Marquis of, xxv. 252, 273, 278, 430-433; xxvi. 73, 87, 105, 106, 107.
Tunis, Crusade of St Louis against, xxvii. 335, 336, 339-341.
Turkey, British Expedition against in 1807, xii. 288; relations of with France and Russia in 1812; xiv. 15-18.
Turn of words, beautiful, from Milton, i. 146.
Turner, Sir James, xxiv. 57, 196, 197, 201, 202.
Tuscany, Grand Duke of, Buonaparte's treatment of, x. 86. 194; ensuing of, to France. xi. 129.
Tweeddale, Marquis of, xxiv. 209; xxv. 77.
Tytler's, Patrick Fraser, 'History of Scotland,' Review of, xxi. 152-198.
Tyrol, attachment of the people of, to the house of Austria, x. 117; the French under

I-chert driven from It in 1797, 207, 208; ceded to Bavaria, xii. 87; insurrection of against Bavaria, xiii. 191, 217-220.

Ulm, capitulation of, xii. 57-61.

Union, failure of proposed between England and Scotland. during James I. xxiii. 266.

—— accomplishment of, by Queen Anne, xxv. 65-105.

Unities, the three, in the drama discussed, vi. 296-315.

Universities of Cambridge and Oxford, James VII.'s conduct to, xxiv. 308-310.

Urquhart, Sir Thomas, account of Francis Stewart, Earl of Bothwell, by, vii. 162, n.

Urry, Sir John (a Dugald Dalgetty). xxiv. 3, 6, 9, 81.

Usher, Captain, xv. 235-237, 240, 246.

Valais, the, annexed to France, xiii. 355.

Valoutina, battle of, xiv. 92, 93.

Vandamme, General, defeat and surrender of, at Culm, xiv. 351-357; xv. 418, 434.

Vanburgh, reviews Fletcher's comedy of ' The Pilgrim,' i. 366.

Vane, Sir Henry, xxiv. 38, 40.

—— Lady, the ' Lady of Quality,' of Smollett's ' Peregrine Pickle,' iii. 132.

Vanhomrigh, Miss Esther (Vanessa), Dean Swift's acquaintance and friendship with, ii. 200-231; two odes written by her. 222, 223.

Varillas's ' History of Heresies,' intended to have been translated by Dryden, i. 286; abandoned, and why, 288.

Vendée, sketch of the war in La, from 1793 to 1796, ix. 141, 173; insurrection in, in 1815, xv. 412, 413.

Vendemiaire, revolution of the 13th, ix. 388-393.

Venice, negotiations of the government of, with Buonaparte, x. 81-84, 194-197; breaks the neutrality and attacks the French, 209; Buonaparte's letter to the Doge, 223; war declared against, by Buonaparte, 226; means adopted by, to avert his vengeance, 227; subsequent measures of, 228; treaty of with the French, 232, 233; transfer of to Austria, by the treaty of Campo Formio, 248-254; cession of by Austria, xiii. 88.

Venus Vaga, mischiefs of the worship of, in early youth, vi. 22.

Versailles, the water-works of, a great display of human power, xxi. 86-87.

Victor Amadeus III. King of Sardinia. See Sardinia.

——, Marshal, Duke of Belluno, x. 184, 188; xi. 108, 112-114, 116; xiii. 282, 283; xiv. 166, 167, 173, 198-201, 204-210, 213, 382, 384; xv. 47, 53, 60, 61, xvi. 69.

Vienna, capture of, by Napoleon in 1805, xii. 67; again in 1809, xiii. 186.
——, Congress of, xv. 333, 367.
Vienne, John de, Admiral of France, xxii. 231-238; xxvii. 252-254, 256.
Villeneuve, Admiral, xii. 103-113.
Vimeiro, battle of, xiii. 115-118.
Vipont, Allan, xxii. 209.
Virgil, Dryden's translation of, i. 325-342.
Vittoria, battle of, xiv. 319, 421.

Wade, Field Marshal, xxvi. 2-9, 183, 202-206, 217, 259.
Wagram, battle of, xiii. 212.
Walcheren, British Expedition to, xiii. 230-235.
Walkinshaw, Miss, mistress of the Pretender, xxvi. 417, 418.
Waller, Edmund, 'the father of English numbers,' i. 14, n. 98; his lines on Cromwell's death, xxiv. 147.
Wall of Severus, description of, vii. 20-22.
Wallace, Sir William, character of, xxi. 175-178; story of, xxii. 77-96.
Walpole, Sir Robert (afterwards Earl of Orford), conduct of, in the affair of Wood's copper coinage, ii. 261, 270; interview of Dean Swift with, 281; satirized by Swift in Gulliver, 290; their subsequent relations, 308-312; Swift's lampoon on him, 310, n. xix. 199; Fielding's verses to, soliciting his patronage, ii. 83, n. See also vol. xxvi. 53-55.
WALPOLE, HORACE (Earl of Orford), BIOGRAPHICAL SKETCH OF, iii. 299; details of his personal history and character, 301-312; remarks on his ' Castle of Otranto,' 313-324; anecdote of Fielding by, 100, 101, n.; errors in his ' Reminiscences' corrected, xix. 199, 200; letter from, to Lady Suffolk, 211.
Walsingham, Sir Francis, xxiii. 177, 179.
Walton, Isaac, quoted, 10, n.; his life of Donne, 13, n.; his ' Angler,' and Davy's ' Salmonia,' parallel between, xx. 261-273.
Warriston, Lady, case of, for murdering her husband, xxi. 260-263.
Warton's, Reverend Thomas, ' History of English Poetry,' characterised, xvii. 4, 19.
Waryng, Miss Jane (Varina), Dean Swift's earliest attachment, ii. 44-46.
WATERLOO, BATTLE OF, v. 99-145, 340-354; xvi. 1-40, 343-379.
—— Visit to the Field of, v 146-162.
Waverley Novels, remarks on the earlier, xix. 2-21.
We are Seven, a characteristic anecdote, xxi. 317.

Weber, Henry, 'Northern Antiquities,' edited by, and R. Jamieson, v. 358; vi. 193; his 'Metrical Romances of the 13th, 14th, and 15th centuries, vi. 99, n.; 144, 209.

Webster, the dramatist, i. 3.

Weissemberg, Baron, xv. 172.

Wellington, Honourable Sir Arthur Wellesley, afterwards Lord, and now Duke of, xii. 296; xiii. 108-118, 281-284, 296-302, 380-383, 385; xiv. 23-25, 266, 319, 335, 421, 422; xv. 77, 85-89, 408, 421-423, 427-438; xvi. 4-40. See also vol. v. 64-145.

Wemyss, Earl of, xxv. 147; xxvi. 142, 188.

Westphalia, kingdom of, xii. 203.

Wharton, Sir George, duel between, and Sir James Stewart, xxiii. 254, 255.

—— Thomas, Earl (afterwards Duke) of, Lord Lieutenant of Ireland, ii. 17, n.; 83, n.; satirized by Swift, 113, 114; moves the House of Lords against Swift, 106, 107; Swift's remarkable advice to him, 386, n.

Whig and High-churchman, characters seldom united in the same person, ii. 81.

Whigs and Tories, xxiv. 285-289.

Whigamores' Raid, xxiv. 59.

Whitefoord, Colonel, xix. 7; xxvi. 162.

White-Knights, seat of the Duke of Marlborough xxi. 91.

Whiteway, Mrs, cousin of Dean Swift, ii. 390, et passim.

Whitshed, Lord Chief Justice, infamous conduct of, on a jury trial, ii. 230; similar conduct of to a grand jury, 266.

Whittingham, Archdeacon, insult offered by, to Dean Swift, ii. 9, n.

Whitworth, Lord, British Ambassador at Paris, xi. 251-259.

Wiazma, battle of, xiv. 161.

Widdrington, Earl of, xxv. 297, 388, 391.

Wild, his 'Iter Boreale,' a poem, i. 33.

'—— Gallant,' by Dryden, i. 68, 413.

Will's coffee-house, the resort of the wits of the day, in Dryden's time, iv. 284, 315, 348, 362, n.

William, Duke of Normandy, afterwards King William I. of England, xxii. 31-34; xxvii. 118-121; conquest of England by, 142-151; death of, 154.

—— II. (Rufus) King of England, xxvii. 154, 180-182.

—— III., liberality of, to Charles Montague, i. 284, n.; patronises Shadwell the poet, 301; his short-lived popularity, 313; scheme of Tonson to make Dryden inscribe his Virgil to, 330; visits of, to Sir William

Temple, ii. 22, 462; cause of his rejecting the Triennial Parliament bill, 463; his share in the massacre of Glencoe, xxv. 1, 9, 10, 19, 20; his conduct in the Darien affair, 34-37, 44, 47-49. *See* Orange.

William the Lion, King of Scotland, notice of the reign of, xxi. 163; xxii. 52-57.

—— Clito, son of Robert Curthose, Duke of Normandy, xxvii. 184-186, 190-194.

Willis, General, xxv. 375-381.

——, Sir Richard, a spy of Cromwell, xxiv. 146.

Wilson, Sir Robert, xiv. 162, 188.

——, a Glasgow mechanic, anecdote of, and Oliver Cromwell, xxiv. 98.

'Windsor Prophecy,' by Dean Swift, ii. 144.

Winton, Seton, Earl of, xxv. 286, 288, 289, 322-391. *See* Seton.

Winzingerode, the Russian General, xiv. 126, 149, 151, 155, 177; xv. 41, 76, 77, 108, 110, 137.

Wirtemberg. Prince Royal of, xiv. 419; xv. 51, 122, 149, 155, 173.

Wishart, George, the protomartyr of the Scottish Reformation, xxiii. 62-64.

——, Dr George, chaplain and biographer of Montrose, xxiii. 391, 394-395, 398; xxiv. 2, 5, 9, 24, 73-79.

Witchcraft, Trials for, in Scotland, xxiii. 125-143.

Wittgenstein, General, xiv. 71, 88, 167, 172-174, 198, 199, 205, 206, 296.

Wogan, the enthusiastic cavalier, notice of, xxiv. 111.

——, Charles, xxvi. 56.

Women, great respect paid to, by the northern nations, vi. 22-26.

'——, or Pour et Contre,' a novel by Maturin, Review of, xviii. 172-208.

Wood, William, controversy to which his patent for a copper coinage in Ireland gave rise, ii. 253-268.

——, Sir Andrew, xxii. 335-337.

——, Anthony, his '*Athenæ Oxonienses*' quoted, i. 6, n.

Worcester, battle of, xxiv. 103.

Works of Art, seizure of, as prize of war, x. 58-68.

Wrede, General, afterwards Prince, xiv. 172, 173, 229, 339, 409-412.

Wright, Captain, xi. 334, 335.

Wurmser, Marshal, Austrian Commander in Italy, in 1796, x. 33, 96, 102-184.

Wynd, Henry (*Gow Chrom*), the blacksmith of Perth, xxii. 244-248.

Wynnes of Wyonesslay, family of, xxv. 63.

Xavier, St Francis, Life of, translated by Dryden, i. 288-291.

Yorck, General D', Prussian

Commander, xiv. 234–237, 307; xv. 51, 53, 56, 107, 113, 151.
York Buildings Company, xxv. 427.
——, Duchess of, verses addressed to, by Dryden. i. 48; dedication of 'The State of Innocence' to, 150.
——, Duke of, Dryden's verses on the victory gained by, i. 48; a convert to the Roman Catholic faith, 125, passim 204, 207, 244; administration of affairs in Scotland, xxiv. 249; recalled to London, 269. *See* JAMES VII.

York, Frederick, Duke of, Characteristic Sketch of, iv. 400.
——, Henry Benedict, Cardinal Duke of, xxvi. 68, 425.
Young, Dr Edward, anecdote of Dean Swift. by, ii. 387; character of, iii. 289, *n*.

Zaragossa, Siege of, by the French, xiii. 94–98.
Ziethen, General, xv. 423, 425.
Zimri, character of the Duke of Buckingham under the name of, in Dryden's 'Absalom,' i. 123, *n*.
Zosim, armistice of, xiii. 218.

THE END.

www.ingramcontent.com/pod-product-compliance
Lightning Source LLC
Chambersburg PA
CBHW020305240426
43673CB00039B/712